PARTY POLITICS IN REPUBLICAN CHINA

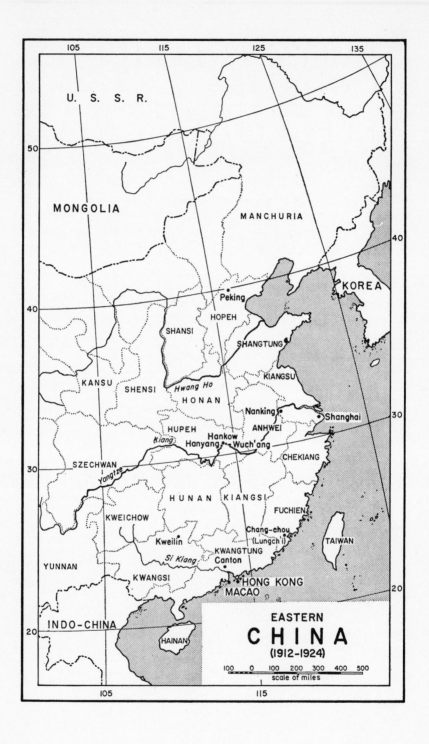

EASTERN
CHINA
(1912-1924)

100   0   100   200   300   400   500
scale of miles

PARTY POLITICS IN

REPUBLICAN CHINA

THE KUOMINTANG, 1912-1924

by George T. Yu

UNIVERSITY OF CALIFORNIA PRESS

BERKELEY AND LOS ANGELES 1966

University of California Press, Berkeley and Los Angeles, California
Cambridge University Press, London, England

Foreword

THE TENDENCY for conflict between borrowed political systems and indigenous social structures has been one of the most complex and fascinating problems confronting the emerging societies of the twentieth century. For most of these new nations, political modernization at certain stages has involved a substantial degree of "Westernization." Political values and institutions conceived and developed in the West have been discovered and subsequently championed by *avant-garde* elements throughout the non-Western world. In many cases, indeed, these values and institutions have at some point become the embodiment of *Truth*, an essential part of the inevitable wave of the future, and hence articles of faith.

It was not always thus, and it does not remain invariably so. The first response toward Westernism by those elites representing the high cultures of traditional Asia was essentially one of rejection. The extensively developed, strongly self-sufficient, and basically closed nature of such societies produced deep feelings of cultural and racial superiority and an intense xenophobia. The trials and tribulations of prolonged contact with the West, moreover, served to sustain some of these emotions. Western colonialism and the advent of Western supremacy throughout the world stirred up sentiments of outrage, bitterness, and enmity. These sentiments could easily interact with traditional anti-foreignism, but they were present also among many of the new elite who in impersonal terms were the most "Westernized" elements of their societies.

This fact beckons us to move toward still more fundamental considerations. Surely, future historians will find that the most significant accomplishment of the West in its age of global domination lay in its universalization of certain values that had previously been parochial, confined merely to the peripheries of Western Europe and the United States. These values can be symbolized by four words: progress, science, industrialization, and democracy. By the mid-twentieth century, what political elite—whether in the Western or the non-Western world—did not covet for itself and its society such designations as progressive, scientific, industrialized, and democratic? For the first time in human history, rival forces argued over the right to use the same words, debated over the most appropriate methods to be used in achieving the same ends.

This universalization of Western values, however, paradoxically presented a new and formidable challenge to the West. Understandably, the advent of Western growth and power abetted that ethnocentric force which lies within every cultural unit. While there were some notable exceptions, Western attitudes after the beginning of the nineteenth century were generally characterized by the assumptions—explicit or implicit—that the values and institutions of the "advanced West" were vastly superior to all others *and* that the modernity, progress and very capacity of non-Western peoples should be judged by the degree to which they accepted and successfully operated the Western value-institutional complex. Such doctrines, however, placed a heavy premium upon the workability of that complex in societies having different cultural traditions, different timings of development, and, hence, different socio-political proclivities.

Suddenly, the political elites of Asia and Africa were faced

with a series of complicated psychological and political challenges. Burdened with their own strongly ethnocentric traditions, they were now forced to deal with a powerful, ethnocentric
West that sought—consciously or unconsciously—to substitute
its culture for theirs. Accustomed to their own deeply-entrenched
beliefs in racial and cultural superiority, these elites were now
threatened, and in many cases humbled, by Western doctrines of
racial and cultural superiority, doctrines that rode on the wings
of Western power.

The first Asian efforts to come to terms with Westernism were
often painful and undertaken unwillingly. When containment
of the West by isolation failed, men deeply steeped in tradition
tried containment by compartmentalization. By relegating Westernism to the realm of technology, they hoped to preserve tradition in values and institutions. Such an approach, of course, was
too artificial and too unrealistic to have more than fleeting meaning. The ultimate answer to the Western challenge had to be
found in the quest for a thorough synthesis in which each people
sought to utilize selected elements of its past in building toward
modernity, while adjusting borrowed techniques, institutions,
and values to the current needs and nature of its own society.
And that ultimate answer, in turn, provided certain serious
challenges to the original premises, values, and power of the
West. Indeed, we are living in the age of that challenge.

At an earlier point, however, it was natural that some Asians,
committed to radical change in the political patterns of their
society, would, in the course of events, move toward a wholehearted, unrestricted acceptance of Western-style parliamentarism. Such an acceptance did not necessarily erase all doubts
about Western political behavior. Nor did it automatically remove various formidable personal and cultural barriers separat-
ing Asians from the West and the Westerner. It was, however, a
logical expression at some point in the far-reaching search for
methods of wiping out the stigma of backwardness, asserting
with full force the principles of independence and power, and
catching up with the West.

Yet, as has already been suggested, in most cases this total com-

mitment to Western-style parliamentarism was short-lived. Repeated failures brought disillusionment and retreat. Ultimately,
attention was focused mainly upon how to modify Western
theory and practice in such a manner as to make it meaningful. This process was not confined to the issue of parliamentarism. Within a few decades at most, full commitment to
Westernism could be expressed differently by a radical, *avant-
garde* element in Asia. We can regard the wholehearted allegiance to Soviet-style communism as another manifestation of
the same basic phenomena. And, once again, the inevitable retreat came eventually, and the quest for a synthesis.

George T. Yu's study of the formative years of the Kuomintang
illustrates some of the basic problems suggested here as they
related to China during the first two decades of this century.
One of its merits is that it focuses upon certain aspects of the
political modernization problem in China previously minimized
or ignored. Two central threads run through this work: the
movement from political traditionalism to political modernity
within the revolutionary group itself; and the movement first
toward Western-style politics and then, in the aftermath of failure, toward authoritarian, mass-mobilization politics.

The most immediate predecessor of the Kuomintang, the
T'ung Meng Hui, as Professor Yu points out, not only con-
sorted with the traditional secret societies, but in its own structure and program illustrated the continuing force of traditionalism within the Chinese revolutionary movement. Its methods
of political recruitment, its organizational and procedural rules,
and its policies—so notably oriented to a nationalism that emphasized an overt racial appeal—all underlined the fact that the
T'ung Meng Hui's links were almost as much with the *Chinese*
past as with the *universal* future. At the same time, however, the
influence of Western political values was already clear in the
commitment to republicanism and to such concepts of social
reform as Henry George's single tax scheme. Even in the T'ung
Meng Hui, one could witness the extensive allegiance of the
young Chinese radicals to the themes of progress (via revolution), science, industrialization, and democracy.

The adherence to "classical" Western values and institutions
was to reach its zenith in the years between 1912 and 1914. It was
in this period that the Kuomintang emerged as a party dedicated
to two basic political principles: nationalism and republicanism.
Its wholehearted espousal of Western-style parliamentarism, its
strong support for immediate constitutional government, and its
willingness to compete in the political market-place with other
parties symbolized the buoyant optimism of Sun and his followers in the aftermath of the 1911 Revolution, and their complete dedication to the basic principles of Western liberalism.
In this era, indeed, the vague socialist doctrines advanced by the
revolutionaries earlier were generally missing from new Party
pronouncements. With the political tasks largely accomplished,
would not economic development, abetted by the advanced West
and by Japan, follow as a matter of course?

Scarcely two years later, the scene was vastly different, and
even the perpetually optimistic Dr. Sun was forced to fight
against recurrent periods of dark despair. Chinese parliamentarism had been crippled by corruption, military intervention,
and the chaotic factionalism and divisions within and among all
political groups. Constitutionalism had become a mockery. The
Kuomintang, like other parties, without military strength or a
mass political base, lay at the mercy of men like Yuan Shih-k'ai.
The dreams of a few years earlier lay in ruins.

It is not surprising that Sun and his followers, sitting once
more in exile, engaged in much soul-searching. Mutual recrimi-
nations and new factional cleavages were prominently displayed,
as they always are in the aftermath of defeat. Slowly, however,
plans for the rebuilding took shape, with certain new emphases.
One theme was *discipline*. Had not the failures of the past proven
that all party members should pledge themselves to unswerving
allegiance to the leader, so that the factionalism and anarchy
which had earlier decimated the Kuomintang could be eliminated? Another theme was *stages of development*. Was it not
clear that the abandonment of earlier concepts of tutelage, and
the attempt to launch full-fledged constitutionalism immediately, had been disastrous mistakes?

Once again, Sun and his followers returned to a theme of previous years: the immediate aftermath of any successful revolution would be characterized by military rule. It was essential, however, that such rule be replaced quickly by the rule of the party, with the Kuomintang assuming full political powers and acting as tutor to the Chinese people, preparing them for eventual constitutional democracy. Such preparation, based upon a province-by-province development, necessarily placed a high premium upon party leaders and cadres. Under a temporary party dictatorship, a modernizing elite, composed largely of those with Westernized education, had to guide the masses, shaping both their values and their capacities, and readying them for their future role as sovereigns. If the preparatory stage was to be successful, many vital tasks had to be undertaken by the party: mass education, fundamental social reforms, and far-reaching economic development.

This revolutionary new approach to power and responsibility inevitably caused Kuomintang leaders in time to turn their attention strongly to organizational issues. If the party was to establish and maintain control, it would need both a strong military arm and a broad political structure based upon the full mobilization of the Chinese people. The old elitist approach, characterized by the secret society or the intellectual club, was totally insufficient. A realization of these facts, to be sure, did not come immediately. By 1923–1924, however, Sun and other Kuomintang leaders were prepared in some measure to accept the organizational implications of their radical new approach to Chinese political modernization.

Another society and another party, moreover, were now prepared to interact with this new approach. The intertwined fate of those two backward giants of the early twentieth century, Russia and China, is one of the intriguing stories of our times. In Russia, as in China, liberal forces had gone from moments of hope and triumph to periods of deep despair in the course of the struggle for political modernization. Here, too, a great variety of forces had vied for the privilege of conducting the revolution, with traditionalist and modernist, foreign and indigenous elements being involved. It is not essential to trace here the events whereby those forces representing Western-style parliamentarism went down to defeat. It is not even important to detail the contrasts and the similarities with China. It is sufficient to note that by the close of World War I, Russia like China was in full retreat from liberal premises and methods.

Sun's Kuomintang and Lenin's Bolshevik Party operated from different ideological positions and aimed at different political goals. There was, however, a certain logic in the alliance that ultimately developed between them as the Kuomintang struggled to reorganize itself in accordance with its new premises. It is true, of course, that this alliance was partly the result of repeated refusals by the West and Japan to grant economic or political support to Sun and his movement; hence it was, in certain terms, an act of desperation. But it is equally clear that the Kuomintang leaders and the Soviet Communists had a wide range of organizational principles and challenges in common.

Both the Chinese and the Russian parties were now committed to the concepts of tutelage, the educative state, and party dictatorship. These concepts in turn demanded a highly disciplined party with some fountainhead of authority; a military force sufficient to coerce dissident elements who, for whatever reason, were not prepared to accept party guidance; and a broad political base resting upon the fullest possible mobilization and indoctrination of the people, so that persuasion could be substituted wherever possible for coercion, and maximum use could be made of the society's human resources.

The Kuomintang was dedicated to the achievement of constitutional democracy. The Communist Party was committed to the creation of a classless society in which the state would wither away, a vastly more utopian goal. Yet each of these parties, in its own way, heralded the new age, an age of unprecedented challenge to Western-style parliamentarism and liberal values. For every emerging society of the non-Western world, the gap between borrowed ideologies and institutions and indigenous social capacities has loomed up, as it did in the case of China and Russia, and the quest for some meaningful syntheses has become a necessity. In most cases, the techniques ultimately employed by these new societies bear a close resemblance to those pioneered by the Kuomintang after 1920. They involve a concept of tutelage, a single or dominant party system, and a wide range of socio-economic reforms, including programs for popular education, legal reform, and economic planning. The mobilization and commitment of the masses to party objectives are primary goals. Yet at the same time, among most political elites there is a genuine desire to avoid the type of totalitarianism implicit in the more rigorous Communist model.

In the light of these developments and the vital stake which all men have in their outcome, Professor Yu's well researched and authoritative monograph has a clear contemporary significance. The Kuomintang made pioneer efforts to seek out a new path toward political modernization without abandoning democratic goals, and this study concentrates upon the critical period when its principles and tactics were constantly being tested and reformulated. During those dramatic years, the Kuomintang, in its own way, symbolized the great political issues which still characterize this revolutionary age.

ROBERT A. SCALAPINO

Preface

THE PARTY MOVEMENT in China has been a neglected field of study. Yet, in the history of China since the founding of the Republic in 1912, political parties have occupied a central role in the political development of the country. Certainly, the struggle between the Chung-kuo Kung-ch'ang Tang (Chinese Communist Party) and the Chung-kuo Kuo-min Tang (Chinese Nationalist Party) since the early 1920's is an example. While the Chung-kuo Kung-ch'ang Tang has been subject to scholarly scrutiny, no detailed study has been completed on the Chung-kuo Kuo-min Tang (referred to hereafter simply as the Kuomintang).

This work consists of an examination of the Chinese party movement with special emphasis upon the Kuomintang in its formative period. The Chinese scene offers an unique opportunity to study a party that was both a parliamentary and a revolutionary movement. Furthermore, the Kuomintang presents an excellent example of a party movement in an emerging society. Studies of Asian party movements are too few to permit valid generalizations encompassing the non-Western world. But if we are to give meaning to existing theories and formulate new ones, the experiences of political parties in non-Western societies should be examined.

There is another reason for undertaking such a study. The record of the Kuomintang in attempting to organize itself, to capture power, and to reconstruct China has contemporary significance. Certainly the failure of the party movements and democratic governments in Burma, Pakistan, and other newly emerging nations has much in common with the Chinese experience. Furthermore, the Kuomintang's concept of "political tutelage" and the idea of "guided democracy" practiced in many of the new nations express a common thought. Indeed, to a degree, the Chinese experience is being repeated in the Afro-Asian world. The Chinese record, therefore, can help to explain the developments in the new nations.

I should like to express my sincere thanks to those who made this study possible. I wish to thank Robert A. Scalapino, Joseph R. Levenson, and Conrad Brandt for their advice and criticism. I am especially indebted to Professor Scalapino, who first suggested that I undertake this study and who has seen the study through its various stages. I am also deeply grateful to him for writing the Foreword. Thanks are due to Dr. Leo Rose for reading an earlier draft of the manuscript. My sincere thanks go to my former senior colleague at the University of North Carolina, Frederic N. Cleaveland, whose assistance was very much appreciated.

The East Asiatic Library, the Interlibrary Borrowing Service, and the Newspaper Room of the University of California Library, Berkeley have greatly aided me in my search for materials. I am indebted to the Chinese Collection at the Hoover Institution, Stanford University. I would like to acknowledge the financial assistance received from the University Research Council of the Graduate School and the Institute for Research in Social Science of the University of North Carolina. Finally, I am grateful to my wife, Priscilla, who has helped and sustained me throughout the writing of this book.

Urbana, Illinois   GEORGE T. YU

Contents

INTRODUCTION

MODERN POLITICAL PARTIES are the product of Western environment, usually associated with the rise of constitutional government in the seventeenth century. Political parties first came into prominence in Great Britain, the prototype of democratic government. However, even British parties did not spring up overnight as full-blown, cohesive organizations. Indeed, the development of political parties and the party system was a long and arduous process anywhere. A civil war came to pass before parties in Britain became a reality. Even then, parties were deemed undesirable, and were identified with factions and interests believed to be disruptive of the harmony and unity of a nation. In the United States, George Washington, in his Farewell Address of September, 1796, cautioned against the "mischiefs of the spirit of party." Nevertheless, by the mid-nineteenth century political parties had become fully accepted and integrated into the British and American political systems. Parties and party politicians had replaced monarchies and aristocracies as the instruments and contestants of power.

The concept of political parties soon spread to other lands

and continents. Their popularity, as a key instrument of democratic government, was primarily the result of Western expansion and the demonstrable success of the Western political
system. The prestige acquired by the major Western democ-
racies led to the imitation of Western institutions, including
that of democratic government. The impact of the West was
felt in Asia, particularly in China. Beginning with the Opium
War in 1839, China's contact with the West had shown increasingly her own internal weakness, both military and political. China's defeat in the war of 1894-1895 at the hands of
Japan, an Oriental nation which culturally was a child of China
but which had earlier adopted Western methods, brought demands for governmental reforms on the Western model followed by demands for revolution. The revolution of 1911
resulted in the overthrow of the old imperial regime and the
establishment of a new government based upon the Western
model. Political parties, as part of the conversion to Western
methods, were similarly introduced.

The concept of a political party and of a party system is
foreign to the traditional political system of China. From the
third century B.C. until the founding of the Chinese Republic
in 1912, China had been governed by a monarchy, which ad-
hered to the teaching of Confucianism. The monarchy, headed
by an emperor who was known as Son of Heaven, reigned
supreme, exercised arbitrary power, governed by a monopoly
of power and by moral suasion, and tolerated no opposition.

What elements in the political thought and institutions of
traditional China conflicted with the development of political
parties? What was the nature of political opposition in pre-
Republican China? Two features which contributed to the
nondevelopment of political parties were the concepts of faction
and loyalty. The Confucian concept of loyalty began with the
ideal that the emperor as Son of Heaven represented *the* final
source of authority, and by implication made correct decisions.
To differ with the emperor's wishes and policies was tantamount
to disagreeing with the will of Heaven. Thus the concept of
loyalty became in practice that of loyalty to the emperor's will.

This ideal was strengthened by the Confucian ideal of society; for society to be well-balanced the most important factor was "the rectification of names."

The concept of rectification of names held that things in actual fact should be made to accord with the implication attached to them by names. Thus it is reported that when asked the right principles of government, Confucius answered: "Let the ruler be the ruler, the minister the minister." Confucius meant that each person occupied a specific station in life and that each name should agree with the attached meaning. Thus the emperor should behave in the way of an emperor, and the minister in the way of a minister. Each name carried certain duties and responsibilities. For the emperor-minister relationship, the rectification of names meant that the minister had the responsibility and duty of being loyal to the emperor. If every category of names was to fulfill its responsibility and duty, then each had the obligation of supporting the emperor's policies and hence of being loyal. Thus the concept of loyalty meant undivided and complete loyalty to the throne.

The idea of total loyalty to the emperor with no allowance for difference of opinion was even more explicit in the traditional concept of factions or parties. Traditionally, factional rivalry has always been interpreted as selfish competition among groups, each endeavoring to advance its private interests. In turn, the fall of dynasties has been attributed to factionalism. The perpetuation of this concept is exemplified by an edict by the Ch'ing emperor Yung-cheng: "Factionalism is an extremely bad pattern of behavior. At the end of the Ming [dynasty], cliques were set up and plotted against each other, with the result that all suffered injury together. . . ."[1] Aside from condemning factions, the Ch'ing emperors took positive steps to prevent their establishment. In 1652 the formation of societies and other groups with large numbers of members was forbidden.

---

[1] Quoted in David S. Nivison, "Ho-shen and His Accusers: Ideology and Political Behavior in the Eighteenth Century," *Confucianism in Action*, ed. by David S. Nivison and Arthur F. Wright (Stanford, 1959), p. 224.

On rare occasions attempts have been made to defend factionalism. Perhaps the most famous was Ou-yang Hsiu's address to
the Sung emperor in 1044.[2] Ou-yang submitted his petition to
the throne at the height of factional contention at the Sung
court. He took the realistic position that factions constituted
a part of government and were to be accepted as such. The real
problem was to distinguish between "virtuous men and unworthy persons." Factions made up of unworthy persons who
shared a common interest were not lasting, for they were based
on expediency. In contrast, the factions composed of virtuous
men who held to the same principle represented a real and permanent bond, for its members abided by "principles and righ-
teousness" and behaved in "accordance with loyalty and hon-
esty." Whereas factions composed of unworthy persons sought
merely their own interests, factions of virtuous men had but
one goal, that of serving the state. Ou-yang thus petitioned the
emperor to dismiss the unworthy and rely upon the "genuine
faction of virtuous men."

According to Ou-yang, the Sung emperor was not the first
ruler called upon to choose between factions, bad and good. The
emperors Yao and Shun (two of the legendary model emperors)
and King Wu of Chou governed a tranquil world because they
relied upon factions consisting of virtuous men, whereas the
last emperors of the Han and T'ang dynasties witnessed the
collapse of their empires because of their refusal to heed the
counsel of virtuous men. The moral was clear. Good and bad
factions had existed since ancient times. The important consideration was not their presence but the ability to distinguish
between good and bad. If the emperor relied upon virtuous
men, the empire would prosper, but if unworthy persons
secured the confidence of the throne, the empire would perish.
Such was Ou-yang Hsiu's "new theory" on factions.

Notwithstanding Ou-yang's appeal, factions continued to be
regarded as groups contributing to the disharmony of the em-

---

[2] Ou-yang Hsiu, "On Factions," *Ou-yang Yung-shu chi* (Collective Works
of Ou-yang Yung-shu) (Shanghai, 1933), I, 22-23.

pire. In 1724 the traditional view was reiterated. In that year
the Ch'ing emperor, Yung-cheng, wrote a long discourse entitled *P'eng-tang lun* (On Factions).[3] The Ch'ing emperor
leaned heavily upon tradition, especially upon the Confucian
teachings. He asserted that, just as Heaven and Earth each had
its place, so were the roles of emperor and minister established.
The sole duty of a minister was to be loyal to the emperor,
sharing his likes and dislikes. The minister was to harbor no
other interest but the emperor's. The Ch'ing emperor characterized Ou-yang's "new theory" as perverse. Ou-yang had
claimed that virtuous men formed factions because they shared
common principles. Not so, retorted the emperor. There could
be no common principle among those who denied their sover-
eign. Those who formed factions did so merely to advance their
private interests. Thus, concluded the Ch'ing ruler, only unworthy men formed factions; the virtuous (as Confucius once
remarked) did not join factions. Yung-cheng, like past and
future Chinese rulers, demanded the total loyalty of all his
ministers. Parties or factions which disrupted governmental
harmony and challenged the emperor's authority were not
tolerated, for they might usurp the dominant position of the
throne.

Politically speaking, minority rights in imperial China did
not exist. The absence of any recognized political groups that
could hold views contrary to the throne's meant that political
protest was, of necessity, both total and illegal. Opposition to
the ruling dynasty usually began as an illegal and sometimes
secret movement and, if successful, resulted eventually in the
founding of a new ruling house. Malcontents were forced to
seek the complete overthrow of the existing regime. No other
roads were open. Success, of course, offered unlimited reward—
that of the rule of China—but one risked one's life in challenging the emperor's authority. The price of defeat was death. This
all-or-nothing attitude undoubtedly discouraged organized political opposition.

---

[3] Nivison, *op. cit.*, pp. 225-227.

Secret societies came to serve as the chief vehicle for opposition to the ruling house. This was a logical outcome of the political pattern which tolerated no division within the ruling elite, and recognized no legal difference of opinion. In general, the secret societies were outside the accepted political and social structure. In ordinary times they were economic protective organizations, which offered no real challange to the ruling house, but in times of stress they could become a focus for antigovernment forces. Although at times the secret societies contributed to the overthrow of governments, and even constituted the "mass" bases of revolutions, their chief contribution to the revolutionary cause was to offer a model of an organizational weapon for those who sought to challenge the ruling house.

Against the background of the demand for absolute allegiance to the throne and the refusal to allow factions, one can understand why political parties never developed in imperial China. The concept of parties, connoting the existence of two or more competing political groups, was alien to the very basis of traditional Chinese political thought and practice. Political protest existed only in the form of secret societies, illegal and underground. It was into this political environment that Western-modeled political parties were thrust in 1912. This study constitutes an investigation of one Western-inspired Chinese party, the Kuomintang.

I PARTIES OF TRANSITION:
THE HSING CHUNG HUI

THE BEGINNINGS of the Kuomintang in the late nineteenth century can be traced to the founding of the Hsing Chung Hui
(Revive China Society). This was the first of what was to become a series of organizations organized to overthrow the Ch'ing
dynasty and reform China. After the turn of the century, the
movement to capture power and the revolutionary organization
gathered strength with the founding of the T'ung Meng Hui
(Common Alliance Society). In the T'ung Meng Hui, as in
the Hsing Chung Hui, Sun Yat-sen served as the rallying center;
he was both midwife and guardian to these antidynastic bodies.

The founding and activities of the Hsing Chung Hui can be
attributed primarily to one man, for the society represented the
ideas, promotion, and determination of one person. Sun Yat-
sen, who devoted his life to the cause of reforming China, gave
birth to the Kuomintang through the establishment of the
Hsing Chung Hui.

Sun Yat-sen was a product of both Western environment and
traditional Chinese society. He was born on November 12, 1866,
in the district of Hsiang-shan (since changed to Chung-shan),

Kwangtung province, in southern China.[1] Sun's provincial birth ties benefited him greatly in his later activities, when he derived much support from his fellow countrymen residing abroad. Sun's family were farmers by profession. As in many other Kwangtung households of the peasant class, a member of the family had gone abroad to make his fortune. This provided Sun's introduction to the Western world.

Sun Mei (Sun Te-chang), an older brother, played a decisive role in Sun Yat-sen's introduction to Western culture and his revolutionary ventures.[2] At seventeen Sun Mei had migrated to Hawaii in 1871; after several years as a hired hand on the island of Oahu, Sun Mei moved to the island of Maui, where he secured land for farming and was successful in raising cattle as well. In 1878 Sun Mei returned to Hsiang-shan, to recruit workers for the Hawaiian government. After several months at home, during which he was married and made arrangements for the transportation of laborers, Sun Mei returned to Hawaii. It is said that Sun Yat-sen wanted to go to Hawaii with his brother, but that his parents refused.

Sun Yat-sen did not have long to wait for his first venture into the foreign world—a world in which he was to travel widely and to know well in subsequent years. A year after his brother's return to Hawaii, Sun's mother decided to visit her son in Hawaii, taking Sun with her. In June, 1879, Sun and his mother left China for the new world of Hawaii, along with a second group of workers recruited by his brother.

---

[1] Lo Chia-lun, ed., *Kuo-fu nien-p'u ch'u-kao* (Taipei, 1958), p. 6. All subsequent dates relating to Sun, unless otherwise noted, follow this source. Sun's original name was Sun Wen, and his courtesy name I-hsien. A Cantonese pronunciation of the Chinese characters I-hsien is Yat-sen. Hence Sun Yat-sen. In 1897, when he fled to Japan, Sun assumed the name Chung-shan-ch'iao (woodcutter of Chung-shan), and thus became known as Sun Chung-shan. While Sun is commonly known in the Western world as Sun Yat-sen, in China he is more familiarly referred to as Sun Chung-shan.

[2] Kao Liang-tso, *Sun Chung-shan hsien-sheng ch'uan* (Chengtu, 1945), pp. 18-20; Lo Chia-lun, *op. cit.*, p. 11.

At home in Hsiang-shan, Sun Yat-sen had been introduced to the classical Chinese system of education at the age of six which continued until he went abroad at the age of thirteen. In Honolulu, Sun was enrolled in the Iolani College in Honolulu, a school for boys fostered by Bishop Willis of the Church of England.[3] When Sun's mother returned to China, he was placed in the care of his brother. After graduating from Iolani College in 1882, Sun entered Oahu College, a local American missionary school, to prepare him for college in America. However, Sun did not set foot in the United States until 1896. Instead of continuing his education at Oahu College in Honolulu, he returned to China in the summer of 1883.[4] Much debate has centered on Sun's sudden decision to return home when he was still in the midst of his schooling. Perhaps it was partly his concern for his parents, whom he had not seen for four years. However, the immediate issue seems to have arisen out of a conflict between Sun and his brother over the question of whether Sun should become a Christian.

The Christian influence upon Sun Yat-sen, beginning with his education at Christian schools in Honolulu, played an important role in his life. In the years to come, Sun derived much support from his fellow Christians. In 1883, however, Christianity came between Sun and his brother. The years spent in missionary schools had prepared Sun for an acceptance of Christianity, but his brother would not countenance this.[5] He not only withheld his consent, but ordered Sun to return to China. According to one account, Sun at first moved from his brother's home to Oahu College. When no reconciliation was forthcoming, Sun purchased a ticket with the aid of the College pastor and returned to China.[6] But the seeds of Christianity

[3] Kao Liang-tso, *op. cit.*, pp. 21-22.

[4] *Ibid.*, p. 27.

[5] Lo Chia-lun, *op. cit.*, p. 27; Feng Tzu-yu, *Ke-min i-shih* (Taipei, 1953), II, 10-18; Ch'en Shao-pai, "Essentials of the Hsing Chung Hui's Revolutionary History," *Chien-kuo Yueh-k'an*, I, No. 3 (July 15, 1929), 16-24.

[6] Ch'en Shao-pai, *ibid.*

had been planted. No longer restrained by his brother, Sun was baptized a Christian in Hong Kong in 1885.[7]

The years following Sun's return to China represent what he calls the period of revolutionary propaganda,[8] when his ideas regarding the reform of China began to crystallize. He enraged the villagers by mutilating the village god, and was forced to leave Hsiang-shan in the fall of 1884.[9] Sun then enrolled in the diocesan school of the Church of England in nearby Hong Kong; he changed to Queen's College in the spring of 1885. In 1886 he enrolled in the Po-chi Hospital School at Canton. Here Sun was brought together with fifteen other students of various backgrounds. One of them was Chen Shih-liang, also from Kwangtung. Chen shared a somewhat similar background with Sun; he had attended a German missionary school and was a Christian,[10] and they became fast friends. Chen introduced Sun to the secret societies of which he was a member,[11] and during this period we first learn of Sun's revolutionary ambition.[12]

In 1887 Sun transferred to the newly founded Hong Kong College of Medicine for Chinese, where he found further support for his revolutionary ideas. Among those who were influenced by Sun was Ch'en Shao-pai, a fellow Cantonese student at the college. Together with two others who shared similar views on reform, they became known as the "Rebel Quartet."[13] The period of "revolutionary propaganda" continued until 1892 when Sun, at the age of twenty-six, graduated with great distinction from the medical school in Hong Kong.[14] The

---

[7] Lo Chia-lun, *op. cit.*, p. 31; Feng Tzu-yu, *op. cit.*, II, 10-18.

[8] Kuomintang, *Kuo-fu ch'uan-chi* (Taipei, 1957), I, 32. Hereafter cited as *Kuo-fu ch'uan-chi.*

[9] Lo Chia-lun, *op. cit.*, p. 29.

[10] Feng Tzu-yu, *op. cit.*, I, 24-25.

[11] *Kuo-fu ch'uan-chi*, I, 32.

[12] *Ibid.*

[13] *Ibid.*

[14] Lindsay Ride, "The Antecedents," *The First 50 Years*, ed. by Harrison Brain (Hong Kong, 1962), pp. 5-22.

period of formal education and propaganda now ended, and the era of active participation was about to begin.

The seeds of the Hsing Chung Hui, parent organization of the Kuomintang, were sown in the years following Sun Yat-sen's graduation from medical school. Sun set up practice, first in Macao and then in Canton; he also entered the pharmaceutical business. However, his prime interest still seems to have been political. He continued to participate actively in discussions with Chen Shih-liang, Ch'en Shao-pai, and others who became familiar with his reformist ideas on domestic conditions. Tsou Lu, Kuomintang party historian, traced the founding of the Hsing Chung Hui by Sun to this period in Macao.[15] However, all other accounts attribute the founding of the Hsing Chung Hui to a later date in Honolulu.[16] Sun seems to have conceived of an organization consisting of those who shared similar reformist views in Macao, Hong Kong, and Canton. He might have suggested to his friends the formation of such a group as the Hsing Chung Hui, but nothing came of it, and the first revolutionary organization did not formally come into being until years later.

---

[15] Tsou Lu, *Chung-kuo Kuo-min Tang shih-kao* (Chungking, 1944), I, 1. Tsou Lu bases his assertion primarily upon the account given by Sun after his release from captivity by the Ch'ing legation in 1897. Sun wrote, "It was in Macao that I first learned of the existence of a political movement which I might best describe as the formation of a 'Young China' party. Its objects were so wise, so modest, and so hopeful, that my sympathies were at once enlisted in its behalf, and I believed I was doing my best to further the interests of my country by joining it. The idea was to bring about a peaceful reformation, and we hoped, by forwarding modest schemes of reform to the Throne, to initiate a form of government more consistent with modern requirements. . . . " Sun Yat-sen, *Kidnapped in London* (Bristol, 1897), pp. 12-13.

[16] Chih Kuei, in a careful examination of various records, rejected the claim that the Hsing Chung Hui was founded in Macao, and attributed the confusion to Sun's inconsistency. Chih Kuei, "Problems Regarding . . . the Founding of the Hsing Chung Hui," *Chien-kuo Yueh-k'an*, IX, No. 1 (July, 1933), 1-4. For others sharing a similar view see Lo Chia-lun, *op. cit.*, p. 51; Ch'en Shao-pai, *op. cit.*; and Feng Tzu-yu, *op. cit.*, I, 14-17.

In February, 1894, Sun traveled with Lu Hao-tung, a child-hood friend and converted Christian revolutionary, first to Shanghai, and in May to Tientsin where he submitted a letter to Li Hung-chang, Manchu grand secretary and patron of things Western.

Sun's letter to Li Hung-chang, one of his earliest writings, indicates the trend of his ideas during this period. It was concerned primarily with strengthening of China and catching up with the West.[17] For this Sun proposed a four-point program for China's salvation: utilizing human resources to the full, deriving full benefits from the land, exploiting natural resources to the utmost, and promoting commerce. Sun considered these elements as the principal sources of wealth and power. He was especially concerned with the land, for he regarded the improvement of agriculture as most urgent. Sun wrote that, although China had attempted to adopt Western knowledge, he had never heard of any program using Western agriculture methods. Neither had he known of any Chinese going abroad to study agriculture nor of the employment of an agriculture expert by the government. He proposed the establishment of a central agriculture institute with branches in the provinces to advise and instruct farmers. Provincial agriculture services for the exchange of information were also recommended. Perhaps as a dramatic gesture, Sun announced his own plans to go abroad to investigate agricultural conditions, to be followed upon his return by a study of agriculture in China. Sun seems to have been preoccupied with technological improvement. Except for a passing reference to the plight of the peasant and China's pressing land problem, Sun demonstrated little interest in social reorganization, and did not mention political principles.

Sun failed to secure support from Li Hung-chang, but he did obtain from Li an official endorsement entitling him to raise funds to establish an agricultural association.[18] He then returned to Shanghai and sailed for Honolulu. No explanation

---

[17] *Kuo-fu ch'uan-chi*, V, 1-12.
[18] Tsou Lu, *op. cit.*, I, 16; Lo Chia-lun, *op. cit.*, p. 51.

is given for Sun's decision to travel to Hawaii. Probably he saw no hope for his plans in China nor did he find his friends in Hong Kong overly enthusiastic. Perhaps Hawaii was merely intended as a stepping stone to his proposed world journey.

The formation of the Hsing Chung Hui in Honolulu on November 24, 1894,[19] had an inauspicious beginning. Sun found the Hawaiian Chinese a conservative lot. The local Chinese population turned a deaf ear to his proposal for reforming China. They saw in Sun's condemnation of the ruling Ch'ing house a scheme to "destroy the family and extinguish the race."[20] Sun wrote in his biography that only after months of persuasion was he able to win the support of his brother and a score of friends and relatives.[21] Among those present at the first meeting were the Chinese manager of a local bank, a Chinese teacher, a Chinese interpreter employed by the local government, a farm owner, Sun's brother and uncle, and several hired hands of Sun's brother. Included in the group were a number of Christians. Sun, as chairman of the meeting, proposed that the group be known as the Hsing Chung Hui and that its aim should be the revival of China. This was agreed to by all present. Officers were elected, and the bylaws of the society were drawn. Sun then asked those present to take an oath by placing their left hand on the Bible, raising their right hand, and asking heaven to serve as their witness.

The manifesto of the Hsing Chung Hui, which Sun formulated in rather vague and indirect terms, drew attention to the decadence of China.[22] It condemned the corruption and weakness of the Ch'ing government and noted the encroachment of the foreign powers upon China. It declared that the purpose of

---

[19] Lo Chia-lun, op. cit., p. 51; Feng Tzu-yu, op. cit., I, 15.

[20] Feng Tzu-yu, loc. cit.

[21] Kuo-fu ch'uan-chi, I, 32. The reluctant participation of the Hawaiian Chinese is well described by Feng Tzu-yu, op. cit., IV, 1-24. A further indication of the small size of the group in terms of the Chinese population is the fact that in 1894 there were over 16,000 Chinese in Hawaii. See R. Adams, The People of Hawaii (Honolulu, 1933), p. 8.

[22] For a full text of the manifesto see Kuo-fu ch'uan-chi, IV, 55-56.

the society was to oppose Ch'ing repression and foreign aggression, and to encourage the revival of China. The Hsing Chung Hui manifesto was essentially a reformist document and a call for self-strengthening. In this respect it differed little from Sun's letter to Li Hung-chang earlier in the year. The two documents together represent an attempt to focus attention on the state of affairs in China and to propose a remedy for their improvement. Sun's ideas on democracy and social reform were still in process of formulation.

The rules of the Hsing Chung Hui provided for a president, vice-president, two secretaries, one treasurer, nine directors, and two minor deputies.[23] Weekly meetings were to be held which either the president or the vice-president must attend. Decisions were to be based upon majority rule. The membership fee was $5, which was to be used for the sole purpose of "aiding the country." New recruits were to be introduced by a member of the society. Thus the Hsing Chung Hui was launched in the free environment of Hawaii among overseas Chinese. But the nature and activities of the Hsing Chung Hui soon transferred it into a totally different setting and structure.

Although the Hsing Chung Hui was founded in Hawaii, its operational base shifted to China. After the establishment of the Honolulu society, Sun Yat-sen had expected to continue to the United States.[24] However, the Sino-Japanese War, which broke out in August, 1894, forced a change in plans. Sun felt that China's repeated defeats at the hands of the Japanese revealed the corruption and weakness of the Ch'ing government, that there existed popular dissatisfaction toward the government, and that a spirit of unrest prevailed. A comrade in China had written Sun urging his return, no doubt sharing Sun's anxiety. All these factors must have had an influence upon Sun's decision to return to China. Sun returned to Hong Kong in January, 1895, with a small group of comrades he had recruited in Ha-

23 Feng Tzu-yu, *op. cit.*, IV, 1-24.
24 *Kuo-fu ch'uan-chi*, I, 32.

waii, as well as a thousand dollars he had collected from the reluctant Hawaiian Chinese.[25]

Sun immediately sought out his former comrades. Ch'en Shao-pai, Sun's schoolmate at the Hong Kong College of Medicine for Chinese, has written that at the time of Sun's return he was at his home in Canton, where Sun found him on Chinese New Year's Day. That same evening Sun and Ch'en returned to Hong Kong to make plans for a revolt in Canton.[26] Another former comrade, Chen Shih-liang, who was living in nearby Macao, and a number of other friends also came to Sun's aid. New recruits were also sought. Members of a patriotic group known as the Fu-jen Wen-she (Fu-jen Literary Society) joined Sun's group.

The Fu-jen Wen-she had been organized by Yang Ch'u-yun, Hsieh Tsuan-t'ai, and fourteen others in Hong Kong in 1892.[27] Its aim was the enlightenment of the people, and its motto was "Ducit Amor Patriae." The group, however, did not participate in direct political activity. They joined Sun and his followers under the banner of the Hsing Chung Hui, a process repeated several times subsequently in Chinese revolutionary history.

The formal union of the Fu-jen Wen-she and the forces of Sun Yat-sen was concluded on February 18, 1895.[28] The Hong

---

[25] Lo Chia-lun, ed., *Ke-min wen-hsien* (Taipei, 1953-1960), III, 284-310. Hereafter cited as *Ke-min wen-hsien*.

[26] Ch'en Shao-pai, *op. cit.*

[27] Yang Ch'u-yun, head of the society, was from Fuchien. He had come to Hong Kong at an early age hoping to become a marine engineer, but had to abandon his career when an accident caused the loss of three right-hand fingers. He learned English, and subsequently taught high school, served as a chief shipping clerk, and in 1895 was an assistant manager in a British shipping company. Hsieh Tsuan-t'ai was an overseas Chinese from Australia, where his father had been in business. Hsieh returned to China in 1887 and while studying in Hong Kong met Yang. See Feng Tzu-yu, *op. cit.*, I, 4-6, and II, 23-25.

[28] On the union of the Fu-jen Wen-she and Sun's forces see C. Hsueh, "Sun Yat-sen, Yang Ch'u-yun, and the Early Revolutionary Movement in China," *Journal of Asian Studies*, XIX, No. 3 (May, 1960), 307-318.

Kong Hsing Chung Hui thus came into being. A manifesto
similar in content to that of the Honolulu Hsing Chung Hui
was issued.[29] All members took an oath "to drive out the Manchu barbarians, restore China to the Chinese, and create a
republic."[30]

The regulations of the Hong Kong Hsing Chung Hui represent a growth and elaboration of the organization and activities
of the revolutionary movement. Some of the more important
provisions were as follows:[31] the Hsing Chung Hui was to have
headquarters in China, with branches to be formed at any place
where there were at least fifteen members; such enterprises as
newspapers and schools were to be provided to educate the
masses; there were to be yearly elections of officers, including
a chairman, a vice-chairman, a treasurer, one Chinese-language
and one English-language secretary, and ten directors; decisions
were to be reached on the basis of full agreement among ten
directors and five members; the membership fee was $5; new
recruits were to be admitted upon the recommendations of two
members.

The Hong Kong Hsing Chung Hui was a fully formed organization, very different from its Honolulu counterpart. The
Honolulu society was an isolated organization; the Hong Kong
society called itself the headquarters of the Hsing Chung Hui
and provided for branches. The Honolulu organization mentioned no activities except the raising of funds; the Hong Kong
group referred to specific activities (e.g., newspapers and
schools) in which the society would engage. The rules and regulations of the Hong Kong Hsing Chung Hui seem to express
a definite policy.

When plans were made to stage the uprising in Canton,[32]
contacts were established with the local Canton secret society,

---

[29] For the full text of the Hong Kong Hsing Chung Hui manifesto see
Ke-min wen-hsien, III, 3-6.

[30] Feng Tzu-yu, *op. cit.*, IV, 64; Lo Chia-lun, *Kuo-fu nien-p'u ch'u-kao*,
I, 56.

[31] *Ke-min wen-hsien*, III, 3-6.

[32] Ch'en Shao-pai, *op. cit.*

which promised to support the revolt with 3,000 men. The brigands around Canton also promised aid. While Sun took personal charge in that area, affairs in Hong Kong were in the hands of Yang Ch'u-yun. The final decision to take Canton was reached on March 16, 1895, but preparations were not completed until October. At the last meeting of the society before the Canton revolt, Sun proposed the immediate election of the president of the society (which had been postponed previously) to whom full authority would be delegated.[33] Sun was elected. However, a division within the ranks almost led to a cancellation of the planned uprising.

The trouble was caused by Yang Ch'u-yun's own presidential ambitions. A few days before the date of the revolt, Yang suddenly ask Sun to relinquish the post of president to him,[34] promising that upon the success of the revolt he would return the position to Sun. According to Ch'en Shao-pai, Sun was stunned.[35] After heated debate, Sun agreed to Yang's demand and relinquished the office, to avoid internal conflict and delay.

The Canton revolt, planned for October 26, 1895, never took place. The plot was discovered by the Ch'ing authorities, and Sun and other members of the group had to flee for their lives. In Hong Kong, Sun, Ch'en, and Chen took the first available ship, which happened to be destined for Japan. Yang left for Southeast Asia, then India, and finally settled in South Africa; everywhere he established branches of the society.[36] The Hong Kong Hsing Chung Hui thus came to a dramatic end, and was not revived until 1899.

Sun, Ch'en, and Chen reached Kobe on November 12, where they read the news of the arrival of "Sun Wen [Sun Yat-sen] of the Chinese Revolutionary Party."[37] Ch'en Shao-pai writes that hitherto they had thought merely in terms of staging an uprising

---

[33] *Ibid.* The president would serve as head of the provisional government if the revolt succeeded.

[34] *Ibid.*

[35] *Ibid.*

[36] Feng Tzu-yu, *op. cit.*, IV, 1-24.

[37] Ch'en Shao-pai, *op. cit.*

to seek reforms. Only those who wanted to become emperors engaged in revolutions. But from that day the word *ke-min* (revolution) became implanted in their minds.[38] The trio moved on
to Yokohama.

In Yokohama, Sun and company soon met a number of Chinese residing in the city. Among them were the Feng brothers,
who owned foreign stationery stores and one of them a printing
plant as well.[39] The eldest, Feng Ching-ju, father of Feng Tzu-
yu, was appointed head of the Yokohama Hsing Chung Hui, and
his younger brother the treasurer. This Hsing Chung Hui seems
to have been another of Sun's independent organizations. Like
the Honolulu and Hong Kong societies, the Yokohama organization was autonomous, with a very loose structure. Indeed,
upon Sun's departure the Yokohama Hsing Chung Hui was to
fall into oblivion.

Sun arrived in Japan a defeated man; he was also a marked
rebel with a price on his head.[40] His first venture in Canton had
ended in failure, and the Ch'ing government sought his capture.
At this critical juncture in his career, from which there was no
turning back, Sun cut his queue, a symbol of submission to the
Ch'ing government, and changed to Western clothing.[41] In effect, he committed himself to the overthrow of the Ch'ing dynasty and the modernization of China.

Sun remained in Japan for only a week.[42] After organizing
the Yokohama Hsing Chung Hui and installing Feng Ching-ju
as head, Sun and Ch'en Shao-pai prepared to leave for the
United States. At the United States consulate, Sun and Ch'en
were informed of the difficulties faced by Chinese who wanted
to enter the United States. The Chinese Exclusion Act of 1882
barred Chinese laborers from entrance into the United States.
According to Ch'en, Sun told the American consul that he was
born in Hawaii and immediately was issued papers to enter the

---

[38] *Ibid.*

[39] Feng Tzu-yu, *op. cit.*, IV, 1-24.

[40] One thousand *yuan* was offered for Sun's capture.

[41] Ch-en Shao-pai, *op. cit.*, I, No. 4 (August 15, 1929), 26-30.

[42] *Ibid.*

United States. Ch'en, having no such excuse, was forced to remain in Japan. However, Sun had one more obstacle to overcome. Apparently Sun, Ch'en, and Chen had come to Japan in a
state of poverty and had been cared for during their stay in
Japan by the local Chinese. Financing the trip to the United
States posed a major problem. In the end Sun secured a loan of
$500 from members of the Yokohama Hsing Chung Hui, a de-
velopment that caused a split in the membership.[43] Sun gave
$100 of this sum to Chen Shih-liang, who subsequently returned
to Hong Kong, another hundred to Ch'en Shao-pai, who remained in Japan, and with the remainder departed for Honolulu on his way to the United States.

The life span of the Yokohama Hsing Chung Hui proved as
brief as that of its Hong Kong counterpart, and evoked little
popular support.[44] The majority of the local Chinese were not
unlike the Hawaiian Chinese in their attitude and viewed with
suspicion and apathy Sun's activities against the Ch'ing government. Fewer than thirty members were recruited. After Sun's
exodus, the society soon became dormant. Ch'en Shao-pai writes
that in the period immediately after Sun's departure the local
members were still enthusiastic. The Feng brothers, one of
whom had been head of the Yokohama Hsing Chung Hui, continued to be active. The death blow, however, was not long in
coming.

The return to Yokohama of the Ch'ing consulate in the spring
of 1895, after the Sino-Japanese War had ended, caused a sudden change in the attitude of the Hsing Chung Hui members.
Fearing interference by the Ch'ing consulate, members severed
their connections with the society. To avoid even guilt by association, the ex-members urged Ch'en to move from Yokohama.[45]

---

[43] Feng Tzu-yu, *op. cit.*, IV, 1-24.

[44] According to Feng Tzu-yu (*ibid.*,), membership was less than thirty.
The exact number of Chinese in Yokohama in 1895 is not known, but it
was estimated at a thousand. See Harley F. MacNair, *The Chinese Abroad*
(Shanghai, 1924), p. 36.

[45] Ch'en felt especially bitter toward the Feng brothers, whom he mentioned by name. Ch'en moved near Tokyo where he lived with a Japanese

Thus the first phase of the Yokohama Hsing Chung Hui and the revolutionary movement in Japan came to an almost ludicrous conclusion.

Meanwhile, Sun Yat-sen was on an extended world tour seeking support for the revolutionary movement. Sun's first port of call was Honolulu. News of his participation in the abortive Canton uprising seems to have caused much excitement in Honolulu, for he soon became a popular speaker, no doubt to relate his revolutionary adventures,[46] but he found few supporters. The Hsing Chung Hui which he had organized in Honolulu in 1894 had long since disintegrated. Most of the old comrades were discouraged because of the Canton failure, and an atmosphere of reaction prevailed among the Hawaiian Chinese. However, an attempt was made to revive the society, and more than a hundred Chinese responded to Sun's call. Most of the new recruits were members of the younger generation, many of whom were Christians. An oath of allegiance was required of new recruits. Their military training consisted of marching with wooden rifles twice weekly. Preparations were made to return to China to engage in the revolutionary movement. Young recruits were plentiful, but the older generation would not offer financial support.[47] After a half-year's stay in Hawaii, during which his family joined him in Honolulu, Sun departed for the United States, and arrived in San Francisco on June 18, 1896.

Sun Yat-sen's first experiences in the United States proved disappointing. He soon discovered that the Chinese in the United States were even more conservative that the Hawaiian Chinese. Commenting on his unresponsive reception, Sun relates: "I crossed the continent from San Francisco to New York. On my

---

friend. Ch'en Shao-pai, *op. cit.*, I, No. 4 (August 15, 1929). Feng Tzu-yu, the son of one of the Feng brothers, accused Ch'en of being unsociable, and thereby contributing to the death of the Yokohama Hsing Chung Hui. See Feng Tzu-yu, *op. cit.*, IV, 1-24.

[46] *Ke-min wen-hsien*, III, 6-12.

[47] When Sun left Hawaii for the United States he had raised only $6,000 from the local Chinese (*ibid.*).

way I stopped at various places for a few days—for ten days at the most—everywhere preaching that to save our mother-country from threatening destruction we must overthrow the Tai-Tsing [Ch'ing] dynasty, and that the duty of every Chinese citizen was to help to reconstruct China on a new democratic basis."[48] He attempted to secure support from the Chinese secret societies in America, but he found that these societies which had originated as anti-Ch'ing organizations in China, had lost their political character and became little more than mutual-aid societies in the free environment of America.[49] Only the Chinese Christians, a small but independent-minded group, sympathized with Sun. In addition to their moral support, Sun received material benefits of food and housing during his sojourn in America.[50] Sun's supporters in the United States were thus few in number.[51]

On September 23 Sun boarded the *S.S. Majestic* for England. His stay in England was dramatized by his imprisonment in the Ch'ing legation in London during October, 1896, and by Sun's own account of it published the following year.[52] As a result, he became an international figure, and the attention of the world was drawn to the Chinese revolutionary movement. From this time on, Sun personified the movement to overthrow the Ch'ing dynasty.

Sun's sojourn in England had its less glamorous phase, that of self-study and observation. After his release from the Ch'ing

[48] Sun Yat-sen, *Memoirs of a Chinese Revolutionary* (Taipei, 1953), p. 147. This is a reprint of the original edition published in Great Britain, 1918.

[49] *Ibid.*

[50] Feng Tzu-yu, *Chung-hua min-kuo k'ai-kuo ch'ien ke-min shih* (Taipei, 1954), p. 37.

[51] The United States was one country where Sun had thus far not established a Hsing Chung Hui organization, although in California alone more than 70,000 Chinese residents were reported in 1890, over 25,000 of whom were in San Francisco. See State of California, Bureau of Labor Statistics, *Eleventh Biennial Report* (Sacramento, 1904), p. 73.

[52] Sun Yat-sen, *Kidnapped in London.*

legation, he spent many hours reading in the British Museum in London.[53] During this period, in Sun's words, ". . . arose my so-called 'san-min chu-i,' or the idea of democracy based upon the three principles."[54]

In England we have the beginning of Sun Yat-sen's three peo-ple's principles. The platforms of the Honolulu and Hong Kong Hsing Chung Hui were restricted to the three slogans of expel-ling the Manchus, restoring China to the Chinese, and creating a republic. The socio-economic reforms hinted at in Sun's letter to Li Hung-chang were not stressed. During his stay in London, Sun systematically developed his socio-economic and political principles against the background of Western environment. Eu-rope in the late nineteenth century was at the height of the democratic movement. In England the rise of Liberal Labour and Fabianism was evident. Sun was also introduced to the single-tax theory of Henry George during this period. Contact with other revolutionary exiles played its part in the develop-ment of Sun's political and economic theories.[55] This was a period of observation and absorption of Western ideas.

Upon his departure from England in May, 1897, Sun re-turned to Japan via Canada, arriving in Yokohama early in

---

[53] Lo Chia-lun, *Chung-shan hsien-sheng Lun-tun pei-nan shih-liao k'ao-ting* (Shanghai, 1930). Lo's work contains the full report (in English) on Sun by Slaters' Detective Association, which was hired by the London Ch'ing legation to observe Sun's movements. Reporting on Sun's activities between February 16 and March 2, 1897, Slaters' noted ". . . he has on each day invariably proceeded to the British Museum where he remains the greater part of the day, taking his meals in the Refreshment Room" (pp. 134-135).

[54] Sun Yat-sen, *Memoirs of a Chinese Revolutionary*, p. 150.

[55] There is no record of such contacts in England. Many years later, Sun related the following story: "When I was in Europe I met a certain mem-ber of the Russian Revolutionary Party. He asked me how many years it would take for the Chinese revolution to succeed. I answered him that it would take thirty years. . . . I then asked him how long it would take for the revolution in Russia to succeed. He replied . . . that even if he were to engage in revolution day and night from that time on, it would take all of a hundred years," See *Kuo-fu ch'uan-chi*, III, 260-261.

August. The Yokohama Hsing Chung Hui which Sun had helped organize in 1895 had become inactive. Sun's return did not cause an immediate regeneration of enthusiasm among the local Chinese. During Sun's absence in America and England, Ch'en Shao-pai had remained in Japan and had come into contact with a group of Japanese interested in China.[56] Upon Sun's return, the relationship between the Chinese revolutionary movement led by Sun and the Japanese adventurers became more intimate.[57] Miyazaki Torazo became a long-time supporter of Sun and participated actively in the revolutionary movement. A close relationship also developed between the revolutionary movement led by Sun and the antidynastic movement of the Chinese secret societies.

The history of the Chinese revolutionary movement from the founding of the Hsing Chung Hui to the 1911 revolution can be recorded partly in terms of the activities of the Chinese secret societies in alliance with the predecessors of the Kuomintang, both within China and among the overseas Chinese. Secret societies have had a long history in China. Their origins have been traced to the alliance among Lu Pei, Chang Fei, and Kuan Yu of the Three Kingdoms period (220-264 A.D.). A secret society of more recent origin is the Hung-meng (Hung Society), which began during the Ch'ing dynasty in the late seventeenth century.[58] The Hung-meng was divided into a number of in-

---

[56] Ch'en writes that he met the Japanese adventurers through Sugawara Den, a Japanese Christian minister whom Sun had met in Hawaii in 1894. Through Sugawara, Ch'en was introduced to Sone Toshitora, a former naval officer. Sone in turn introduced Ch'en to Miyazaki Torazo. See Ch'en Shao-pai, *op. cit.*, I, No. 5 (September 15, 1929), 13-18.

[57] For an account of the relation between Sun and the Japanese adventurers see Marius B. Jansen, *The Japanese and Sun Yat-sen* (Cambridge, 1954).

[58] An extensive literature, both Chinese and English, is available on the Hung-meng. In Chinese, Chu Lin's *Hung-meng chi* (Shanghai, 1947); Hsiao I-shan, ed., *Chin-tai pi-mi she-hui shih-liao* (Peking, 1935); and Wei Chu-hsien, *Chung-kuo ti pang-hui* (China's Secret Societies), (Chungking, 1949). In English the most detailed is John S. M. Ward and W. G. Stirling, *The Hung Society or the Society of Heaven and Earth* (London,

dependent groups. In central China, covering most of the central and lower portions of the Yangtse River region, the Hung-meng was popularly known as the Ko-lao Hui; in south China, Kwangtung and Fuchien, and among the Chinese in Southeast Asia, it was referred to as T'ien-ti Hui, San-ho Hui, or San-tien Hui; in the Americas and Hawaii it was generally known as the Chih Kung T'ang. It was with these and other secret societies that the Hsing Chung Hui and its successor the T'ung Meng Hui became associated.

Since no ruling house in traditional China tolerated opposition, its opponents have had recourse only to secret societies. The Hung-meng seems to have originated as an antidynastic movement.[59] Its history is usually traced to a group of Ming remnants who in the late seventeenth and early eighteenth centuries organized it as an anti-Ch'ing secret society with the slogan of "Overthrow the Ch'ing, Restore the Ming." The Hung-meng derived its major support from the nonliterati social classes in Chinese society, as well as from the overseas Chinese. However, with the passage of time the Hung-meng, while engaging in sporadic revolts and retaining its slogan, lost much of its vigor and purpose. This was especially true of the overseas groups. In the Americas, the Hung-meng Chih Kung T'ang became more of a mutual-aid society than an antidynastic revolutionary organization. Nevertheless, such secret societies remained popular among the lower classes. The Hung-meng was thus a potential source of support to any organization or person who could provide leadership and redirect it toward its original goal. The Hsing Chung Hui sought to become such an organization.

The alliance between the Hsing Chung Hui and the Chinese secret societies dates from the Canton coup of 1895. Contact with the secret society was sought as a source of popular support. However, since the revolt failed, nothing came of this brief al-

---

1925-1926). For a recent work see L. F. Comber, *Chinese Secret Societies in Malaya* (Locust Valley, New York, 1959).

[59] Chu Lin, *op. cit.*; Hsiao I-shan, *op. cit.*

liance. Some of Sun's original supporters, among them Chen Shih-liang, were members of secret societies and had introduced Sun to them and to their history.[60] The real beginning of co-operation between the revolutionary forces of the Hsing Chung Hui and the secret societies, both in China proper and among the overseas Chinese, took place toward the end of the nineteenth century.

This period witnessed a renewal of the revolutionary activities of the Hsing Chung Hui. This renewed burst of energy may be in part attributed to the appearance of a force which competed with the Hsing Chung Hui for the loyalties of the Chinese and, more important, for the leadership in the race to reform China. This rival force was headed by K'ang Yu-wei and his disciple Liang Ch'i-ch'ao, who appeared on the scene in Japan after the abortive Hundred Days' Reform in 1898. When K'ang Yu-wei arrived in Japan, talks were held between the Sun and K'ang forces on the possibility of an alliance.[61] But K'ang considered himself "obligated" to the young emperor who had initiated K'ang's reforms. No cooperation between the two groups was thus possible. The Pao-huang Hui (Emperor Protection Society), founded by K'ang, soon began to compete actively with Sun's Hsing Chung Hui for support of forces both within China and abroad. This struggle became world-wide in scope. In the Chinese communities in Canada, the United States, and Southeast Asia, the followers of Sun and K'ang battled with words and sometimes with their fists for the support, chiefly financial, of the overseas Chinese. For a while the K'ang forces held the upper hand, threatening to drive Sun and his supporters into oblivion. However, the challenge of the Pao-

---

[60] Sun possessed a full knowledge of the role of secret societies in Chinese history and did not hesitate to pay them homage. In his *Hsin-li chien-she* (Psychological Construction), he credited the Hung-meng with keeping alive the idea of nationalism among the people. See *Kuo-fu ch'uan-chi*, II, 83.

[61] The Japanese adventurers who had been instrumental in bringing K'ang Yu-wei and Liang Chi'i-ch'ao to Japan were also seeking to bring K'ang and Sun together. See Jansen, *op. cit.*, pp. 74-81.

huang Hui only sparked the fire of revolution within Sun and
his followers. Thus, toward the end of the nineteenth century,
with divisions within and challenge from without, the revolutionary movement under the Hsing Chung Hui banner renewed
its drive toward its goal—the overthrow of the Ch'ing dynasty
and the reform of China.

The revival of the revolutionary movement was initiated on
two fronts: contacts with secret societies were renewed and a
propaganda organ was set up. The Hong Kong Hsing Chung
Hui's regulations of 1896 called for the establishment of newspapers for the dissemination of revolutionary propaganda. With
Japanese assistance, the *Chung-kuo Jih-pao* was started by Ch'en
Shao-pai in Hong Kong in 1899.[62] Ch'en also reorganized the
old comrades while recruiting new supporters in preparation
for a second uprising. To obtain support from the secret societies Ch'en found he had to become a member, and joined the
local Hung-meng society, the San-ho Hui, in Hong Kong.[63]

Pi Yung-nien, a Ko-lao Hui "dragonhead," a title given to
secret society leaders, had joined the Hsing Chung Hui in Japan
in 1898.[64] It is reported that he informed Sun on the activities
and strength of the secret society in central China. In 1899 Pi
and Hirayama Shiu, a Japanese adventurer and friend of Sun's,
were dispatched to investigate the true strength of the secret societies in central China. Their report, highly favorable, resulted
in Pi's return to China, where he secured the support of leaders
of the Ko-lao Hui in Hunan and Hupeh.[65] In November, 1899,
Pi brought a group of seven Ko-lao Hui "dragonheads" from
Hunan and Hupeh to Hong Kong, where they were entertained
by Ch'en Shao-pai and introduced to leaders of the southern
San-ho Hui. Later in that same month the Hsing Chung Hui,
the San-ho Hui, and the Ko-lao Hui combined to found the

---

[62] Ch-en Shao-pai, *op. cit.*, II, No. 3 (January, 1930), 46-51.

[63] *Ibid.*

[64] Feng Tzu-yu, *Ke-min i-shih*, I, 73-76.

[65] For a report on the Chinese secret societies see Hirayama Shiu, *Chung-
kuo pi-mi she-hui shih* (Shanghai, 1934). This is a Chinese translation of
the Japanese original.

Hsing Han Hui (Revive Han Society) with Sun Yet-sen as its leader.[66] By obtaining the support of the San-ho Hui and the Ko-lao Hui, the arm of the Hsing Chung Hui reached into central as well as southern China. But this alliance proved a brief one, owing to competition from the Pao-huang Hui group for support of the secret societies. The Ko-lao Hui leaders in Hunan and Hupeh deserted the Hsing Han Hui to join K'ang's camp. With this change the Hsing Chung Hui lost its contacts in central China, not to be reestablished until the founding of the T'ung Meng Hui in 1905.

Besides losing the support of the Ko-lao Hui in central China to the followers of K'ang Yu-wei, Sun and the Hsing Chung Hui met defeat on the battlefield. A planned uprising at Waichow Kwangtung, in October, 1900, ended in failure.[67] An attempt to persuade Li Hung-chang, then governor-general of Kwangtung, to declare the province independent from the Manchus was also without results.[68] The Hsing Chung Hui suffered further losses among its overseas supporters to the Pao-huang Hui. Feng Tzu-yu reports that by 1903 in Yokohama, where Sun was residing, the Hsing Chung Hui had less than twenty members,[69] for the majority of the local Chinese supported K'ang's Pao-huang Hui. Similar conditions prevailed in other overseas Chinese communities.

In 1903 Sun left Japan for another trip to Hawaii and the United States. With the Waichow failure and the loss of supporters in Japan behind him, Sun arrived in Hawaii in October, 1903. In Honolulu, where he had established the first Hsing Chung Hui in 1894, Sun found that the local Chinese had deserted it for K'ang's Pao-huang Hui.[70] Sun attempted to reacti-

---

[66] Ch'en Shao-pai, *op. cit.*, II, No. 3 (January, 1930).

[67] The Waichow revolt was carried out under Chen Shih-liang. It was supported by bandits and secret society members. Initially successful, it failed when aid from the Japanese did not materialize. See Feng Tzu-yu, *Ke-min i-shih*, V, 16.

[68] Ch-en Shao-pai, *op. cit.*, II, No. 3 (January, 1930).

[69] Feng Tzu-yu, *Ke-min i-shih*, IV, 1-24.

[70] In part this was Sun's own doing. When Liang Ch'i-ch'ao went to

vate the local Hsing Chung Hui, but, except for a number of
Christians, few answered his call. Sun also looked for assistance
from a more traditional source: a Chinese secret society. In December, 1903, Sun took the oath of "Overthrow the Ch'ing, Restore the Ming" and became a member of the Chih Kung T'ang,
the Hung-meng secret society as it was known in the Americas
and Hawaii.[71]

After five months' stay in Hawaii, Sun departed for the
United States. In San Francisco, where Sun arrived on March
31, 1904, he was immediately imprisoned by the American custom authorities.[72] However, through the efforts of the San Francisco Chinese Christians and the secret society Chih Kung
T'ang, Sun was released. He proceeded to recruit members for
the Hsing Chung Hui. His first objective was the local Chinese
Christian community which had just rescued him from the
American customs. At a meeting held at the Chinese Presby-
terian Center on Stockton Street,[73] Sun explained his principles,
and sold revolutionary bonds. Each bond sold for ten dollars,
which would be repaid ten times upon the success of the revolution; the purchaser would automatically become a member in
the Hsing Chung Hui. Sun raised $4,000 in this way. However,
even the Chinese Christians were unwilling to associate openly
with Sun and his movement, and refused to become members
of the Hsing Chung Hui. Only one member was recruited,
K'uang Hau-t'ai, better known as Walter N. Fong, who had
served as a Chinese assistant in Oriental languages at the University of California, Berkeley, between 1900 and 1902.[74]

Honolulu in 1899 he had asked Sun for a letter of introduction. Soon
Liang won over the local Chinese to the cause of the Pao-huang Hui. Feng
Tzu-yu, *Ke-min i-shih*, IV, 1-24.

[71] Lo Chia-lun, *Kuo-fu nien-p'u ch'u-kao*, pp. 127-128.

[72] Feng Tzu-yu, *Ke-min i-shih*, II, 101-124.

[73] *Ibid.*; Feng Tzu-yu, *Hua-ch'iao ke-min tsu-chih shih-hua* (Taipei,
1954), p. 25.

[74] K'uang Hau-t'ai (Walter N. Fong) and Sun were already acquainted,
perhaps having met during Sun's first trip to the United States in 1896.
This is confirmed by two letters intercepted by the detective agency hired

Sun turned next to the Chih Kung T'ang, the Chinese secret society in the Americas. Although preserving the slogan of "Overthrow the Ch'ing, Restore the Ming," it had lost most of its political compulsion. Transplanted into the free American society, the Chih Kung T'ang, as Sun recalled, "had been reduced to little more than mutual-aid clubs."[75] What was supposed to have been a tightly controlled structure had become a loosely organized body. In theory the branches scattered throughout the United States were subject to the jurisdiction of the society's headquarters in San Francisco. In fact the Chih Kung T'ang branches had become independent entities. No doubt Sun saw that the Chih Kung T'ang could greatly assist the revolutionary movement, especially financially, if it were properly organized. This he set out to do. Having become a member in Honolulu, Sun had direct access to the secret society. His proposal to reorganize and register members was accepted by the San Francisco Chih Kung T'ang leaders. Sun estimated that if each member would pay the two-dollar registration fee,

by the London Ch'ing legation. Passing through Montreal, Canada, on his way to Japan on July 12, 1897, Sun wrote to two friends in the United States. The first, addressed to a Mr. Chew in Boston (?), asked, "Can you do anything in Boston and New York with our patriots to help us in China?" Sun said he would be continuing on to Vancouver and hoped to hear from Chew. However, "I cannot give you my address now and you can post them [Chew's letters to Sun] in care of Mr. Walter N. Fong, 916 Washington St., San Francisco. He will forward [the letters] to me when he gets my address in Vancouver." The second letter was addressed to K'uang (Fong):

"I arrived here this morning from England en route for Vancouver and the Far East. I did not accomplish anything of importance during my sojourn in England but our members in China have done a good deal for the cause and call to join them there to plan the future movement.

"How are you getting on with the members in San Francisco? Can you do anything to help us in China?

"I should like to hear from you. . . .

"When I get to Vancouver I shall send you my address so that we can exchange a few messages during my stay there."

See Lo Chia-lun, Chung-shan hsien-sheng . . . , pp. 157-158.

[75] Sun Yat-sen, Memoirs of a Chinese Revolutionary, p. 147.

over $20,000 could be raised.[76] Sun also reorganized the society's newspaper, the *Ta Tung Pao*.[77] New regulations called for the assertion of headquarters' authority over the branches and a unity of purpose by all. Sun sought to reawaken the American Chih Kung T'ang to its original political objective; he also introduced his socio-economic principles. The object of the reorganized Chih Kung T'ang was to "expel the Manchu barbarians, restore China to the Chinese, establish a republic, and equalize land rights."[78] However, at a meeting sponsored by the San Francisco Chih Kung T'ang, Sun emphasized the traditional nationalistic sentiment on a theme of patriotism.

In San Francisco's Chinatown, on May 3, 1904, speaking before a crowd of several thousand on the issue of the Han (Chinese) people versus the Manchu race, Sun declared that the Han people should be loyal to China and not to the Ch'ing government.[79] Several days later he repeated his plea for a union of the Han people to overthrow the Ch'ing government and to restore China to the Chinese.[80] A third speech by Sun, on May 15, was a call to arms.[81] Manchu rule, Sun claimed, was leading to the partition of China by foreign powers; the tide of revolution was increasing daily, and all loyal Chinese should join the revolutionary party. The *Chung-sai Yat-po* reported that on this occasion Sun had an even larger audience with standing room only.[82]

In May, 1904, Sun departed on a campaign tour which took

---

[76] Feng Tzu-yu, *Hua-ch'iao ke-min tsu-chih shih-hua*, pp. 25-26.

[77] *Ibid.* The *Ta Tung Pao* had been edited by a member of the Paohuang Hui. Sun changed this; he wrote Feng, who introduced Liu Ch'eng-yu, a Hupeh student who had just been expelled from Japan for partaking in anti-Ch'ing activities by the Ch'ing minister to Tokyo. Liu later served as intermediary between Sun and the Hupeh students in Europe.

[78] Feng Tzu-yu, *Ke-min i-shih*, I, 136-164.

[79] *Chung-sai Yat-po*, May 9, 1904, p. 2.

[80] *Ibid.*

[81] *Ibid.*, May 16, 1904, pp. 1-2.

[82] *Ibid.*

him into Chinese communities from California to New York.[83] Traveling with Sun was Huang San-te, a San Francisco Chih Kung T'ang leader. Together they spent five months in an attempt to awaken the Chinese in America to the evils of the Ch'ing government, the need for its overthrow, and the necessity of organizing to achieve the desired goal. But Sun's attempt to secure the backing of the Chinese secret society ended in failure.

Sun's failure has been attributed to the popularity of K'ang Yu-wei's Pao-huang Hui among the Chinese in America during this period.[84] Huang San-te blames Sun's "lack of knowledge and poor speech."[85] However, other factors also were responsible: the separation of the Chinese in America from their former environment while busily engaged in earning a livelihood in a new surrounding; and the traditional political apathy of the Chinese peasant (from which the American Chinese were derived). The tour was a complete financial fiasco as well. When Sun left the United States for Europe in December, 1904, he had to be assisted financially.[86]

While the Hsing Chung Hui met defeat on the battlefield and was being challenged by the Pao-huang Hui, Sun Yat-sen had failed in his overseas mission. However, this discouraged neither Sun nor, apparently, his small band of followers. With support from the growing body of Chinese students studying abroad, a new revolutionary organization was soon founded.

The Hsing Chung Hui period represented the embryonic stage in the development of the Kuomintang. The Hsing Chung Hui was the work of only a handful of men and, in particular, the promotion of one man, Sun Yat-sen. Those who

---

[83] Feng Tzu-yu, Ke-min i-shih, I, 136-164; for a personal account of the tour see Huang San-te, Hung-meng ke-min shih (n.p., 1936).

[84] Feng Tzu-yu, Ke-min i shih, I, 136-164.

[85] Huang San-te, op. cit., p. 12.

[86] It is not certain who paid for Sun's European tour. Huang maintains that he did. Feng says that the Chinese students in Europe assisted Sun, but the students claim no such thing.

participated in the founding of the Hsing Chung Hui shared
one characteristic; a Western background. Almost every member of the party had received a foreign education or was a
Chinese residing abroad. Many were also Christians. The overwhelming extrinsic nature of the membership was reflected in
the goal of the society. From the beginning, the Hsing Chung
Hui sought to break the dynastic pattern and establish a republican form of government.

If the membership composition of the new party was "foreign," the Hsing Chung Hui as a party further strengthened this
characteristic. The party was founded overseas, first in Honolulu and then in Hong Kong, Japan, and wherever a sufficient
number of Chinese abroad responded. The organization of the
party was very simple. However, there seems to have been no
connection among the various units; each was independent of
the other. The primary link among the several Hsing Chung
Hui's and their members was Sun Yat-sen.

The Hsing Chung Hui, being primarily an "overseas" party
with a membership of overseas Chinese, was forced at a very
early date to seek assistance. While the Hsing Chung Hui as a
party cooperated with the secret societies, individual Hsing
Chung Hui members also joined them. Foreign assistance was
also sought. Nevertheless, the Hsing Chung Hui failed in its
endeavors to overthrow the Ch'ing and establish a republican
form of government. One reason for the Hsing Chung Hui's
failure was the lack of response to its mission, both among the
Chinese abroad and in China.

II PARTIES OF TRANSITION:
THE T'UNG MENG HUI

THE FOUNDING of the T'ung Meng Hui in 1905 represented the beginning of popular participation by China's intelligentsia in the revolutionary movement and an expansion of the revolutionary basis. Hitherto, the mainstay of the movement to overthrow the Ch'ing government had been the secret societies and the overseas Chinese. Both proved to be undependable and unresponsive. Indeed, on the eve of Sun Yat-sen's departure for Europe in December, 1904, the revolutionary movement seemed to have failed. Yet, by the fall of 1905, new groups had come to the support of Sun's activities, a new alliance had been formed, and new vigor had been injected into the movement.

The new vitality of the revolutionary movement came primarily from the student class. The attitude of the Chinese intelligentsia in general and Chinese students in particular during the years when Sun and the Hsing Chung Hui were staging uprisings and planning revolts was perhaps best exemplified by Wu Chih-hui. Wu, trained in the classics and a *chu-jen* (second degree graduate), at first scorned Sun because he was not a classical scholar and a man of letters; he regarded Sun's movement

as little more than the work of brigands.[1] When Wu was in
Japan in 1901, friends invited him to meet Sun. Recalling the
episode years later, Wu remarked that he was rather startled at
the invitation, no doubt feeling that men of learning should not
lower themselves by associating with "illiterates." Wu replied
that he was not even going to call upon Liang Ch'i-ch'ao, who
was also in Japan at the time, so why should he consider visiting
Sun? The attitude of China's learned class toward Sun explains
in part K'ang Yu-wei's and Liang Ch'i-ch'ao's initial success,
both among China's intelligentsia and the overseas Chinese.
Both were members of the traditional, prestigeful, scholarly
class. However, K'ang and Liang found themselves defending an
"alien" government upon which all the ills of China were
blamed. China's exposed weaknesses, her "partition" by the
Western powers and defeat by Japan, inflamed the hearts of
men. The increasing exposure of China to world currents—democracy, socialism, science, and many others—speeded up the
tempo for China's modernization.

At the turn of the century, political consciousness was increasing among China's intelligentsia, especially the rise of nationalism. The traditionally aloof scholarly class became vocal in
expression and militant in conduct. Under the watchful eye of
the Ch'ing government, students in Hupeh and Hunan gathered secretly, some under the protection of the Catholic Church,
to plot against the "alien" dynasty.[2] Meanwhile, in 1902 Chang
Ping-lin, Ts'ai Yuan-p'ei, and other members of the intelligentsia founded the Ai-kuo Hsueh-she (Patriotic Society) in Shanghai which became a center for revolutionary ideas. In 1903
Chou Yung, a Szechwan student recently returned from Japan,
published the famous inflammatory anti-Manchu pamphlet, *Ke-
min chun*,[3] which landed him in prison. However, if members

---

[1] Chang Wen-pe, *Chih-lao hsien-hua* (Taipei, 1952), p. 24.

[2] Chu Ho-chung in *Ke-min wen-hsien*, ed. by Lo Chia-lun (Taipei,
1953), II, 251-270. Hereafter cited as *Ke-min wen-hsien*.

[3] For a reprinted copy see Chou Yung, *Ke-min chun* (Revolutionary
Army) (Shanghai, 1958).

of the Chinese intelligentsia in China were outspoken against
the Ch'ing government and plotted for its overthrow, Chinese
students abroad became even more violent in their hatred of the
Manchus.

Between 1872 and 1900 select students had been sent overseas[4] by the central government and the provincial administrations to gain Western knowledge.[5] However, it was not until the
turn of the century that the Ch'ing government sanctioned
study abroad on a wide scale. Soon Chinese students were to be
found in major centers of learning in Japan, Europe, and America. Certain provincial administrations also ordered known
"radicals" abroad to relieve political pressure at home.[6] Whereas
their associates in China gathered in secret, Chinese students
abroad could meet openly in defiance of the Ch'ing government. Japan eventually became the center for Chinese students
abroad, and subsequently the headquarters for the revolutionary movement. However, Sun Yat-sen's first open support from
the intelligentsia came from the student radicals in Europe.

Chu Ho-chung and Ho Chih-ts'ai, two students from Hupeh
who had been ordered to Europe, learned of Sun's presence in
England through Liu Ch'eng-yu, who was also from Hupeh and
who was serving as editor of the San Francisco *Ta Tung Jih Po*.
According to Chu Ho-chung, who was in Berlin, Liu wrote that
Sun was staying with Dr. Cantlie in London and was in a state

---

[4] For an account of Chinese students studying abroad see Shu Hsin-
ch'eng, *Chin-tai Chung-kuo liu-hsueh shih* (Shanghai, 1933).

[5] Between 1872 and 1881, selected Chinese youths were sent to the
United States for foreign training, but the program was terminated when
the Ch'ing authorities learned that the students were becoming too Westernized. From 1881 to 1900 a limited number of students were sent abroad
by provincial administrations (e.g., Hupeh and Szechwan) and by the
military.

[6] A group of so-called radicals from the provinces of Hupeh and Hunan
were ordered overseas by local authorities in the winter of 1903 for partaking in antigovernmental activities. According to Chu Ho-chung, the
"extremists" were ordered to Europe, and the "moderates" were dispatched
to Japan. Chu was ordered to Germany. See Chung Ho-chung, *op. cit.*; also
Feng Tzu-yu, *Ke-min i-shih* (Taipei, 1953), II, 132-141.

of poverty.[7] Liu hoped that Chu and other Chinese students in Europe could assist Sun financially. Chu sent 1,200 marks to Sun, and Ho Chih-ts'ai in Belgium also dispatched funds and invited Sun to travel to the continent.[8] Sun accepted the invitation and with funds provided by the Chinese students in Europe arrived in Brussels in the spring of 1905.[9]

Chu Ho-chung, who had come from Berlin to welcome Sun, reports that a meeting of Sun with a group of Chinese students lasted three days and three nights.[10] This was an important gathering which decided the new strategy of the revolutionary movement, which was to place less dependence upon secret societies and increased reliance upon the intelligentsia. Sun, arguing that neither the intelligentsia nor the military were dependable revolutionary sources, stressed the importance of secret societies. The students countered by referring to the conduct of the secret societies as mere plundering. Chu Ho-chung questioned the use of illiterate secret societies, and attributed Sun's repeated failures to his lack of support among the intelligentsia. Sun, however, pointed to Shih Chien-jo and Lu Hao-tung as examples of revolutionary members who were scholars.[11] Chu replied that a few scholars would not help the cause, but if the assistance of the majority of the intelligentsia were obtained, half of the work of the revolution would have been achieved. On the third day, Sun decided that henceforth the revolution-

---

[7] Chu Ho-chung, op. cit.

[8] Feng Tzu-yu, op. cit., II, 132-141.

[9] No record exists of the date of Sun's arrival in Belgium from England in 1905. Indeed, the whole of his stay in Europe is unaccounted for in terms of precise dates. Lo Chia-lun, ed., Kuo-fu nien-p'u ch'u-kao (Taipei, 1958), I, 140 (hereafter cited as Kuo-fu nien-p'u ch'u-kao), merely lists Sun's stay in Europe as the spring and summer of 1905.

[10] Chu Ho-chung, op. cit.

[11] Lu Hao-tung was one of Sun's early supporters in Hong Kong; he was arrested and put to death after the failure of the Canton uprising of 1895. Shih Chien-jo was introduced into the Hsing Chung Hui by Ch'en Shao-pai. In 1900 he attempted to assassinate the governor-general of Kwangtung. The plan failed and Shih was captured and put to death.

ary movement would concentrate on the overseas student
groups. He asked those who agreed with him to take an oath "to
expel the Manchus, restore China to the Chinese, establish a
republic, and equalize land rights."[12] Over thirty Chinese students at Brussels complied. A new revolutionary alliance thus
came into being.

Students in England, Germany, and France also joined the
revolutionary ranks. After Sun's successful visit to Brussels, he
returned to London, but only one student answered Sun's call.
Upon the invitation of Chu Ho-chung, Sun traveled next to
Germany. In Berlin, as in Brussels, he held discussions with the
students. After questioning him at length about his principle of
equalization of land and the five-power constitution,[13] some
twenty students took the oath.[14] Sun concluded his European
recruiting adventures with a trip to Paris, where ten students
were converted to the revolutionary cause.

In forming the student revolutionary alliances in Europe, it
is significant that Sun did not utilize the name of the still-exist-
ing Hsing Chung Hui. Nor was the T'ung Meng Hui, which
was introduced later in the year in Japan, mentioned. Perhaps
the students objected to the close ties between the Hsing Chung
Hui and the secret society groups. To be associated with, not to
mention dominated by, the secret societies had always been considered degrading by the Chinese intelligentsia. The European
Chinese students were well aware of the influence of the secret
societies on the Hsing Chung Hui which Sun had stressed during his first encounter with the students in Brussels. No doubt
to placate them, no mention was made of the Hsing Chung Hui
when the student alliances were established; they were called
simply "revolutionary parties."

Disaster almost immediately struck the newly organized student revolutionary groups in Europe. Wang Fa-k'o, who had

---

[12] Feng Tzu-yu, *op. cit.* II, 137; Chu Ho-chung, *op. cit.*

[13] Chu Ho-chung, *op. cit.*

[14] *Ibid.*; Liu Kuang-ch'ien, in *Kuo-fu nien-p'u ch'u-kao*, I, 142-143.

joined the alliance in Berlin, influenced other members to withdraw from the clandestine group.[15] In Paris they sought to re-
tract their membership certificates, which were in Sun's possession. Certain that Sun would reject their request, Wang and
his companions broke open Sun's briefcase and took back their
membership certificates. The briefcase contained also a full
record of the student revolutionary groups in Europe, with a
membership list, and correspondence between Sun and the
French governmental authorities concerning possible French assistance to the revolutionary forces in Indo-China. Not satisfied
with regaining their own certificates, Wang and the others stole
the various documents and delivered them to Sun Pao-ch'i, the
Ch'ing minister in Paris.[16] The revolutionary activities which
Sun and the students had labored over were thus threatened.

The disclosure of the European revolutionary activities created a crisis within the ranks. Sun considered the affair the most
serious setback to the revolutionary cause since his kidnap in
London in 1896. He was concerned over the disclosure of the
membership lists of student groups to the Ch'ing authorities,
for the lives of several scores of comrades were at stake. He was
also apprehensive that the negotiations with the French government would elicit a strong protest from the Ch'ing government.
Above all, he feared that the recently established contact with
the intelligentsia-student class might be lost.[17]

The student revolutionary groups were badly shaken by the
defection of their members and the disclosures to the Ch'ing
minister. A re-registration of members was begun, and, as a
result of the incident, membership in the student revolutionary
groups fell off. A small band of diehards, chiefly students from
Hupeh, remained loyal to Sun and the revolutionary cause.[18]
Two of them, Ho Chih-ts'ai and Shih Ch'ing, students ordered

[15] Chu Ho-chung, *op. cit.*, pp. 120-126; Feng Tzu-yu, *op. cit.*, II, 136-137.

[16] Sun Pao-ch'i, after taking down the information contained in the various documents, ordered them all returned to Sun Yat-sen. See Feng Tzu-yu,
op. cit., II, 139.

[17] *Ibid.*

[18] The re-registration after the reorganization of the student revolutionary groups found the following remaining members: in Belgium, 10 of the

to Europe from Hupeh, later founded a revolutionary organ known as the Kun-min Tang in Belgium.[19] The Kun-min Tang served as a contact and training organization for prospective members. Except for the provision calling for the equalization of land rights, the Kun-min Tang shared the principles of the parent organization: "expel the barbarians, restore China, [and] found a republic."[20]

The revolutionary movement gained momentum with the support of the Chinese students in Japan. By 1906 nearly 10,000 Chinese, either government-dispatched or privately supported, were studying in Japan.[21] Geographical propinquity, financial considerations, cultural kinship, and Japan's success in modernization made Japan the first choice for Chinese seeking to acquire Western knowledge. The Chinese students in Japan were from a varied background, ranging from sons of Manchu nobles to descendants of Chinese peasants.[22] Politically their background was equally diverse. There were government officials as well as leaders of revolutionary societies who had taken part in anti-Ch'ing revolts. Some concentrated on their studies without regard to political events; others participated in meetings and demonstrations. And while a number of them worshiped everything Japanese, some found Japan disappointing and looked to the political system and culture of Europe and the United States. However, within this mass of diversity, the majority of the Chinese students agreed on the need for the reformation of China.

The political outlook of the Chinese students in Japan had

original group of more than 30; in France, only 1 of the original more than 10; in Germany, 3 of the original more than 20. See Feng Tzu-yu, *op. cit.*, II, 139.

[19] *Ibid.*, II, 140.

[20] *Ibid.*

[21] Shu Hsin-ch'eng, *op. cit.*, pp. 46-71, 279. According to Saneto Keishu, the number of Chinese studying in Japan was largest in 1905 and 1906, when 8,000 Chinese students were reported studying at Japanese institutions of learning. See Saneto Keishu, *Chukokujin Nihon ryugaku shi* (Tokyo, 1960), pp. 55-62.

[22] The following account is taken primarily from *Ke-min wen-shien*, III, 385.

undergone a radical transformation between 1900 and 1905. In 1899 Chinese students in Japan had organized the Li-chih She (Determined Society), which engaged primarily in translations of foreign works.[23] In 1900 a dispute occurred within the Li-chih She between students advocating revolution as the means of reforming China and those who opposed such a solution. The revolutionary faction formed a separate student association, the Ch'ing-nien Hui (Young Men's Association), which began to challenge Ch'ing authority openly. In August, 1902, a group led by Wu Chih-hui marched on the Ch'ing legation in Tokyo, demonstrating against the Ch'ing minister's refusal to recommend private students to military academies.[24] The police dispersed the students and Wu was banished from Japan for "disturbing the peace."[25] In January, 1903, more than a thousand students gathered to celebrate Chinese New Year's Day. Both the Ch'ing minister and the student supervisor were present. Ma Chun-wu, a student from Kwangsi, delivered a speech on "the history of the Manchu annexation of China."[26] Then Liu Ch'eng-yu argued that nothing less "than the expulsion of Manchu absolutism and the restoration of Han sovereignty" could save China. For his speech against the Manchus, Liu was subsequently dismissed from school by the Ch'ing minister.[27] The students also published a number of journals strongly nationalistic in tone and anti-Manchu in sentiment.[28] Journalistic propaganda combined with open defiance of the Ch'ing authorities soon led to direct action against the Ch'ing government.

---

[23] Chang Chi, *Chang P'u-ch'uan hsien-sheng ch'uan-chi* (Taipei, 1951), p. 232; Feng Tzu-yu, *Chung-hua min-kuo k'ai-kuo ch'ien ke-min shih* (Taipei, 1954), I, 55.

[24] Chang Wen-po, *op. cit.*, pp. 13-14; Shu Hsin-ch'eng, *op. cit.*, p. 27.

[25] Chang Wen-po, *op. cit.*, p. 14.

[26] Feng Tzu-yu, *Chung-hua min-kuo . . .* , p. 56.

[27] *Ibid.*; see also Liu Ch'eng-yu's account of the episode abstracted in *Kuo-fu nien-p'u ch'u-kao*, I, 117.

[28] For a sample of the student journals (published in Tokyo), consult *Hupeh Hsueh-sheng Chiai* (Hupeh Students' Circle), 1902; *Chekiang Ch'ao* (The Tide of Chekiang), 1903; *Chiangsu*, 1903; *Erh-shih Shih-chi Chih Chih-na* (The Twentieth Century China), 1905.

The spirit of nationalism was aflame and the Manchus as alien rulers of China became the center of student attacks. Although the students were united in their hatred of the Manchus, they were divided organizationally. The most active groups were the provincial student associations, and a small number of multiprovincial societies also functioned. But they were limited in membership and restricted in their influence. The largest following, which cut across provincial loyalties, was the constitutional movement vigorously promoted by K'ang Yu-wei and Liang Ch'i-ch'ao after their exile from China. The *Ch'ing-i Pao* (Public Opinion) and the *Hsin-min ts'ung-pao* (New People's Magazine), which Liang edited in Japan beginning in 1898, enjoyed wide circulation among the Chinese students.[29] Indeed, many of them were introduced to "revolutionary thought" through the pages of the *Hsin-min ts'ung-pao*.[30] As the students became increasingly aware of China's plight and demanded immediate action, the moderate approach of reforming China through a constitutional monarchy proved unsatisfactory.

Sun Yat-sen's arrival in Japan on July 19, 1905, provided the means by which the frustrations of the students could be released. Sun immediately commenced organizing the large body of Chinese students in Japan. On July 28 he visited the popular Twentieth Century China Society clubhouse, one of the few multiprovincial student societies. According to Sung Chiao-jen,[31] one of the founders of the society and a participant in an abortive Hunan uprising of 1904, Sun was accompanied by Miyazaki Torazo, a close friend and one of the earliest Japanese collaborators. Sun appealed for unity among the revolutionary groups. He cited the support of the revolutionary movement among the people and secret societies of Kwangtung and

---

[29] The *Ch'ing-i Pao* was published from 1898 to 1902, the *Hsin-min Ts'ung-pao* between 1902 and 1907, both in Yokohama.

[30] Chu Ho-chung (*op. cit.*, p. 253) writes that the *Hsin-min Ts'ung-pao* was read by Hupeh students in 1902 and 1903, the height of the journal's influence.

[31] Sung Chiao-jen, *Wo-chih li-shih* (Hunan, 1920), II, 27A-27B.

Kwangsi. However, owing to lack of leadership, the movement was confined to petty acts of banditry. If, Sun continued, men of ability were recruited, the work of destruction as well as construction would be properly managed, and eventually a civilized government could be established. China's problem was not so much partition by foreign powers as it was internal strife. Uncoordinated and separate provincial uprisings would surely bring chaos, not unlike the end of past Chinese dynasties, and lead to foreign intervention. China's extinction would follow.

On July 30, 1905, more than seventy Chinese students met with Sun to discuss the founding of a new revolutionary party to overthrow the Ch'ing dynasty.[32] Sun discussed the form and strategy of the revolution[33] and again stressed the necessity for one organization to direct the revolutionary activities of the various groups. One student suggested that the new party be called the Tui Man T'ung Meng Hui (Common Alliance Association to Oppose the Manchus), but Sun rejected the proposal. He felt that the aim of the revolution was not only the overthrow of the Manchus but also the abrogation of absolutism and the establishment of republicanism. Instead, Sun suggested the name Chung-kuo Ke-min T'ung Meng Hui (Chinese Revolutionary Common Alliance Association). However, the word *ke-min* (revolution) raised doubts among some of the students, who felt that, since the organization was secret, the word *ke-min* was unnecessary. Huang Hsing, a much respected Hunan student leader, feared that it might restrict their activities. The issue was decided with the acceptance of Chung-kuo T'ung Meng Hui (Chinese Common Alliance Association) as the name for the new revolutionary organization.

Sun next introduced his famous four-point declaration of objectives: the expulsion of the barbarians, the restoration of China to the Chinese, the creation of a republic, and equalization of land rights. The students questioned Sun regarding the "equalization of land rights," even to the extent of demanding

---

[32] Feng Tzu-yu in *Ke-min wen-hsien*, II, 147.

[33] For an account of the preparatory meeting see Sung Chiao-jen, *op. cit.*, II, 28A; Feng Tzu-yu in *Ke-min wen-hsien*, II, 147-148.

that this provision be eliminated. According to Feng Tzu-yu,[34] who represented the Hsing Chung Hui at the gathering, Sun defended his "equalization of land rights" as the first step toward the solution of social issues. As the world's newest revolutionary party, the Chung-kuo T'ung Meng Hui should not confine itself to racial and political issues. Rather, the new revolutionary party needed to solve the foremost social problems. Only thereby could China become a wealthy and strong nation. Sun's appeal must have impressed the students, for they dropped their objections to the "equalization of land rights" provision. However, judging from their past behavior and subsequent conduct, the majority were anything but social reformers. The primary factor which brought the students and Sun into union was their common hatred of the Manchus. But whereas Sun saw nationalism and the overthrow of the Manchus as a means to an end, the majority of the students regarded this as their ultimate goal. These differences were now put aside, and the meeting ended harmoniously with the appointment of a committee to draft rules for the new organization.[35] The following oath was pledged by those present:

The person joining the alliance from ——— province, ——— district, by name ———, has sworn before heaven to drive out the Manchu barbarians, restore China to the Chinese, create a republic, and equalize land rights, and keep his good faith, and maintain his loyalty from beginning to end. If he should break his promise, he will be punished by other members as they see fit.[36]

The formal founding of the Chung-kuo T'ung Meng Hui, commonly referred to as the T'ung Meng Hui, took place on August 20, 1905, in a private home in Tokyo.[37] Among the several hundred students present, every Chinese province except

---

[34] Feng Tzu-yu, *ibid.*, II, 148.

[35] Among those appointed to the committee were Huang Hsing, Ch'en T'ien-hua, Sung Chiao-jen, and Wang Ching-wei.

[36] For a full text of the oath see Tsou Lu, *Chung-kuo Kuo-min Tang shih-kao* (Chungking, 1944), I, 47.

[37] Sung Chiao-jen, *op. cit.*, II, 31A.

Kansu was represented.[38] After the party's constitution had been
approved, Huang Hsing nominated Sun as *tsung-li* (director-
general) of the new revolutionary group. The constitution provided for the subsequent inclusion of other revolutionary groups
which shared the aims of the T'ung Meng Hui.[39] Three separate
departments were established at headquarters: a department of
general affairs, a judicial department, and a deliberation department. A council of thirty was to be elected to govern the
party. Local branches were to be established on a provincial
level, supervised by the Tokyo headquarters. Five internal divisions covering the whole of China were set up to govern party
activities and four external divisions were founded to carry out
party activities overseas. Each division head was to be appointed
by the director-general.

Following the election of officers, Huang Hsing announced
that since half of the members of the Twentieth Century China
Society had joined the T'ung Meng Hui, they were prepared
to turn over the Society's journal, the *Erh-shih Shih-chi Chih
Chih-na*, to the new organization.[40] The offer was immediately
accepted.

The manifesto or revolutionary program of the T'ung Meng
Hui[41] of 1905 unquestionably symbolized the crystallization of
Sun Yat-sen's ideas.[42] Aside from defining the four aims of ex-
pelling the Manchus, restoring China to the Chinese, establishing a republic, and equalizing land rights, it introduced the
concept of political tutelage. The traditionally politically apathetic Chinese masses were to be trained for a constitutional

---

[38] No students from Kansu were studying in Japan at the time.

[39] For a full text of the regulations see Tsou Lu, *op. cit.*, I, 47-50.

[40] Sung Chiao-jen, *op. cit.*, p. 31A.

[41] For the full text of the manifesto see Tsou Lu, *op. cit.*, I, 53-55. An
English translation is available in Teng Ssu-yu, John K. Fairbank, *et al.*,
China's Response to the West (Cambridge, Mass., 1954), pp. 227-229.

[42] On the development of Sun's revolutionary principles, see Wang Te-
chao in *Chung-kuo hsien-tai shih ts'ung-k'an*, ed. by Wu Hsiang-hsiang
(Taipei, 1960), I, 65-188.

democracy. The first stage would be government by military law. During this period of three years the evils of the Manchus would be exterminated. The second stage, lasting six years, would be government by provisional constitution. While the national government would remain in control of the military government, the people would be trained in the art of self-government on the local level. The final stage of government under a democratic constitution would then begin, with all governmental powers, local and national, transferred to the people. The manifesto concluded with a call to the Chinese masses to arise and overthrow the Ch'ing dynasty.

Writing many years later regarding the founding of the T'ung Meng Hui, Sun said:

After the creation of the "United League" [T'ung Meng Hui], I began to believe that a new era of the Chinese Revolution was opening before us. Previously, I had more than once met with great difficulties, I had been spat upon and ridiculed by all. I more than once suffered defeats, but I audaciously moved forward, although I must confess that I did not dream of the accomplishment of the overthrow of the Manchu dynasty still in my lifetime. However, from the Autumn of 1905 onwards, after the creation of the revolutionary "United League," I became convinced that the great cause of the Chinese Revolution would be accomplished during my lifetime.[43]

The composition of the T'ung Meng Hui had an important effect on the future of the party and the revolutionary movement. Most of the seventy or more students who attended the July 30 meeting were members of one of the anti-Ch'ing groups. Indeed, one of the distinctive characteristics of the T'ung Meng Hui was that it came to represent a union of various revolutionary groups. Two groups predominated at the July 30 meeting: the Hsing Chung Hui, Sun Yat-sen's group; and the Hua Hsing Hui (Restore China Society), established by Japan-returned students from Hunan.

---

[43] Sun Yat-sen, *Memoirs of a Chinese Revolutionary* (Taipei, 1953), p. 158.

The Hua Hsing Hui was founded by Huang Hsing, Liu K'uei-i, Sung Chiao-jen, Ch'en T'ing-hua, and others in December, 1903, in Hunan. Huang Hsing,[44] who had first arrived in Japan late in 1902, led the group. Between 1902 and 1903, he had been active in student activities in Japan and was one of the organizers of the student volunteer corps to protect China and fight the Russians after Russian occupation of Manchuria in 1903. Like most students in Japan, Huang was first and foremost a nationalist. He blamed China's ills upon the Manchus, whom he sought to overthrow. According to Liu K'uei-i, Huang believed that the success of the "racial" revolution (i.e., Han versus Manchu) required the support of the students as well as of the military. However, to win an early victory the secret societies had to be utilized.

Huang proposed that the movement to overthrow the Ch'ing government begin at the provincial level. He rejected the so-called capital revolutions of France and England—movements centered in Paris and London, which he considered unsuitable to conditions in China. According to Huang, the population of Peking sought nothing but comfort and were generally apathetic. Further, there was little chance that the Manchu troops guarding the capital could be induced to join the revolutionary forces. Huang thus conceived of regional revolutions under which each province would rise separately and cast off the Ch'ing yoke. Hunan would be secured as the main base, and assistance would then be extended to provinces which had not risen. Students were recruited and members of the local Western-trained army were enlisted.[45] The T'ung-ch'iu Hui (Common Enemy Society) was formed to make alliances with secret societies. An uprising in Hunan was arranged for November 16, 1904, the day of the Empress Dowager's birthday. However, through an indiscreet comment by one of the participants, the plot was revealed to the authorities. The revolt never mate-

---

[44] Liu K'uei-i, *Huang Hsing ch'uan-chi* (Taipei, 1952), p. 3. This work, first published in 1929, was written by a close follower of Huang's.

[45] *Ibid.*, pp. 4-5.

rialized and Huang, Sung, and other leaders fled to Japan to avoid arrest.[46]

In January, 1905, preparations were made by the exiled Hunanese in Japan to publish a journal to spread the revolutionary gospel.[47] On June 3, Sung Chiao-jen, T'ien T'ung (a recent arrival from Hupeh), and others, after great difficulties, began to publish the *Erh-shih Shih-chi Chih Chih-na*, which, like the earlier student journals, stressed the now familiar theme of nationalism. The opening statement deplored the backwardness of China and lamented the absence of signs of progress.[48] China was being partitioned by foreign powers and yet the people remained apathetic because of the limited development of means of communication. Whereas in the Western nations and even in Japan thousands of periodicals were published which informed as well as incited the people, no such publications existed to arouse the Chinese masses. The *Erh-shih Shih-chi Chih Chih-na* thus proclaimed as its objective the instillation of the idea of patriotism among the peoples of China.

In an article on "A History of the Encroachments of the Han People," the former glories of the Han people were analyzed.[49] Why was it, asked the author, that in recent times the Han people had repressed their sense of patriotism and abandoned their spirit of militarism? They had been conquered by the Manchus and sold as slaves to foreigners. Why was it that the Hans "possess a cultural strength but are wanting in collective powers . . . possess the ability to propagate in abundance but lack the capacity to compete . . . ?"[50] The ability of a race to unite and found a nation depended upon two factors: antiforeignism and a policy of progress. The so-called "national imperialism"

---

[46] *Ibid.*, pp. 5-6; Sung Chiao-jen, *op. cit.*, I, 1A-7A.

[47] Sung Chiao-jen, *op. cit.*, II, 1B-2A.

[48] Wei-chung, "Opening Words of the Twentieth Century China," *Erh-shih Shih-chi Chih Chih-na*, No. 1 (June 3, 1905), 1-14. All essays in this journal are individually paginated.

[49] Kung-ming (Sung Chiao-jen), "Han-tsu ch'in-lioh shih" (A History of the Encroachments of the Han People), *ibid.*, pp. 1-12.

[50] *Ibid.*

of the Europeans was cited as an example. However, nationalism
and xenophobia as means of securing independence and freedom
were beyond the comprehension of the Chinese people. But if
the masses were reminded of the glories of their ancestors and
the future plight of their children they would become angry
and ready for revolution.

While the Hua Hsing Hui and the Hsing Chung Hui were the
primary groups participating in the new revolutionary party,
others joined the T'ung Meng Hui. One, the Kuang Fu Hui
(Restoration Society) had been founded in 1904 in Shanghai.[51]
Ts'ai Yuan-p'ei, a prominent scholar, was elected chief, and
other important members included Kung Pao-ch'uan, Hsu Hsi-
lin, and T'ao Ch'eng-chang. The Kuang Fu Hui's greatest
strength was in the province of Anhwei and Chekiang, whence
came most of its members. Membership consisted mainly of
student intellectuals, and secret society support was also obtained. The Kuang Fu Hui was strongly nationalistic, dedicated
to the overthrow of the Ch'ing dynasty. Some of its members
also promoted socialist principles. The Kuang Fu Hui maintained close ties with the Hua Hsing Hui. In 1904 it promised
to support the Hua Hsing Hui's Hunan revolt and planned an
uprising in Chekiang province to follow the Hunan revolt, but
neither endeavor materialized.

Another important group, the anarchists, later joined the
new revolutionary party.[52] Although never organized formally,
the anarchists were an identifiable and closely knit group which
came into being during 1906 in Paris. Members were drawn
chiefly from the Chinese students in France. Leading members
included Chang Ching-chiang, Ch'u Min-i, Li Shih-tseng, and
Wu Chih-hui. Their principal activity was the publication in
France of a weekly, between 1907 and 1910, which championed

---

[51] Feng Tzu-yu in *Hsin-hai ke-min*, ed. by Ch'ai Te-keng (Shanghai,
1957), I, 515-520 (hereafter cited as *Hsin-hai ke-min*); Chang Huang-ch'i,
ibid., I, 521-529.

[52] Robert A. Scalapino and George T. Yu, *The Chinese Anarchist Movement* (Berkeley, 1961).

the causes of anarchism and revolution, universal and anti-Ch'ing.

Although the majority of the groups disbanded after they became parts of the T'ung Meng Hui, a few continued to function, and members retained membership in their old group. Some members of groups which had been dissolved maintained their former ties among themselves informally. This gave rise to a system of dual membership, constituting blocs within the T'ung Meng Hui which was a cause of friction. Perhaps it was to be expected that factionalism should emerge because of prior loyalties, diversity of goals, differences in ideology, divergencies in tactics and strategies, and the conflict of strong-willed personalities. The full implications of the composite nature of the new revolutionary party were not considered at the founding of the T'ung Meng Hui. After all, the groups which joined the T'ung Meng Hui shared a goal which cut across all differences: the overthrow of the Ch'ing dynasty.

Immediately after the founding of the T'ung Meng Hui in Tokyo, the infant group narrowly escaped being classified as anti-Japanese. The second issue of the *Erh-shih Shih-chi Chih Chih-na*, the journal published by the Twentieth Century Chinese Society which had been accepted as the official organ of the T'ung Meng Hui, included an article criticizing Japanese activities in China.[53] On August 27, Japanese police suddenly descended, ordered the journal to cease publication, and confiscated all printed copies. Sung Chiao-jen was questioned at length by police concerning the journal's views and the anti-Japanese essay. Only by claiming that the objectionable essay had been contributed by a writer from Hong Kong and that other members of the journal had since returned to China did Sung escape arrest.

The crisis brought about a change in the plans of the T'ung Meng Hui. To dissociate the T'ung Meng Hui from the *Erh-*

---

[53] According to Sung Chiao-jen (op. cit., II, 32A-33B) the article dealt with the development of China by Japanese politicans.

shih Shih-chi Chih Chih-na, it was decided to change the title of their official organ to *Min-pao* (People's News),[54] and to refrain from printing articles that would arouse the suspicion of the Japanese authorities. Chang Chi, a T'ung Meng Hui member from Hopeh with years of experience in Japan and fluent in the language, was appointed publisher of the *Min-pao.*[55] In registering with the Japanese police to secure a permit for the new journal's publication, Chang was asked the principles which the *Min-pao* proposed to disseminate. Chang Chi recited the famous six principles of the *Min-pao*: (1) to overthrow the corrupt Manchu government, (2) to establish a Chinese republic, (3) to maintain true world peace, (4) to nationalize land, (5) to promote cooperation between the Chinese and Japanese people, and (6) to obtain the support of the nations of the world for the revolutionary task of China.[56] When the police questioned him regarding the meaning of "cooperation between the Chinese and Japanese people," Chang's answer was that "People are eternal, but governments are transitional."[57] This reply must have been satisfactory, for a permit was granted. The first issue of the *Min-pao*, which included the six principles, was published on November 17, 1905, in Tokyo.

Writing many years later, Chang Chi stated that the six points which he presented were formulated by him personally to satisfy the police.[58] They did not represent the policy of the T'ung Meng Hui, but were based on expediency. The first four points did not differ radically from the four basic principles included in the T'ung Meng Hui oath, but points five and six were departures, and point five was especially novel. While Sun was known to be pro-Japanese, the students were gravely disturbed by Japan's increasing interest in Manchuria. But if *Min-pao's* six principles, especially point five, are viewed in terms of the existing circumstances (i.e., the *Erh-shih Shih-chi Chih*

---

[54] *Ibid.,* II, 34A-37B.
[55] Chang Chi, *op. cit.,* p. 235.
[56] *Ibid.*
[57] *Ibid.*
[58] *Ibid.*

Chih-na incident), Chang Chi's explanation may be substantially correct. At any rate, the six principles were adopted by the *Min-pao*, and the T'ung Meng Hui freed itself from suspicions that it harbored anti-Japanese sentiments.

Before the end of 1905, another crisis confronted the T'ung Meng Hui. While the *Erh-shih Shih-chi Chih Chih-na* incident had served to strengthen the T'ung Meng Hui, a succession of events beginning in November caused a serious rupture within the ranks. It arose from the attempt of the Japanese government to impose new regulations over the ten thousand or so Chinese who were studying in Japan. While a number were attending leading Japanese universities, the vast majority were enrolled in institutions established expressly for their education.[59] These schools were lax regarding entrance requirements, and it is alleged that Chinese students passed from one school to another without observing any formalities. There were even reports that certain schools sold diplomas to Chinese students.[60] Student living conditions were deplorable. These and other factors led the Japanese Ministry of Education to issue new rules in November, 1905, which gave the Japanese government powers to approve institutions open to Chinese, control private schools which admitted Chinese, and select and supervise housing for Chinese students. The students in Japan immediately protested against the regulations.

The issue split the T'ung Meng Hui in Japan into two factions.[61] One, led primarily by students from Hupeh and Hunan, including Sung Chiao-jen, Ch'en T'ien-hua, T'ien T'ung, and Hu Ying, advocated a mass withdrawal of Chinese students from Japanese institutions and their immediate return to China to engage directly in the revolutionary movement. Taking the opposite viewpoint was the group from southern China, led by Hu Han-min, Chu Chih-hsin, and Wang Ching-wei, who viewed

[59] Saneto Keishu, *op. cit.*, pp. 64-75.

[60] *Ke-min wen-hsien*, III, 390.

[61] *Ibid.*, III, 390-392; Feng Tzu-yu, *Ke-min i-shih*, II, 129-131; Feng Tzu-yu, *Chung-hua min-kuo . . .* , I, 198.

the transfer to China of the T'ung Meng Hui headquarters and
the recently founded *Min-pao* as certain to have grave consequences, and considered premature the idea of returning to
China to participate directly in the revolutionary movement.
Those advocating a return to China were in the majority. The
struggle was given even greater impetus by the death of Ch'en
T'ien-hua, a student from Hunan and leader of the return-to-
China group, who was so infuriated at the Japanese regulations
that he committed suicide. To further complicate matters, both
Sun Yat-sen and Huang Hsing, the leading members of the revolutionary organization, had left Japan to obtain financial assistance and recruit new members. No one of comparable status
remained in Japan to mediate the internal strife, and yet the
activities of the revolutionary movement forced the leaders
to be constantly away from the Japan headquarters. The problem of leadership became a chronic weakness of the T'ung Meng
Hui. Instead of a tightly knit revolutionary group centrally
directed, the T'ung Meng Hui increasingly became an organization of loosely associated factions, with various centers of
power each independent of the others. The future of the T'ung
Meng Hui hung in the balance. The immediate crisis subsided
when the Japanese government decided not to enforce the regulations. Nevertheless, deep cleavage had been created within the
revolutionary ranks, even though on the surface the T'ung
Meng Hui remained intact.

Between 1905 and 1911 the T'ung Meng Hui was engaged in
various activities designed to achieve the overthrow of the
Ch'ing dynasty, primarily through military uprisings.[62] Members
of the T'ung Meng Hui returned to China to participate in this

---

[62] The more important military adventures of the T'ung Meng Hui include the P'ing-hsing, Kiangsi, and Liu-yang, Hunan, uprisings of December, 1906; the Huang-kang, Kwangtung, uprising of May, 1907; the Waichow, Kwangtung, uprising of June, 1907; the An-king, Anhwei, uprising
of July, 1907; the Ch'in-chou, Kwangtung, uprising of September, 1907; the
Cheng nan-kuan, Kwangsi, uprising of December, 1907; the Hokow, Yunnan, uprising of April, 1908; the Canton, Kwangtung, new army uprising
of February, 1910; the Canton, Kwangtung, uprising of April, 1911.

task. The abortive December, 1906, uprisings in P'ing-hsiang, Kiangsi, and Liu-yang, Hunan, were in part the results of a conspiracy hatched by T'ung Meng Hui members recently returned from Japan. To instigate revolt, journalistic propaganda sought to inflame the people on the evils of the Manchus.[63]

Besides serving as the revolutionary organ, calling upon the populace to arise and overthrow the Manchus, the *Min-pao* elucidated the San Min Chu I principles (Three Principles of the People). *Min-sheng chu-i*, the principle of people's livelihood, was fully discussed in the pages of the *Min-pao*.[64] To support these and other revolutionary ventures, extensive fund-raising campaigns were undertaken among the overseas Chinese. Thus, the T'ung Meng Hui operated on two fronts: military insurrections and journalistic propaganda to overthrow the Ch'ing dynasty, and fund-raising campaigns among overseas Chinese to finance the revolutionary movement.

The T'ung Meng Hui was confronted also with internal dissension. A number of the disagreements involved Sun Yat-sen and his newly-acquired colleagues. A dispute concerning the revolutionary flag nearly resulted in the withdrawal of Huang Hsing from the T'ung Meng Hui.[65] Sun insisted upon retaining the design of the original Hsing Chung Hui flag, a round white circle with twelve points against a blue background. Huang, however, disagreed, and proposed a flag with the character *ching*, denoting socialism, as the new revolutionary banner.[66] Sun maintained that Huang's design gave the impression of a desire to restore the past. Huang angrily announced that he would withdraw from the T'ung Meng Hui, but he finally bowed to Sun's will. Regarding the incident, Huang wrote to

---

[63] See Kao Liang-tso, "Record of Revolutionary Books and Periodicals of the Hsing Chung Hui and T'ung Meng Hui Periods," *Chien-kuo Yueh-k'an*, II, No. 2 (August, 1934), 1-14.

[64] See R. A. Scalapino and H. Schiffrin, "Early Socialist Currents in the Chinese Revolutionary Movement," *Journal of Asian Studies*, XVIII, No. 3 (May, 1959), 321-342.

[65] Sung Chiao-jen, *op. cit.*, VI, 12B; *Ke-min wen-hsien*, III, 393-394.

[66] Huang's *ching* referred to the *ching-t'ien* or "well-field" system.

Hu Han-min, " . . . for the sake of the party and general interest,
I have constrained myself to obey Sun's wish."[67]

A more serious dissension erupted soon thereafter. The activities of the T'ung Meng Hui in staging uprisings in China
and proselytizing among the Chinese students in Japan led to
protests from the Ch'ing government, culminating in Sun's expulsion from Japan in March, 1907.[68] Sun's decision to accept
60,000 yen[69] from Japanese government sources without prior
consultation with T'ung Meng Hui members caused a split in
the party. Sun also accepted 10,000 yen from a private Japanese
source.[70] Other than designating 2,000 yen for support of the
Min-pao, Sun contributed the remainder to the Huang-kang
and Waichow uprisings.[71] Members of the T'ung Meng Hui
headquarters in Tokyo had been displeased with Sun's acceptance of Japanese funds without their approval. With the failure
of the Huang-kang and Waichow revolts, displeasure turned into
open rebellion. Chang Ping-lin, editor of the Min-pao, Chang
Chi, Sung Chiao-jen, and others attempted to oust Sun as T'ung
Meng Hui tsung-li. The rebels sought to elect Huang as head
of the revolutionary alliance. Liu K'uei-i, who was serving as
acting tsung-li in Sun's absence, sought to prevent the dispute
from becoming a struggle between Sun and Huang over the
"empty" post of tsung-li, thereby placing the whole revolutionary movement in jeopardy.[72] To placate the Tokyo rebels,
Liu wrote Feng Tzu-yu and Hu Han-min in Hong Kong, asking
them to advise Sun to admit his wrongdoing publicly and accept
the blame. Meanwhile, Liu informed Huang of the Tokyo

---

[67] Quoted in Ke-min wen-hsien, III, 394.

[68] According to Jansen, while the Japanese wanted no trouble from the
Ch'ing government, they realized the importance of keeping on good terms
with Sun, and asked him to depart voluntarily. Marius B. Jansen, The
Japanese and Sun Yat-sen (Cambridge, 1954), pp. 128-129.

[69] This is the amount given by Jansen (ibid., p. 129). However, the sum
given by Liu K'uei-i (op. cit., p. 16) is 5,000 in gold.

[70] Liu K'uei-i, op. cit., p. 16; Jansen, op. cit., p. 129.

[71] Liu K'uei-i, op. cit., p. 16.

[72] Ibid.

events. Sun, however, attributed the unrest to the lack of revolutionary activities among the Tokyo members, and saw no reason why he should accept the blame.

Sun's expulsion from Japan had a second important consequence in that it resulted in a shift of the T'ung Meng Hui's center of operations. With Sun's departure and the increasingly direct participation of the students in the military uprisings, the function of the Japan T'ung Meng Hui headquarters became largely nominal. The real centers of power were Sun's constantly shifting headquarters and the numerous T'ung Meng Hui branches in and about China, the latter frequently established independently. Thus power and leadership became increasingly diversified.

In 1907 southeast Asia became the center of Chinese revolutionary activities. Between 1907 and 1909, revolts staged in southwest China were planned and directed from headquarters in Indo-China and Singapore, where Sun, Huang Hsing, Hu Han-min, Wang Ching-wei, and other party comrades sought to overthrow the Ch'ing dynasty through military uprisings. Sun and company did not neglect party work, however. T'ung Meng Hui branches were established in Hanoi, Indo-China; in Penang, Malaysia; in Rangoon, Burma; in Bangkok, Siam; in Singapore, and throughout Southeast Asia. Though new members were recruited, the primary purpose of the branches in Southeast Asia was to secure the financial backing of the overseas Chinese. However, the revolutionary organization was not alone in attempting to draw upon the support of the Southeast Asian Chinese. The Pao-huang Hui, Sun's rival from the Hsing Chung Hui days, had long been active. Fierce competition for the allegiance of the overseas Chinese ensued.[73]

For many of the student T'ung Meng Hui members who followed Sun from Japan, this was the first encounter with overseas

---

[73] For one aspect of this battle see Kao Liang-tso, "Battle of Words between the Revolutionists and the Constitutional Monarchists before the Republic," *Chien-kuo Yueh-k'an*, VII, No. 3 (August, 1932); VIII, No. 5 (May, 1933); No. 6 (June, 1933).

Chinese. Hu Han-min, who traveled throughout Southeast Asia rallying the Chinese to the revolutionary cause while combating the Pao-huang Hui forces, charged the overseas Chinese with "a desire for glory and for wealth." They were, moreover, ignorant regarding "racial" matters and political principles, and hence were easily influenced by the Pao-huang Hui and even the Ch'ing government with promises of official positions in exchange for their support.

The difficulties of the revolutionaries were not confined to competition from the Pao-huang Hui and the ignorance of the overseas Chinese. Intraparty strife hampered the T'ung Meng Hui fund-raising campaigns. The chief source of contention was Sun's rivalry with the faction led by Chang Ping-lin and Tao Ch'eng-chang. The latter had long been active in the Dutch colonies of Southeast Asia.[74] As early as 1905 he had organized branches of the Kuang Fu Hui in Java and elected Chang head of the group. Though he later joined the T'ung Meng Hui in Tokyo, Tao continued to promote the Kuang Fu Hui. The conflict between the Sun group and the forces of Tao and Chang broke out in 1908 after the Japanese government had forced the *Min-pao* to cease publication. Chang and Tao accused Sun of using revolutionary funds for private use:[75] that when he was in Japan Sun would claim that all the wealthy Chinese in southeast Asia were supporters of his revolutionary cause; when he was in Southeast Asia he would claim that all the students in Japan were members of the T'ung Meng Hui, and yet, according to Chang and Tao, the *Min-pao* had received not one penny of assistance from Sun. Another accusation was that Sun was prejudiced against anyone not from Kwangtung. These allegations were widely circulated and aroused the suspicion of overseas Chinese. During a fund-raising campaign in the Netherlands East Indies in 1908, Wang Ching-wei encountered fierce opposition from the local Chinese.[76]

---

[74] Feng Tzu-yu, *Ke-min i-shih*, V, 61-75; Chang Huang-ch'i, *Hsin-hai ke-min*, I, 521-529.

[75] Tsou Lu, *op. cit.*, I, 77-78.

[76] Feng Tzu-yu, *Ke-min i-shih*, V, 61-75.

Many overseas Chinese, in the Americas as well as in southeast Asia, were reluctant to support the revolutionary cause. The crisis led Sun to appeal to Wu Chih-hui, then editor of the Paris Chinese anarchist journal *Hsin Shih-chieh* (The New Century), to explain and defend Sun's position.[77] Despite external competition and internal disputes, some financial support from the Southeast Asian Chinese was obtained for military uprisings and other party activities. Subscribers were promised a fourfold repayment within a year after the establishment of the military government; commercial, mining, and other rights were offered as inducements to contributors.[78] Whether from sheer patriotism or for a good investment or both, many Chinese in Southeast Asia and the Americas gradually came to support the T'ung Meng Hui.

The repeated uprisings in southwest China, instigated by revolutionary headquarters in Indo-China and Singapore, led to a curtailment of the T'ung Meng Hui and the expulsion of Sun Yat-sen by various authorities in Southeast Asia. In May, 1909, Sun left Singapore for Europe and subsequently the United States on a world fund-raising campaign. During Sun's fourth world journey, branches of the T'ung Meng Hui were established in New York, San Francisco, and other overseas Chinese communities.

With Sun absent, the burden of the revolutionary movement fell upon Hu Han-min and Huang Hsing. Huang returned to Japan, where with the aid of Japanese officers, he trained more than a hundred Chinese students in warfare and the manufacture of explosives. Meanwhile, the command of party activities in south China was assigned to the south China division in Hong Kong, headed by Hu Han-min, which provided guidance for the abortive Canton "new army" uprising of February 12, 1910.[79]

---

[77] See Sun's letters to Wu Chih-hui in Kuomintang, *Kuo-fu ch'uan-chi* (Taipei, 1957) V, 82-85, 86-88, 89-93 (hereafter cited as *Kuo-fu ch'uan chi*).

[78] Tsou Lu, *op. cit.*, I, 112. In 1908, during the Hokow, Yunnan, uprising, Sun promised the exclusive mining rights to Yunnan for ten years in exchange for a 10,000 yuan contribution. See *Kuo-fu ch'uan-chi*, V, 53.

[79] *Ke-min wen-hsien*, III, 31-34.

The year 1910 marked a new low in the revolutionary movement. The failure of the T'ung Meng Hui in its last attempt to
oust the Manchus by a military uprising discouraged the party
members. Complaints had been voiced that the strategy of staging uprisings in the southern coastal provinces, far from the
Ch'ing capital of Peking, was ill-conceived.[80] An article in the
Chung-kuo Jih-pao, the party's organ in Hong Kong, outlined
the advantages of an uprising in Peking.[81] In an absolute state,
the capital served as the nerve center. "Capture the capital and
the whole country will be shaken. Take hostage the ruler and the
country will disintegrate."[82] The success of the Manchus in overthrowing the Ming dynasty was attributed to the capture of Peking, the Ming capital. In contrast, the Taiping Rebellion failed
because of its inability to seize Peking, even though the rebellion
succeeded in the outlying provinces. The article also explained
why the Ch'ing government retained its hold over China when
Peking was seized by the Allied Powers during the Boxer Rebellion in 1900. "The answer lies in the fact that the 1900 affair was
a foreign adventure. At the time, the foreign powers had no
plans to demand the surrender of the provincial authorities and
the division of China. The provincial authorities, in turn, felt no
need to surrender. [However], the situation would be vastly different if those who captured Peking belonged to the Han Revolutionary Army."[83] Even if an attempt to seize Peking failed, it
would still make a greater "impression within the hearts of men"
than the abortive uprisings in the outlying provinces. On another occasion it was proposed that the T'ung Meng Hui should
divide its activities between uprisings in the outlying provinces
and creating ferment at the Manchu seat of power, Peking.[84]
However, in 1910 there was a need for immediate action. The
frustration of repeated failures culminated in the abortive as-

[80] Feng Tzu-yu, *Ke-min i-shih*, II, 153.

[81] "The Rumor That the Revolutionary Party Intends to Take Peking,"
Chung-kuo Jih-pao, March 2, 1907, p. 2.

[82] *Ibid.*

[83] *Ibid.*

[84] Feng Tzu-yu, *Ke-min i-shih*, II, 160.

sassination attempt on the life of the Manchu regent, Tsia-feng, by Wang Ching-wei on April 2, 1910.

Wang Ching-wei's failure increased the despair within the ranks of the T'ung Meng Hui. Some daring event was needed to rejuvenate the party lest the T'ung Meng Hui fall into oblivion. Two separate plans, destined to have far-reaching effects upon the future of the party, were formulated. Sun Yat-sen, originator of the first plan, summoned Hu Han-min, Huang Hsing, and other party leaders to a conference in Penang, Malaysia. Sun, in his usual optimistic frame of mind,[85] informed Hu that he intended to instigate a new military uprising. Huang Hsing, Hu, and others had not forgotten the failure of the Canton revolt in February, but Sun assured them that the revolutionary tide was rising in China, that the overseas Chinese also were embracing the revolutionary movement, and that, if the revolutionaries had a definite plan and the determination to carry it through, it would succeed. Again Sun's will triumphed, and plans were begun for the famous Canton uprising of April 27, 1911.[86]

As Li Chien-nung has noted, the careful planning of the Canton uprising should have insured a high degree of success for the revolutionaries.[87] Huang Hsing was designated commander of the operation, and the full resources of the T'ung Meng Hui were mobilized.[88] Contact with the Canton "new army" was renewed and headquarters established at Hong Kong. To finance the uprising, the overseas Chinese communities would be divided into districts, each with a quota to fulfill.[89] To avoid interference by local governmental authorities, money was to be raised ostensibly for a Chinese educational fund. Within a

---

[85] *Ke-min wen-shien*, III, 407-408.

[86] In China this uprising is more commonly known as the March 29 uprising, the lunar calendar date.

[87] Li Chien-nung, *Chung-kuo chin-pai-nien cheng-chih shih* (Taipei, 1957), I, 290.

[88] See Tsou Lu, *Kwang-chou san-yueh erh-shih-chiu ke-min shih* (Shanghai, 1926).

[89] The Chinese in the British and Dutch colonies in Southeast Asia were

month after the Penang conference, Sun was expelled from Malaysia for partaking in activities "endangering local safety."[90] On December 6, 1910, he set sail for Europe and America, where he remained to settle intraparty disputes[91] and raise funds for the revolutionary cause. During the last few years of the anti-Ch'ing movement, much of the financial burden of party ventures shifted from the Southeast Asian Chinese to those in the Americas, where Sun's many promotional trips must have helped to win their support. At any rate, increasingly the Chinese in Canada and the United States aided the T'ung Meng Hui. Almost half of the funds raised for the abortive Canton uprising of April 27, 1911, came from this source.[92]

---

assigned a quota of $50,000; those in Siam and Indo-China, $30,000. *Ibid.*, p. 4.

[90] *Ibid.*, p. 5.

[91] One of the major disputes was between members of the T'ung Meng Hui and the Chih Kung T'ang in San Francisco. Chih Kung T'ang members considered themselves senior in status, since their parent organization, the Hung-meng, was among the first to oppose the Manchus. It was partly due to the hostility of the Chih Kung T'ang that branches of the T'ung Meng Hui in the United States were not founded until 1909. The San Francisco branch was founded in 1910. The entrance of the T'ung Meng Hui into what had hitherto been an exclusive world of the Chih Kung T'ang created a serious problem: the T'ung Meng Hui was not popular enough to command the loyalty, i.e., financial contribution, of the Chinese in the United States, and the Chih Kung T'ang, angered by the T'ung Meng Hui's intrusion, withdrew its support of the revolutionary cause. The conflict was resolved in June, 1911, by Sun, who negotiated an agreement whereby all T'ung Meng Hui members were invited to join the Chih Kung T'ang. Feng Tzu-yu, editor of a Chinese newspaper in Vancouver, Canada, was called to San Francisco to settle the details. Meanwhile, Sun organized a fund-raising committee. During this period in San Francisco Sun used the designation Chung-hua Kemintang (Chinese Revolutionary Party), which he adopted for the party in 1914. See Feng Tzu-yu, *Ke-min i-shih*, I, 136-164.

[92] Whereas $32,550 (Hong Kong) were raised among the Chinese in the Dutch colonies in Southeast Asia and $47,663 from the Chinese in British colonies in Southeast Asia, a grand total of $77,000 was raised from among the Chinese in the United States, Canada, and the Hawaiian Islands. Tsou Lu, *Kwang-chou san-yueh erh-shih-chiu ke-min shih*, p. 18.

Almost concurrently during preparations for the Canton uprising, a second plan to rejuvenate the revolutionary movement was being formulated in Japan. The Tokyo T'ung Meng Hui headquarters had been inactive since Sun's expulsion from Japan in 1907, although a small nucleus of members remained. The Tokyo remnant of the party had frequently disagreed with the Sun faction. However, away from the center of activity and short of funds, the Japan-based group offered no real challenge to Sun's leadership. Nevertheless, the repeated defeats of Sun and his followers in southwest China led to a movement to shift revolutionary activities to central China. This plan was chiefly the work of a Japan-based group, mostly students from Hunan and Hupeh, many of whom were former Hua Hsing Hui members.

At a meeting of T'ung Meng Hui members in Japan in May, 1910, Sung Chiao-jen, who had remained in Japan except for a brief trip to Manchuria in 1907, proposed that revolutionary activities be concentrated on central China and that a division of the T'ung Meng Hui be established to direct affairs.[93] Party work would be undertaken first in central China and then extended to the north. A time limit of three years was set for the completion of the preparatory work. The banner of revolution would then be raised. When objections were made to the length of the preparatory period, it was decided not to impose a time limit.

Between May, 1910, and July, 1911, members of the Japan-based group returned to China to participate directly in the anti-Ch'ing movement. A delay in the founding of the central division was due primarily to the April 27, 1911, Canton uprising, an all-party venture. Sung Chiao-jen and other comrades from Japan went to Hong Kong to assist in the revolt. When it failed, work in central China was renewed, and the revolutionary center was shifted to Shanghai.

Shanghai, with its foreign settlements, had long served as a

---

[93] Chu Cheng, *Chu Chio-sheng hsien-sheng ch'uan-chi* (Taipei, n.d.), II, 473-535.

base for anti-Ch'ing activities. As early as 1902 the Ai-kuo Hsueh-she (Patriotic Society) had been founded in Shanghai. However, unlike southwestern China, where repeated uprisings were staged, Shanghai served chiefly as a propaganda center until 1911. Yu Yu-jen's series of anti-Ch'ing newspapers did much to undermine the authority of the government.[94]

The Shanghai-based central division of the T'ung Meng Hui concerned itself primarily with revolutionary activities in central China. Branches were established also in Szechwan and Shensi. However, activities were concentrated in Hupeh, especially in the Hankow-Wuch'ang-Hanyang district, more commonly known as the Wuhan cities. The Wuhan region had a long history of revolutionary ferment; the large number of Hupeh students in the T'ung Meng Hui contributed to its selection as a center of activities. Local headquarters were established in the Russian concession in Hankow. T'ung Meng Hui members contacted other anti-Ch'ing groups, and members were recruited among the "new army."[95] On the eve of the October 10, 1911, revolution, the work of the central division had exceeded all expectations.

Plans had been progressing for an uprising in the Wuhan area, but the conspiracy was accidentally discovered when a bomb exploded at the revolutionists' headquarters in Hankow. Seized at headquarters were T'ung Meng Hui membership lists of the new army. Widespread panic ensued, and members of the new army mutinied in self-defense. The uprising, though anticipated by the central division, took the revolutionary leaders by surprise.[96] No T'ung Meng Hui leader was in Wuhan to direct the revolt, and the local revolutionists took matters into their own hands. Li Yuan-hung, assistant commander of the Ch'ing new army in Wuhan, was chosen to lead the local revolt. When the T'ung Meng Hui leaders arrived in Wuhan, the local rebels were already in command.

---

[94] For an account of Yu's role in Shanghai and the Shanghai-based revolutionary movement, see Feng Tzu-yu, *Ke-min i-shih*, II, 74-100.

[95] Chu Cheng, *op. cit.*

[96] *Ibid.*

A successful uprising had finally been achieved, but not even the Shanghai T'ung Meng Hui group led by Sung Chiao-jen exercised any control over the Wuhan revolt. The rebels elected their own leader, Li Yuan-hung, an officer in the Ch'ing new army. Leadership in the revolutionary movement thus passed from the hands of the T'ung Meng Hui. The revolutionists had won the battle but lost the war.

Internally, on the eve of the 1911 revolution the T'ung Meng Hui was undergoing a radical change. With the repeated defeats in southwestern China and his long enforced sojourns abroad, Sun Yat-sen was increasingly challenged by others for leadership within the revolutionary alliance. Indeed, Sun's very strategy was directly challenged with the establishment of the central division of the T'ung Meng Hui in Shanghai to further the revolutionary movement in that region. The Shanghai group represented an entirely independent movement within the T'ung Meng Hui.

Beginning as a one-man operation, the revolutionary movement now included several groups operating under a common banner. While Sun was recognized as the nominal head of the T'ung Meng Hui, actual power was divided among the various factions. Thus the revolutionary movement which Sun had built almost single-handedly had now freed itself from his control. Sun became the party elder but not the party leader.

The party itself had undergone vast changes. The T'ung Meng Hui marked the beginning of the domination of the party's leadership by the intelligentsia-student class. Except for Sun, not a single Hsing Chung Hui member played a leading role in the T'ung Meng Hui. However, the overseas Chinese continued to serve as the party's basis. The T'ung Meng Hui was still organized on the model of a secret society. In spite of efforts to bring the various revolutionary forces under one command, the party suffered increasingly from ineffective leadership. The absence of centralized leadership and the party's subordinated position after the outbreak of the 1911 revolution were the causes of many of the T'ung Meng Hui's ills during the first years of the Republic.

III   THE "SINGLE-ISSUE PARTY"

BETWEEN 1905 AND 1911 numerous abortive insurrections had
been attempted by the T'ung Meng Hui. However, while the
foundation for the Wuch'ang revolt of October 10, 1911, had
been laid by the revolutionary party through these earlier
attempts, intensive propagandizing, and infiltration of the
Ch'ing army, the decision to rise against the Ch'ing dynasty in
this instance was made by a local military unit rather than the
T'ung Meng Hui. Caught by surprise with the sudden realization of a long-sought objective, the T'ung Meng Hui was ill-
prepared to control the events which followed.[1]

In the months immediately following the Wuch'ang revolution, chaos prevailed both within the political realm and on the
military front. Li Yuan-hung, a local Ch'ing military officer,
assumed the revolutionary command, and other former Ch'ing
officials joined the Wuch'ang revolutionary government.[2] Thus,

---

[1] Chu Cheng, *Chu Chio-sheng hsien-sheng ch'uan-chi* (Taipei, n.d.),
pp. 475-505.

[2] The best-known of these in the Wuch'ang government was perhaps
T'ang Hua-lung.

while the T'ung Meng Hui members may have contributed to the movement, the immediate fruits of victory were not theirs to enjoy.

After the Wuch'ang revolt, the T'ung Meng Hui sought to recapture the revolutionary initiative. Huang Hsing, who had remained in Hong Kong after the abortive Canton uprising of April 27, departed for Wuch'ang. During a stopover in Shanghai he met with Sung Chiao-jen and other leaders of the central division.[3] With Sung Chiao-jen, Li Shu-ch'eng, and Liu K'uei-i, Huang arrived in Wuch'ang on October 28, 1911. At a meeting with Li Yuan-hung, Huang emerged as commander-in-chief of the revolutionary forces at Wuch'ang. Fierce battles ensued with the Ch'ing armies. However, the revolutionaries lacked military strength and suffered a series of defeats. Hankow and Hanyang, which had been liberated, were reoccupied by the Ch'ing armies. Wuch'ang was also threatened.

But if the revolutionary future looked bleak in the Wuch'ang area, there was cause to rejoice in other places. Within a month of the October 10 uprising, all the provinces except Hopeh, Honan, Shangtung, and the Three Eastern Provinces had declared their independence from the Ch'ing house. These almost spontaneous revolts served to demonstrate to the Ch'ing ruling house their unpopularity throughout the country. The uprisings also prevented the Ch'ing government from concentrating its armies against the revolutionists. A single defeat on the battlefield, as in the Wuch'ang area, was but an isolated setback, and did not result in the collapse of the revolutionary movement as had been the situation in previous uprisings. Although the Ch'ing government could smash an isolated assault, they were unable to suppress a national revolution.

While the anti-Ch'ing revolution thus achieved national success, the nature of the provincial uprisings illustrated the weakness of the T'ung Meng Hui, which had never operated nationally before 1911. Its activities had been confined mostly to insurrections in southern China. Only in the last years of the

---

[3] Liu K'uei-i, *Huang Hsing ch'uan-chi* (Taipei, 1952), p. 31.

movement had revolutionary agitation been extended to central
China. No serious military efforts were contemplated in northern China. The T'ung Meng Hui thus had very limited national strength. However, indigenous provincial anti-Ch'ing groups
were strong everywhere; these groups initiated most of the provincial revolts without consulting the T'ung Meng Hui. The
1911 revolution thus began as a premature, uncoordinated
affair.

The provincial revolutionists, however, hastened to establish
a central command. But the decentralized character of the
revolution prevented the immediate formation of a united
anti-Ch'ing front. Li Yuan-hung, who had assumed the leadership in Hupeh after the Wuch'ang revolt, circulated a telegram
on November 9 requesting the provinces to send delegates to
Wuch'ang to participate in the establishment of a provisional
national government. Meanwhile, Ch'en Ch'i-mei, the T'ung
Meng Hui military governor of Shanghai, supported by the
military governors of Kiangsu and Chekiang, proposed that a
constitutional conference be held at Shanghai. The conflict
over revolutionary leadership between Shanghai and Wuch'ang
was resolved in Wuch'ang's favor. However, before the provincial delegates reached Wuch'ang, the Ch'ing armies had reoccupied Hankow and Hanyang and were threatening Wuch'ang. The delegates finally met in the British Concession in
Hankow, where the "General Plan for the Organization of the
Provisional Government" was promulgated.[4] A resolution was
adopted that, should Yuan Shih-k'ai defect from the Ch'ing
government to support the revolution, he would be elected
president of the Republic. Nanking, which had just been liberated, was designated as the capital of the provisional government. This expression of unity among the delegates was soon
shattered over the question of the election of a chief executive.

The contest over the leadership of the provisional government was between Li Yuan-hung, the former Ch'ing military

[4] For a personal account of the events see Ku Chung-hsiu, *Chung-hua
min-kuo k'ai-kuo shih* (Shanghai, 1914), pp. 33-40.

official, and the T'ung Meng Hui leader Huang Hsing. In a preliminary move the Shanghai delegates elected Huang Hsing commander-in-chief to head the government, but the Wuch'ang representatives protested. Li Yuan-hung was then elected commander-in-chief of the provisional government and Huang Hsing associate commander. A plan was devised whereby Li would remain in Wuch'ang, and Huang, as associate commander, would head the government in Nanking. Li assented, but Huang refused to assume office. Deprived of the necessary leadership, the provisional government was incapacitated and the success of the revolution was immediately placed in doubt.

The fate of the revolution and the provisional government was temporarily resolved with the arrival of Sun Yat-sen, who had been in the United States on a fund raising campaign at the outbreak of the Wuch'ang revolution. He had proceeded to China by way of Europe in order to secure foreign support for the Chinese revolution. In an atmosphere of personal triumph, Sun arrived in Shanghai on December 25, 1911. The uncertainties of the revolution were swept aside. Sun was elected provisional president and the Chinese Republic was proclaimed. However, a false tranquillity prevailed; beneath the serene surface lay a stormy sea.

The revolution demanded guidance, but the organization capable of providing the leadership was torn with dissension. Between 1905 and 1911 the T'ung Meng Hui had been constantly plagued with internal strife. Ideological differences, personality conflicts, and disagreements over tactics all contributed to intraparty discord, which increased with each military failure. By 1911 there existed two major groups within the T'ung Meng Hui: the southern faction and the Shanghai-based central division. A number of minor factions, such as Chang Ping-lin and his followers, added to the complexities of T'ung Meng Hui politics. Nevertheless, no rival revolutionary parties made an appearance and the various factions continued uneasily under the banner of the T'ung Meng Hui. No doubt each group desired to capitalize upon the name T'ung Meng Hui, which had become synonymous with the

Chinese nationalist movement. Furthermore, they shared the immediate goal of overthrowing the Ch'ing dynasty, for which maximum cooperation would be required. Therefore, prior to the 1911 revolution most differences were put aside temporarily in the struggle to achieve the common goal.

The T'ung Meng Hui underwent a complete transformation after the revolution. The semblance of unity within the revolutionary party came under increasing strain. Factions within the T'ung Meng Hui became clearly delineated, and some groups left to form separate political parties. With the final overthrow of the Ch'ing dynasty, T'ung Meng Hui members considered their mission accomplished. Each was now free to pursue his personal ends.

The major division within the revolutionary party evolved between the central division, the faction which had planned to carry the revolution to central China, and the southern faction, which had been instigating revolts in southern China. The two factions became engaged in an intraparty struggle for control of the T'ung Meng Hui.

The southern faction, or "left wing," as Hu Han-min described it, was represented by Hu, Chu Chih-hsin, Liao Chung-k'ai, Ch'en Chiung-ming, and other southern leaders.[5] After the Wuch'ang uprising, this faction advocated completion of the revolution by military unification of the country. Hu Han-min and company sought to convert Sun Yat-sen to their view during his stopover in Hong Kong on his return to China in December, 1911.

The southern faction argued that, while the Ch'ing dynasty had lost the support of the people, the northern army under Yuan Shih-k'ai was still in the field.[6] Unless this power was eliminated, the revolution could not succeed. The revolution needed a strong base to secure its aims. They feared that once Sun arrived in Shanghai he would succumb to pressure and

---

[5] *Ke-min wen-hsien* Lo Chia-lun ed., (Taipei, 1953), III, p. 53-66. Hereafter cited as *Ke-min wen-hsien*.

[6] *Ibid.*

THE "SINGLE-ISSUE PARTY" 69

accept the presidency of a powerless provisional government at Nanking. Huang Hsing's election and his subsequent forced resignation as commander-in-chief were cited as the likely pattern for any chief executive. The southern faction thus asked Sun to remain in Kwangtung and organize a military force that could unify the country within two or three months. With the conflict between Hupeh and Nanking, there was speculation that Canton might be made the temporary capital. If so, Sun could remain in Kwangtung and yet control the situation.

To their dismay, Sun disagreed. "If I do not proceed to Shanghai and Nanking, there are no others who can assume the task of managing internal and external affairs. . . ."[7] According to Hu Han-min, Sun said that the enemy might have the military strength, but he, Sun, had the support of the people. With internal conflict raging inside the revolutionary camp, he was needed more than ever to aid the revolution. A defensive military policy would surely lead to defeat. What purpose would Kwangtung and the south serve if central China could not be held? Although Sun distrusted Yuan Shih-k'ai, he considered him more valuable than an army of a hundred thousand men. Sun saw in Yuan a means for the final overthrow of absolutism and the Ch'ing dynasty.

The central division of the T'ung Meng Hui, labeled by Hu Han-min the "right wing," was clearly in control in Shanghai.[8] Members of the division included Sung Chiao-jen, Ch'en Ch'i-mei, and Chu Cheng. As Hu and the southern faction had predicted, Sun Yat-sen became increasingly susceptible to the political manipulations of the right wing. After Sun's arrival in Shanghai, a meeting was held to decide between a presidential and a cabinet form of government.[9] The gathering was attended by Sun, Hu Han-min, Wang Ching-wei, Huang Hsing, Ch'en Ch'i-mei, Sung Chiao-jen, Chu Cheng, Chang Ching-

---

[7] *Ibid.*

[8] *Ibid.*

[9] The following account is taken from *ibid.*, III, 56; Chu Cheng, *op. cit.*, p. 529; and Hsu Hsu-erh, "Biography of Sung Chiao-jen," Part III, *Min-li Pao*, April 13, 1913, p. 3.

chiang, Ma Chun-wu, and others. Sun favored a presidential system with powers concentrated in the hands of the chief executive on the ground that a strong chief executive was an absolute necessity in a period of national reconstruction. Hu Han-min supported Sun's position, as did Huang Hsing. The advocates of a cabinet system were led by Sung Chiao-jen, who may have feared that Yuan Shih-k'ai, who had been promised the presidency, would misuse the powers of the chief authority. Sung finally persuaded Sun to approve the cabinet system. Huang Hsing was chosen to head the cabinet as premier.

Since the General Plan formulated by the provisional delegates at Hankow provided for a presidential form of government, an amendment was required to legalize the substitution of a cabinet system. Sung Chiao-jen was unable to persuade the Provisional Parliament in Nanking to make the necessary revision.[10] The presidential system was retained and Sun was duly elected provisional president of the Chinese Republic by the Provisional Assembly.[11]

According to the General Plan, cabinet members were to be appointed by the president with the concurrence of the Provisional Assembly.[12] The cabinet list submitted by Sun to the Provisional Assembly, now the Provisional Parliament, was a combination of former Ch'ing officials and T'ung Meng Hui members.[13] In the former category were Huang Chung-ying (minister of the navy), Ch'en Chin-t'ao (minister of finance), Wu T'ing-fang (minister of judicial affairs), T'ang Shou-ch'ien (minister of communications), and Chang Chien (minister of the army). In the latter category were Wang Ch'ung-hui (min-

---

[10] Hsu Hsu-erh, op. cit.; Ku Chung-hsiu, op. cit., p. 51.

[11] Of the seventeen votes cast, Sun received sixteen and Huang Hsing one.

[12] The original version of the General Plan provided for only five ministries: Foreign Affairs, Interior, Finance, Military Affairs, and Communications (sec. 3, art. 17). When the number of ministries proved inadequate, after the founding of the government, the General Plan was amended to omit any fixed number of ministries.

[13] Chu Cheng, op. cit., p. 531.

ister of foreign affairs), Sung Chiao-jen (minister of interior), and Chang Ping-lin (minister of education). The representatives of the Provisional Parliament, however, rejected the appointments of Sung Chiao-jen and Chang Ping-lin, and sought the appointment of Wu T'ing-fang in place of Wang Ch'unghui as minister of foreign affairs. The representatives were strongly opposed to Sung Chiao-jen's appointment as minister of interior. According to Ku Chung-hsiu, Hopeh delegate to the Nanking Provisional Parliament, Sung had aroused the opposition of the Assembly because of his earlier attempt to amend the General Plan.[14] It was felt that Sun himself was seeking the premiership. As a result of the Provisional Parliament's rejection, Sun withdrew the cabinet nominations.

Sun Yat-sen then delegated the selection of a cabinet to Huang Hsing. Huang devised a system under which three ministries, Army, Foreign Affairs, and Education, would be headed by T'ung Meng Hui members and the rest by former Ch'ing officials.[15] However, the office of the ministers would be primarily titulary. The actual power in the various ministries would be held by the vice-ministers who were to be T'ung Meng Hui members. The Provisional Parliament accepted the revised cabinet nominations. The first cabinet of the Chinese Republic included the following members (the provincial origin of each is included for reference):[16]

	Ministry	
Minister		*Vice-minister*
	Army	
Huang Hsing (Hunan)		Chiang Tso-pin (Hupeh)
	Navy	
Huang Chung-ying (Fuchien)		T'ang Hsiang-ming (Hupeh)
	Foreign Affairs	
Wang Ch'ung-hui (Kwangtung)		Wei Ch'en-tsu (Hupeh)
	Judicial Affairs	
Wu T'ing-fang (Kwangtung)		Lu Chih-i (Yunnan)

---

[14] Ku Chung-hsiu, *op. cit.*, p. 60.

[15] Chu Cheng, *op. cit.*, p. 531; *Ke-min wen-hsien*, III, 57.

[16] *Min-li Pao*; January 5, 1912, p. 2.

Finance

Ch'en Chin-t'ao (Kwangtung)   Wang Huang-yu (Hupeh)

Interior

Ch'eng Te-ch'uan (Szechwan)   Chu Cheng (Hupeh)

Education

Ts'ai Yuan-p'ei (Chekiang)   Ching Yao-yueh (Shansi)

Industry

Chang Chien (Kiangsu)   Ma Chun-wu (Kwangsi)

Communications

T'ang Shou-ch'ien (Chekiang)   Yu Yu-jen (Shansi)

As matters turned out, none of the former Ch'ing officials who were appointed to head the various ministries assumed office.[17] Chang Chien, T'ang Shou-ch'ien, and Ch'eng Te-ch'uan were preoccupied with the formation of their own political party, the T'ung-i Tang. Control of the ministries, therefore, passed into the hands of the vice-ministers, dominated by T'ung Meng Hui members from central and northern China, and in particular from the province of Hupeh. Members from the central region occupied two other important positions. An old revolutionary, Hu Ying, from Hupeh, was appointed secretary-general in the office of the president,[18] while the controversial Hunanese Sung Chiao-jen was subsequently appointed to head the legislative bureau, empowered to draft the new republic's laws.[19] Sung Chiao-jen and the T'ung Meng Hui central division may have failed in their attempt to secure a cabinet system of government, but the control of the Nanking government was certainly in their grasp.

One point of dissension was resolved. However, the contention between the forces of the left (represented by Hu Han-min) and the right (led by Sung Chiao-jen) in the T'ung Meng Hui continued. The leaders of the right and left fac-

---

[17] Except for Chang Chien and T'ang Shou-ch'ien, who actually took office briefly, the others never assumed their ministerial posts in Nanking.

[18] *Min-li Pao,* January 12, 1912, p. 2. Hu subsequently resigned as secretary-general in the office of the president and was succeeded by Hu Han-min.

[19] *Min-li Pao,* January 12, p. 2.

tions differed markedly in their ideas on the form of government.[20] Sung Chiao-jen sought national centralization. He saw the trend toward local autonomy as a threat to the national government, which had become a mere figurehead. If this trend continued, it would end in the downfall of the government. A centralized government was a prerequisite to China's national rejuvenation. He pointed to the example of Japan after the Meiji restoration of 1868, where a strong, centralized government had made Japan into a world power. Hu Han-min, on the contrary, favored a federal system because of China's vast size and underdeveloped communications. China's traditional political system also discouraged the introduction of a centralized government. Hu argued that the situation in Japan was not comparable, for Japan had preserved monarchical institutions whereas China had discarded them for a republican system. Furthermore, the revolution had yet to reach the north. No doubt with Yuan Shih-k'ai in mind, Hu maintained that the Republic must be guarded against those who had been schooled in the age-old principles of absolutism.

Sung Chiao-jen agreed with Hu Han-min that Yuan Shih-k'ai and other former officials must be restrained. However, unlike Hu, who thought that federalism would serve as the method of restraint, Sung's plan called for neutralizing the powers of the presidency through the introduction of the cabinet system. Hu replied that the cabinet system depended upon a parliamentary system, and Chinese inexperience with representative government made the success of the cabinet questionable. He doubted whether the Parliament could resist external pressures. And if Parliament succumbed to outside influences, how could the cabinet be effective? In conclusion, Hu insisted upon the supremacy of the provinces as the sole guarantee for the Republic.

Both Hu Han-min and Sung Chiao-jen were concerned with the problem of containing the entrenched traditional forces represented by Yuan Shih-k'ai while China was being introduced to republicanism. Hu's answer to this problem lay in a

---

[20] *Ke-min wen-hsien*, III, 64-65.

territorial division of powers, while Sung's solution was a functional division of powers within the national government. China's political tradition favored Hu's argument. Weak in the extraconstitutional activities of an effective party organization, a federal structure seemed the only effective restraint upon the central government. Moreover, it would permit a gradual introduction of republicanism in China, allowing for local differences and limited experimentation. In 1912, however, China was eager to discard the old and adopt the new. A unitary state with functional division of powers was sought by a majority of the proponents for a new China. Sung Chiao-jen represented that segment of the new political leaders who dreamed of China as a strong, centralized, and unified state. They were impatient with the inherent rigidities which arise from a territorial division of powers in the federal scheme. Notwithstanding China's total inexperience with a republican form of government, Sung Chiao-jen was confident that with proper guidance and the functional division of powers on a national basis Yuan Shih-k'ai could be neutralized and China guided on the road toward republicanism.

Another area of disagreement between the right wing and the left wing centered on the future of the T'ung Meng Hui. This issue arose from the internal division of the revolutionary party and the complex political conditions after the 1911 revolution. The T'ung Meng Hui was founded chiefly on the basis of an anti-Ch'ing alliance. Under its banner were gathered nationalists, socialists, anarchists, and other groups. The success at Wuch'ang marked the achievement of their common goal; it also signaled the end of a unity based on expediency. Besides the open emergence of clearly distinguishable factions within the T'ung Meng Hui, some members left to form separate political groups. Liu Ch'eng-yu, Sun Wu, Lan T'ien-wei, and other T'ung Meng Hui members joined with elements in Hupeh to form the Min-she (People's Society),[21] which supported republicanism, claimed Rousseau's *Social Contract* as

---

[21] Yang Yu-chun, *Chung-kuo cheng-tang shih* (Shanghai, 1937), p. 53; Hsieh Pin, *Min-kuo cheng-tang shih* (Shanghai, 1928), p. 39.

the basis of its fundamental principles, and elected Li Yuan-hung as its leader. Another group, including Chang Ping-lin and members of the Kuang Fu Hui, established the Chung-hua Min-kuo Lien-ho Hui (Union of the Chinese Republic),[22] composed primarily of men from Chekiang. This group advocated that the T'ung Meng Hui should be dissolved.[23]

Others in the T'ung Meng Hui, while not renouncing their membership, established associations which contributed to the centrifugal tendencies within the party. The Chin-te Hui (Society to Advance Morality) was founded by T'ung Meng Hui members who were connected, directly or indirectly, with the promotion of anarchism. Some of the more prominent were Li Shih-tseng, Wu Chih-hui, Wang Ching-wei, Chang Chi, and Ts'ai Yuan-p'ei.[24] While primarily a nonpolitical organization, the purpose of the Chin-te Hui nevertheless lessened the solidarity of the T'ung Meng Hui. The Chin-te Hui was chiefly a moral regeneration society, which required of its adherents various forms of restraint, such as the avoidance of "immorality," gambling, tobacco, and alcohol. Members in certain categories were supposed to decline election to Parliament or appointments to parliamentary and governmental posts.[25] Wang Ching-wei was reported to have refused first the governorship of Kwangtung[26] and later the position of prime minister under Yuan Shih-k'ai[27] because of his membership in the Chin-te

---

[22] Yang Yu-chun, *op. cit.*, p. 51; Hsieh Pin, *op. cit.*, p. 37.

[23] *Ke-min wen-hsien*, III, 55.

[24] "Special Chin-te Hui Section," *Min-li Pao*, February 27, 1912, p. 8.

[25] The Chin-te Hui was a very complex organization with many rules. Of the five types of members, "general members" agreed not to gamble, practice immorality, or take concubines. "First-level members" agreed also not to become government officials. "Second-level members" added to these rules an agreement not to become members of Parliament and not to smoke. "Third-level members" included all the rules above with the additional stipulations of not drinking liquor and not eating meat. "Supporting members" agreed not to practice immorality and not to gamble. *Loc. cit.*

[26] *Ke-min wen-hsien*, III, 66.

[27] "News from Peking," *Min-li Pao*, March 6, 1912, p. 3.

Hui. [28] The refusal of Chin-te Hui members to participate directly in governmental activities no doubt contributed to the political instability after the revolution. That it furthered the internal division within the T'ung Meng Hui is unquestionable.

The T'ung Meng Hui also encountered strong competition externally from various mushrooming political groups. The new political freedom, hitherto unknown in China, produced a period of unusual political activity. The Chung-kuo She-hui Tang (Chinese Socialist Party) was founded by Chiang K'ang-hu on November 5, 1911.[29] On March 3, 1912, the Chung-hua Min-kuo Lien-ho Hui combined with other groups, chiefly from the provinces of Kiangsu and Chekiang, to form the T'ung-i Tang (Unification Party).[30] Other political groups such as the Kung-ho Tang (Republican Party), the Kuo-min Chieh-chin Hui (People's Progressive Society), the Kuo-min Kung-chin Hui (Joint Citizens' Progress Society), and the Kung-ho Chien-she Tao-lun Hui (Society for Discussing the Reconstruction of the Republic) were founded, all within a six-month period after the October 10 revolution.[31] Each sought the spoils of government, thereby increasingly challenging the leadership of the dissension-ridden T'ung Meng Hui.

The growth of political groups soon gave rise to public concern. Chang Hsin-yen initiated a crusade to correct what he considered an unnatural phenomenon. He had just returned from Great Britain, where he had studied law and politics at the University of Edinburgh. Armed with the teachings of the West, he set out to champion a new political system. Chang insisted that parties should be based upon principles,[32] and cited Edmund Burke's classic definition of a political party: "Party is

---

[28] In Fuchien a Chin-te Hui member declined to head the provinces' educational department and governmental post. "Impact of the Chin-te Hui," *Min-li Pao*, April 20, 1912, p. 2.

[29] Yang Yu-chum, *op. cit.*, p. 212.

[30] *Min-li Pao*, March 3, 1912, p. 10.

[31] Yang Yu-chum, *op. cit.*, pp. 53-56; Hsieh Pin, *op. cit.*, pp. 37-41.

[32] Chang Hsin-yen, "Political Parties and Party Platforms," *Min-li Pao*,

a body of men united for promoting by their joint endeavors the national interest upon some particular principle in which they are all agreed."[33] Surveying the state of political groups in China, Chang asked how many measured up to Burke's definition? How many of the political groups had a platform? Chang stated that it was a political platform that distinguished between a political party and a mere cluster of individuals seeking private gain. Political competition should be between principles and not between men.

Chang Hsin-yen favored a two-party system. The platforms of the two parties must differ, to insure the representation of diverse views. Chang encouraged the emergence of two major parties from among the numerous political factions. He also supported a parliamentary government with a responsible party cabinet.[34] Chang's appeal did not go unnoticed, and a realignment of political groups ensued.

The introduction of Western-inspired political institutions must be examined against the background of the Chinese political tradition.[35] China's monarchical system, in which the emperor held absolute rule, worked against the development of political parties and other democratic institutions. In contrast, modern political parties have been closely associated with the rise of Western democratic constitutionalism.[36] The mainstay of political support for constitutionalism was the mercantile class. It was the commercial middle class which battled against royal absolutism and eventually produced constitutionalism. Nationalism and Christianity, especially Protestantism, which preaches the dignity and responsibility of the individual,

February 24, 1912, p. 2; and "Why Has Shanghai Given Rise to Countless Parties and Factions?" ibid., February 27, 1912, p. 2.

[33] Edmund Burke, Thoughts on the Cause of the Present Discontents, (London, 1951), p. 81. This work was first published in 1770.

[34] Chang Hsin-yen, "On a Strong and Powerful Political System," Min-li Pao, March 1, 1912, p. 2.

[35] See Introduction.

[36] C. J. Friedrich, Constitutional Government and Democracy (Boston, 1950), pp. 19-28; R. M. MacIver, The Web of Government (New York, 1947), pp. 175-183.

also contributed. Even in Great Britain, the mother of democracy and political parties, it took centuries for democratic constitutionalism to emerge. Yet China, which had been governed
continuously since prehistoric times by an absolute monarchy,
had been dominated by a single system of belief, and had never
had a commercial middle class, was expected to adopt overnight
a Western type of political system. The optimism which prevailed among the republican leaders without considering the
realities of the Chinese social and political scene invited disaster. But the catastrophe was hidden by the flush of victory. A
new China was to be built upon the Western democratic image.
And were not political parties the major instruments of democracy?

The principal issue faced by the T'ung Meng Hui after the
founding of the Republic was whether it should continue as a
revolutionary secret society or reorganize as a Western-style
political party. When the provisional government was established, the headquarters were transferred from Shanghai to
Nanking. At a meeting of the party called on January 20, 1912,
more than a thousand members were reported to have attended.[37] Sun, who was serving as president of the Chinese Republic, was preoccupied with affairs of state, and had sent Hu
Han-min to represent him. The major decision of the conference appears to have been the election of Wang Ching-wei as
tsung-li (director-general) of the T'ung Meng Hui.[38] The meeting ended without taking action on the organizational condition
of the party.

Political events, however, had thrust the T'ung Meng Hui
into the limelight. The T'ung Meng Hui could no longer remain a secret society. The politics of the Republic necessitated
the passing away of the traditional secret societies. Legal change
had to follow. Externally, the formation of various political

---

[37] *Min-li Pao*, January 22, 1912, p. 2.

[38] *Ibid.* Wang Ching-wei did not hold the position for long. Whether
out of reverence for Sun Yat-sen or preoccupation with other matters, e.g.,
the Chin-te Hui, Wang resigned from the post of *tsung-li* in February,
1912. *Ibid.*, February 24, 1912, p. 3.

groups increasingly challenged the T'ung Meng Hui's position of leadership and made necessary a reexamination of the party's position. The founding of the T'ung-i Tang as a full-fledged party served as a special impetus. Perhaps more important was the T'ung Meng Hui's consideration of its role under Yuan Shih-k'ai, who had been elected president by the Provisional Parliament in February. All factions of the T'ung Meng Hui distrusted Yuan, and no doubt realized the need of an effective organization to counter his every move. Intraparty affairs also demanded attention. The T'ung Meng Hui's traditional lack of discipline greatly weakened the party at Nanking. Moreover, it lacked a real organizational structure. Chu Cheng reports of individuals posing as T'ung Meng Hui members and falsely recruiting new members, pocketing the five-dollar membership fee.[39] Owing to these and other factors, the T'ung Meng Hui soon acquired a very bad reputation. To be resolved also were the differences between the T'ung Meng Hui members of the Provisional Parliament and the national government; the misunderstanding between Li Yuan-hung's Hupeh Min-she group and Nanking were to be overcome, too.[40]

The T'ung Meng Hui party congress of March 1912 was badly divided.[41] The left wing, represented by Hu Han-min and other southern leaders, sought to continue the secret society role of the T'ung Meng Hui. It argued, as Hu and others had earlier, that the success of the revolution was yet to be achieved. With Yuan Shih-k'ai's assumption of the presidency the future was even more unpredictable. The left wing rejected the idea of transforming the organization into an open political party. The right wing, represented by Sung Chiao-jen and other members of the party's central China division, considered that the military phase of the revolution had been successfully concluded, and that open political parties should engage in constitutional parliamentary activities, represent the people, and act

---

[39] Chu Cheng, *op. cit.*, p. 549.
[40] *Ibid.*, pp. 532-533.
[41] *Ke-min wen-hsien*, III, 63.

as a watchdog over the government. Much to the dismay of Hu Han-min and others of the left wing, their opponents won the day,[42] and the T'ung Meng Hui was transformed from a secret society into an open political party.

The new T'ung Meng Hui proceeded to draft a constitution, set forth its platform, and elect officers. In Western fashion, the constitution began with a statement of purpose:[43] to bring about the consolidation of the Republic and to effectuate the principles of the people's livelihood. A nine-point political program was proclaimed: (1) the achievement of administrative unity, and the development of local government; (2) the fostering of racial assimilation; (3) state socialism; (4) compulsory education; (5) equality of men and women; (6) compulsory military service; (7) financial reorganization and reform of the tax system; (8) support for international equality; (9) emphasis upon the opening and development of wastelands through colonization.

In part this political program was an attempt to combine the pre-Republican goals of the T'ung Meng Hui and the practical needs of the Republic. Certainly the provisions calling for the principles of the people's livelihood and state socialism were consistent with Sun Yat-sen's principles, while the provisions of obligatory military service and financial reforms fulfilled the urgent needs of the time. Nevertheless, the T'ung Meng Hui program of 1912 fell short of the original program expressed in the manifesto of 1905. The important idea of a three-stage process through which China would be gradually introduced to republicanism was omitted. The right-wing T'ung Meng Hui, together with the rest of the country, seemed determined to turn China into a republic immediately.

Membership in the new T'ung Meng Hui was open to all adult Chinese. Prospective members were to be nominated by two members and, upon the official sanction of the deliberation

---

[42] Hu Han-min was so disappointed at the turn of events that he considered retiring and going abroad to study. *Ibid.*

[43] For the full text of the constitution see *Min-li Pao.* March 6, 1912, p. 2; March 8, 1912, p. 2.

department, be accepted into the party. They should possess "a general knowledge" and be willing to adhere to the party's principles and regulations. Members were prohibited from affiliating with other political parties. An entrance fee of one dollar was required of new members, and annual dues of two dollars from all members. The prerequisites of a general education, together with entrance fees and annual dues, greatly limited the membership potential. In a country where education was limited to the few and destitution was common this was inevitable. Thus, while the T'ung Meng Hui became an open political party, it remained an elitist group.

A head office was established at Nanking; branches were to be founded in all provincial capitals and important cities. Sun Yat-sen was elected *tsung-li* to serve as its standard-bearer; Huang Hsing and Li Yuan-hung were associate directors.[44] Both the *tsung-li* and the associate directors were to hold office indefinitely. The constitution provided for the election of a ten-member secretariat. Members of the committee elected at the March 3 party congress included two members from Kwangtung, Hu Han-min and Wang Ching-wei; three from Hupeh, Liu K'uei-i, T'ien, T'ung, and Chu Cheng; and one each from Hunan, Hopeh, Kwangsi, Kweichow, and Szechwan, Sung Chiao-jen, Chang Chi, Ma Chun-wu, Ping Kang, and Li Chao-fu.[45] The secretariat was clearly dominated by the party's right-wing central division. For the five administrative bureaus, the *tsung-li* selected directors from among the ten-member secretariat for a period of one year, with provisions for re-election. Wang Ching-wei was appointed head of the general affairs bureau; Sung Chiao-jen, of the political affairs bureau; Chang Chi, of the social affairs bureau; Li Chao-fu, of the correspondence bureau; and Chu Cheng, of the finance bureau.[46] In addition, a deliberation department at headquarters, composed of representatives from each of the provinces and from the head

---

44 *Ibid.*, March 5, 1912, p. 3.
45 *Ibid.*, March 6, 1912, p. 7.
46 *Ibid.*, March 9, 1912, p. 3.

office, was given authority to pass judgment upon the statutes of
the T'ung Meng Hui.

In the organization of the new T'ung Meng Hui, there is
little doubt that power was intended to concentrate in the
person of the *tsung-li*. The unlimited term of office and control
of the party bureaucracy through the right to appoint directors
of the various bureaus vested decisive powers in the *tsung-li*.
However, Sun Yat-sen never attempted to build the party organization, but attended to other matters such as the propaga-
tion of the principles of people's livelihood. Control of the
T'ung Meng Hui thereby shifted to the ten-man secretariat and
especially the five bureau heads. Within the ten-men secretariat,
the left-wing leader Hu Han-min returned to Kwangtung to
assume the provincial governorship, while Wang Ching-wei left
to "study" overseas. The control of the T'ung Meng Hui, therefore, passed completely into the hands of Sung Chiao-jen and
the right wing. The destiny of the T'ung Meng Hui thus lay
with those who had sought its establishment as an open political
party.

A new political era was ushered in with the inauguration of
the renovated T'ung Meng Hui. Chang Hsin-yen wrote in the
Min-li Pao: ". . . with the declaration of its platform on March
3, 1912, though it underwent no change in name, the old T'ung
Meng Hui passed away and a new T'ung Meng Hui came into
being. . . ."[47] Chang's statement may have been unduly optimistic. Certainly no mere declaration of a platform could re-
make a political group overnight. Nevertheless, there was cause
for celebration, for with the establishment and operation of
Western-style political parties the new Republic could begin to
progress toward a democratic political system. The party became a symbol of China's transition into the republican era.

In many ways, the party's transformation was a direct consequence of its character as an alliance of various anti-Ch'ing
groups. Indeed, the pre-Republican T'ung Meng Hui may even

---

[47] Chang Hsin-yen, "On the T'ung Meng Hui," *ibid.*, March 6, 1912,
p. 2.

be characterized as a single-issue party, once advocated by M. Ostrogorski. The various groups which gathered under the banner of the T'ung Meng Hui had shared one common objective, to overthrow the Ch'ing dynasty. This was achieved with the 1911 revolution. Much like Ostrogorski's ideal single-issue party, the T'ung Meng Hui dissolved after the successful overthrow of the Ch'ing dynasty. However, events after the 1911 revolution demonstrated the need for the T'ung Meng Hui to continue, as an organizational unit to guide the nation on the road to reconstruction. There was even more reason now for the T'ung Meng Hui to reorganize and work toward the achievement of a true Chinese Republic.

IV THE PARLIAMENTARY PARTY:
THE KUOMINTANG

THE T'UNG MENG HUI reorganization of 1912 proved only a temporary measure. The months between the appearance of the new T'ung Meng Hui in March, 1912, and the formation of the Kuomintang in August of the same year witnessed momentous political changes. The resignation of the presidency by Sun Yat-sen in February, 1912, in favor of Yuan Shih-k'ai acknowledged and formalized the existing power relationship. Yuan Shih-k'ai, the Ch'ing war lord turned republican, became the *de jure* and *de facto* head of the infant Chinese Republic. With the transfer of power from Nanking to Peking, Yuan's stronghold, the T'ung Meng Hui was relegated to a secondary position. To regain the helm of government, therefore, became the sole objective of the party. The Kuomintang became the instrument through which the reassertion of power was achieved.

How did the new T'ung Meng Hui fail, thus precipitating the formation of the Kuomintang? There can be no doubt that the factional contention between the right wing and the left wing created a deep cleavage within the new political party. The left wing faction led by Hu Han-min and other southerners withdrew to the south. Hu Han-min assumed the governorship of Kwangtung and proceeded to build a model province. The new T'ung Meng Hui thereafter was dominated by Sung Chiao-jen's right-wing faction.

The political environment during this period and the role of Sun Yat-sen both had a profound impact upon the fortunes of the new T'ung Meng Hui. Within the T'ung Meng Hui, Sun, who had been elected *tsung-li* of the new party, remained the sole alternative force to Sung's faction which was capable of leading the party. But Sun's resignation from the presidency of the Republic in February, 1912, marked his withdrawal from politics. He chose instead the role of the great liberator, the man above politics, and, foremost, the social reformer. As "Father of the Republic," Sun perhaps reached his greatest height of popularity during the first year of the republic. Never again was he so popularly acclaimed.

Sun, after his abdication from office, planned a national speaking tour, leaving the affairs of the party to Sung Chiao-jen and others. He set the theme of his chosen mission in a speech at the farewell meeting of the T'ung Meng Hui at Nanking in April, 1912.[1] "Today with the abdication of the Manchus and the founding of the Chinese Republic, the two principles of nationalism and democracy have been achieved; only the principle of people's livelihood has yet to be realized." Henceforth the goal of the party must be to realize this principle. People tended to believe that political and national revolutions were less difficult to realize than social revolutions. Sun granted that such a thesis might be correct in Great Britain, the United States, and other countries where industry and commerce were fully developed. In those countries the capitalist class would present obstacles, and the realization of a social revolution would be difficult. But in China, where an industrial revolution had not occurred, where the development of commerce was still in its infancy, and a capitalist class had yet to appear,

[1] *Min-li Pao*, April 1, 1912. For the full text of Sun Yat-sen's speech see Kuomintang, *Kuo-fu ch'uan-chi* (Taipei, 1957), III, 21-26. (Hereafter cited as *Kuo-fu ch'uan-chi*).

a social revolution could be achieved with relative ease. In the industrially developed countries force would be required, but China, because of its very backwardness, could realize a social revolution without resort to violence. Said Sun: "If equalization of land rights can be accomplished, 70 to 80 per cent of the social revolution will then have been attained."

In Wuch'ang, Sun renewed his appeal to carry on the work of a social revolution.[2] And in Shanghai he reasserted his position: "Today with the Manchu government eliminated and the republican political system established, the two political platforms of nationalism and democracy have been attained. Henceforth, we need urgently to strive toward the principle of people's livelihood."[3] Again Sun struck out against his adversaries, who questioned the practicality of the principle of people's livelihood for China when even the highly developed Western nations were unable to carry it out. The foremost need of China, according to the opposition, was to encourage Chinese capitalists; only thus could China compete with foreign capitalists and develop industrially. Sun replied that the principle of people's livelihood did not oppose capital; rather, it was against capitalists, against the economic monopoly of the few. Sun summarized the three people's principles as follows: "The principle of nationalism of our Society is the maintenance of our country's national independence against external forces; the principle of democracy is opposition to political monopolization by a minority; and the principle of people's livelihood is the elimination of a capitalist minority so as to allow the people to enjoy in common the fruits of production. Therefore, the principle of people's livelihood is state socialism."[4]

Sun returned to Kwangtung in May, 1912. He had not set foot in his native province since the abortive Canton revolt of 1895, and there was much rejoicing when he visited his birth-

---

[2] Speech by Sun in Wuch'ang, April 10, 1912, *Kuo-fu ch'uan-chi*, III, 28-29.

[3] Speech by Sun in Shanghai, April, 1912, *ibid.*, III, 30-32.

[4] *Loc. cit.*

place, Hsiang-shan. In a series of talks in Canton Sun reiterated
the principle of people's livelihood, emphasizing the equalization of land rights, and defending his program on the score that
it would prevent the accumulation of wealth, in the form of
land, by a minority.[5] If his policy of equalization of land rights
was not implemented now, he warned, China would never have
another opportunity. Sun's urgent appeal seemed to have little
effect on his audience. Toward the end of June, 1912, he returned to Shanghai and engaged in the more modest task of
planning China's railway system.

Sun Yat-sen's endeavor to win support for his principles of
people's livelihood was in marked contrast to the preoccupation
with political affairs of other T'ung Meng Hui leaders. While
party members continued to pay lip service to the principles of
people's livelihood, Sun was the only party leader who actively
sought to make them a reality. Without higher standards of
living, China could not hope to achieve political stability; yet
were not China's political problems also pressing? Should Sun
not have placed equal emphasis upon social and political affairs?
Consciously or unconsciously, he seemed to believe that socio-
economic reconstruction could be divorced from political reconstruction.

If Sun was guilty of concentrating on socio-economic problems to the neglect of China's immediate political needs, Sung
Chiao-jen and other T'ung Meng Hui leaders were guilty of
focusing on political matters to the exclusion of all others.
Sung's almost single-minded determination to introduce Western political institutions into China reached its height with the
formation of the Kuomintang. The proponents who sought
China's institutional transformation dominated the party; Sun's
plans for socio-economic development were disregarded. The
T'ung Meng Hui raced toward the introduction of political
institutions based upon Western models.

The period of Sun Yat-sen's tour coincided with the formal

---

[5] Speeches by Sun in Canton, May 4 and May 13, 1912, *ibid.*, III, 37-40,
45-46.

transfer of power from Nanking to Peking. The affairs of both
government and party were therefore left to the discretion of
those who remained, Sung Chiao-jen's right wing faction. The
right wing well knew the significance of this shift of power.
Consequently, to safeguard T'ung Meng Hui interests and to
restrain the presidential office, a plan was devised to vest control of the government in the legislature. The cabinet was
chosen as the instrument through which the scheme would be
achieved. The cabinet system had been written into the provisional constitution and adopted by the Provisional Parliament in Nanking. Besides the intent to neutralize Yuan Shih-
k'ai, the adoption of the cabinet system was a victory for Sung
Chiao-jen.

When the new government was organized by Yuan Shih-k'ai,
T'ang Shao-i, an old retainer of Yuan, who had become a T'ung
Meng Hui member, was chosen premier,[6] and proceeded to
form a cabinet. T'ung Meng Hui members were appointed to
head four ministries: Ts'ai Yuan-p'ei as minister of education,
Wang Ch'ung-hui as minister of justice, Sung Chiao-jen as
minister of agriculture and forestry, and Ch'en Ch'i-mei as
minister of commerce and industry.[7] The key ministries (Interior, Army, Navy) were filled by Yuan's personal followers,
while Chao Ping-chun, a member of the newly formed pro-
Yuan Kung-ho Tang (Republican Party), was appointed minister of finance.[8] The heterogeneity of the T'ang cabinet ruled

---

[6] T'ang Shao-i was introduced into the T'ung Meng Hui by Sun Yat-sen
and Huang Hsing (Min-li Pao, April 1, 1912, p. 3). T'ang became a follower of Yuan Shih-k'ai while serving as a customs official in Korea. At the
time Yuan was in charge of military affairs in Korea. Upon Yuan's recall to
power after the success of the revolution, T'ang represented him in negotiations with the revolutionaries.

[7] Ch'en Ch'i-mei never took office; the Ministry of Commerce and Industry was directed by Wang Cheng-t'ing, also a T'ung Meng Hui member.

[8] The Kung-ho Tang was formed on May 5, 1912, soon after the opening
of the Provisional Parliament in Peking. It was an amalgamation of the
Min-she (People's Society), the Min-kuo Kung Hui (People's Association),
the Kuo-min Chieh-chin Hui (People's Progressive Society), the T'ung-i
Tang (Unification Party), and the Kuo-min Tang (People's Party). Its

against its success; partisan differences in turn increased the predominant position of the president. Under growing pressures, the T'ang Shao-i cabinet fell in June, 1912.

A period of political instability ensued, and ushered in a wave of antipolitical party sentiment. The failure of the cabinet did not discredit the institution itself. Rather, failure was attributed to the mixed composition of the T'ang cabinet, and a cry for a responsible party cabinet followed. The staunchest supporter of a party cabinet was the T'ung Meng Hui, which had been disillusioned by the "coalition" cabinet experience. Speaking before the quarterly meeting at T'ung Meng Hui headquarters (now in Peking) in July, Wei Ch'en-tsu, acting director of the general affairs bureau, explained the party's position.[9] The T'ung Meng Hui, Wei stated, had voluntarily abdicated the presidency in favor of Yuan Shih-k'ai in the interest of national unity, and had accepted the cabinet posts assigned to its members. It did not insist on the appointment of Huang Hsing, the party's nominee as minister of war. Its decision to join the T'ang cabinet was based upon T'ang Shao-i's four-point program: disarmament, restoration of order, obtaining foreign recognition, and financial reform. The T'ung Meng Hui believed that T'ang's program would contribute to the attainment of the principle of people's livelihood. When T'ang was charged with financial mismanagement, a stalemate developed in the cabinet. T'ang and the T'ung Meng Hui members in the cabinet resigned. Because of this experience the T'ung Meng Hui insisted on a homogeneous cabinet. A party cabinet, however, did not necessarily connote the formation of a one-party cabinet by the T'ung Meng Hui. Rather, explained Wei, it meant the concentration of executive powers (prime minister) within one party, which need not be the T'ung Meng Hui. Other political parties could assume the responsibilities.

---

members included Li Yuan-hung, Chang Chien, Ch'eng Te-ch'uan, and T'ang Hua-lung. The party was pro-Yuan. See Yang Yu-chun, *Ching-kuo cheng-tang shih* (Shanghai, 1937) pp. 56-57.

[9] "Speech of Mr. Wei Ch'en-tsu," *Chung-kuo T'ung Meng Hui Yueh Chih-pu Tsa-chih*, No. 7 (September 1, 1912), 1-4 (individual pagination).

The T'ung Meng Hui would be content to assume the role of a watchful opposition if another party succeeded in forming a cabinet.

The predicament was that neither the T'ung Meng Hui nor the other political parties were capable of forming a party cabinet. None had a majority in the Provisional Parliament, whose consent was required for the appointment of the premier and cabinet. The political complexion of the Provisional Parliament (numbering 121 members) consisted of some forty T'ung Meng Hui members, an equal number of Kung-ho Tang members, twenty-five members of the T'ung-i Kung-ho Tang (the United Republican Party), and a scattering of minor political groups.[10] With neither of the major parties in a majority, balance of power in the Provisional Parliament fell upon the minor T'ung-i Kung-ho Tang. The T'ung Meng Hui, unable to obtain support from the minor parties, could not attain power. Since they saw no possibility of organizing a cabinet of their own, the T'ung-i Kung-ho Tang and the Kung-ho Tang advocated a nonpartisan cabinet, which was intended to block the formation of a government by the T'ung Meng Hui. The T'ung Meng Hui, however, endorsed a nonpartisan cabinet. At a meeting of the Kung-ho Tang, the T'ung-i Kung-ho Tang, and the T'ung Meng Hui to discuss the political crisis on June 21, the T'ung Meng Hui representative, Li Chao-fu, gave his party's full support to "a cabinet organized by another party or even a nonpartisan cabinet."[11] A so-called nonpartisan premier, Lu Cheng-hsiang,[12] was chosen, but his cabinet was unable to obtain the approval of the Provisional Parliament. Only

---

[10] Yang Yu-chun, op. cit., p. 57. It is difficult to break down the party membership in the Provisional Parliament because of the practice of maintaining membership in more than one party concurrently. The China Year Book, 1913, numbers the T'ung Meng Hui membership in the Provisional Parliament as thirty-six. However, six of them are listed as members of the T'ung-i Kung-ho Tang also. See H. T. Montague Bell and H. G. W. Woodhead, The China Year Book, 1913 (London, 1913), p. 504.

[11] Min-li Pao, June 24, 1912, p. 3.

[12] Lu Cheng-hsiang was supported by the Kung-ho Tang and the T'ung-i

through Yuan Shih-k'ai's personal intervention was a cabinet finally formed.

During this period, the political parties discredited themselves in the eyes of the country. Dissensions became increasingly personal in character. The Kung-ho Tang's demand that T'ung Meng Hui members should be excluded from the premiership was considered a new low in party morality.[13] Chang Hsin-yen regarded it as a dangerous precedent when political parties were guided by men instead of principles.[14]

The frustration resulting from the inability of a party to form a cabinet led to a demand for the creation of two major parties. In his famous essays "On the Dissolution of Parties and the Creation of Parties,"[15] Chang Hsin-yen called for the dissolution of current political parties and their replacement by two major political parties based upon principles. Chang put forth the novel idea of convening a meeting of party representatives to study and take positions on all political issues. Two political parties would then be organized upon the basis of their stand on the issues. Platform-based political parties would finally become a reality. Chang's goal of a two-party system subsequently came into being, at least in a rudimentary form.

The T'ung Meng Hui in 1912 was distinguished by its adherence to the principle of people's livelihood. Certainly Sun Yat-sen's national campaign contributed to this image, and the national officers also interpreted the party's goal in terms of the attainment of the principle of people's livelihood. However, long-range goals were one thing; immediate needs, another. Whereas Sun Yat-sen could devote his thoughts to a utopian dream, the national T'ung Meng Hui in Peking, engaged in daily political combat, encountered the reality of politics. Since the T'ung Meng Hui needed a parliamentary majority to attain

---

Kung-ho Tang. He was unacceptable to the T'ung Meng Hui. Lu was a veteran diplomat, but he knew nothing about domestic politics.

[13] Chang Hsin-yen, "Comments on Current Events," *Min-li Pao*, June 23, 1912, p. 2.

[14] *Ibid.*

[15] Chang Hsin-yen, *Min-li Pao*, July 29, August 4, and August 7, 1912.

power, the national party must pursue a course of action to secure a majority in the first parliament.

The internal requirements of the T'ung Meng Hui were also in need of revitalization. The party had lost its purpose for existence.[16] The national party lacked organization and planning, and nothing had been achieved since it moved to Peking. Instead, charged Ts'ai Yuan-p'ei, T'ung Meng Hui members were engaging in self-praise, glorifying their role in the creation of the Chinese Republic. Ts'ai called upon party members to organize into an effective unit and to abide by the decisions of the party.

The T'ung Meng Hui in 1912 was at an embryonic stage of development. Provincial and local branches were only beginning to be established. The party occupied dominant positions in only four provinces.[17] Aside from the lack of organization, a major hindrance to the party's expansion was the shortage of funds. During the early months of the Republic, funds were diverted into governmental channels to meet the continuous financial crisis.[18] The support of the T'ung Meng Hui, therefore, depended chiefly upon voluntary contributions from national party leaders and party provincial governors.[19] In July,

---

[16] "Speech of Mr. Ts'ai Yuan-p'ei," *Chung-kuo T'ung Meng Hui Yueh Chin-pu Tsa-chih*, No. 7 (September 1, 1912), 4-5 (individual pagination).

[17] These were Kwangtung, Hunan, Anhwei, and Kiangsi provinces, governed, respectively, by T'ung Meng Hui members Hu Han-min, T'an Yen-k'ai, Po Wen-wei, and Li Lieh-chun. However, even these T'ung Meng Hui strongholds were no match for Yuan Shih-k'ai's military power.

[18] The most pressing needs were military, for Nanking had to meet both local and provincial demands. Private and public loans were secured, but the financial needs of the government continued to be greater than the available income. Lo Chia-lun, ed., *Ke-min wen-hsien* (Taipei, 1953), III, 58-61 (hereafter cited as *Ke-min wen-hsien*), and Ku Chung-hsiu, *Chung-hua min-kuo k'ai-kuo shih* (Shanghai, 1914), pp. 65-67.

[19] Chu Cheng, the first director of the T'ung Meng Hui's finance bureau, wrote that the party had to rely upon individual contributions from Sun Yat-sen, Huang Hsing, and T'ung Meng Hui provincial governors to subsist. Chu Cheng, *Chu Chio-sheng hsien-sheng ch'uan-chi* (Taipei, n.d.), pp. 550-551.

1912, the Nanking T'ung Meng Hui branch still required a personal contribution from Huang Hsing for its maintenance.[20] The party also suffered from intraparty contention. One such controversary involved the Kwangtung T'ung Meng Hui branch and the national party headquarters,[21] in regard to jurisdiction over the overseas Chinese, a lucrative source of financial support. Both the national party and the Kwangtung branch were organizing their brothers overseas. The Kwangtung branch, however, claimed that it was to have sole jurisdiction over the Chinese abroad. The T'ung Meng Hui, national and provincial, was less a cohesive political organization than an aggregation of individual leaders, and hence did not constitute a dependable source of political power.

As the dominating force within the national party, the Sung Chiao-jen faction assumed responsibility for the destiny of the T'ung Meng Hui. To strengthen the political position of the T'ung Meng Hui and settle intraparty claims, a majority in the new Parliament must be captured. This the national T'ung Meng Hui set out to attain through coalitions and amalgamations with other political groups.[22]

The decision to expand the base of the T'ung Meng Hui had its origin in the T'ang Shao-i cabinet crisis of June, 1912. The idea was first expressed publicly at the July 14 party meeting at Peking.[23] However, the party was in the midst of a power struggle over the issue of a cabinet and it was decided that any reorganization of the party at that moment might be misinterpreted. In the meantime the move to reorganize the T'ung

[20] "Branch Reports—Nanking Branch," *Chung-kuo T'ung Meng Hui Yueh Chih-pu Tsa-chih*, No. 4 (August 11, 1912), n. p.

[21] *Ibid.*

[22] The *Min-li Pao* (June 4, 1912, p. 7) reported the merger of the Ch'uan-kuo Lien-ho Chin-hsin Hui (National United Progressive Society) with the T'ung Meng Hui. Other parties wishing to join the T'ung Meng Hui were to observe its platform, discard their own program, abandon their party designation, turn over their membership list and financial holdings. "Branch Decisions," *Chung-kuo T'ung Meng Hui Yueh Chih-pu Tsa-chih*, No. 4 (August 11, 1912), n. p.

[23] *Min-li Pao*, July 17, 1912, p. 3.

Meng Hui was gathering momentum. In a July 19 editorial of the Shanghai *Min-li Pao*, Hsu Hsu-erh, a Sung Chiao-jen supporter, called upon the party to revitalize itself by absorbing new blood.[24] The T'ung Meng Hui should merge with other political groups and create "a pure and great political party."

The drive to capture a parliamentary majority assumed greater vigor after the assumption of formal control of the T'ung Meng Hui by Sung Chiao-jen. Decisions relating to changes in the national party's command now intensified the T'ung Meng Hui's revisional trend. The five new party bureaus had never become fully operative. Wang Ching-wei, director of the all-important general affairs bureau, second to the office of *tsung-li* in prestige and authority, apparently never assumed office; until the July 21 conference, the bureau was led by an acting director. Chu Cheng, the finance bureau director, was also absent from the national headquarters at Peking. Sun Yat-sen, the elected leader of the T'ung Meng Hui, had chosen the role of a social reformer instead of a party builder. The lack of an organizational sense within the national party, therefore, contributed to its disintegration. At the party's summer quarterly meeting, Sung Chiao-jen was elected director of the general affairs bureau, replacing Wang Ching-wei; Sun Yu-yun, director of the finance bureau, replacing Chu Cheng; and Chang Yao-ts'eng, director of the political affairs bureau, taking the position vacated by Sung Chiao-jen. With a strengthened party, the T'ung Meng Hui prepared for action.[25]

In Sung Chiao-jen's acceptance speech as director of the general affairs bureau, he explained the new role of the T'ung Meng Hui.[26] He first expounded upon the nature of a political party. In a republican environment it was dependent upon

---

[24] Hsu Hsu-erh, "Comments on Current Events," *ibid.*, July 19, 1912, p. 2.

[25] *Ibid.*, July 23, 1912, p. 3; July 28, 1912, p. 7.

[26] *Ibid.*, July 28, 1912, p. 7. "Speech of Mr. Sung Chiao-jen," *Chung-kuo T'ung Meng Hui Yueh Chih-pu Tsa-chih*, No. 7 (September 1, 1912), pp. 5-6 (individual pagination).

public opinion. A political party resulted from majority support given to a specific political program which would contribute to the welfare of the people: "Politics is the life of
political parties and political opinion is its pivot." Sung con-
trasted the earlier secret society system of the T'ung Meng Hui
and the present Western-styled political party with an announced political program. Whereas a secret society was concerned primarily with destroying the old system, a political
party in a republic had to adopt peaceful tactics. The solution
of the major problems confronting the Republic—the financial
condition of the country and the foreign crisis—depended upon
political parties, and only through strengthening the T'ung
Meng Hui could effective means be devised. Sung Chiao-jen
proposed two ways of increasing the influence of the party: to
contact other political parties in basic agreement with the
T'ung Meng Hui, and to concentrate on the parliamentary
elections. If the party won a majority in Parliament, regardless
of the government's position, T'ung Meng Hui members could
control it.

The national T'ung Meng Hui formally undertook measures
to widen its base in August, 1912, when it first approached
representatives of the T'ung-i Kung-ho Tang, one of the minor
parties in the Provisional Parliament, which had much in common with the T'ung Meng Hui.[27] Generally, it sought to limit
the authority of the president. Some of its leaders had served
with the Provisional Parliament at Nanking, and a number of
its members belonged to the T'ung Meng Hui also. While its
membership and popularity could not be compared with that
of the T'ung Meng Hui, the T'ung-i Kung-ho Tang was well
entrenched in the northern provinces, a region in which the
T'ing Meng Hui was particularly weak.[28] The merger offer
gave the T'ung-i Kung-ho Tang an opportunity to assume a

---

[27] The following account of the formation of the Kuomintang is taken
mainly from "Merger of Five Parties," *Min-li Pao*, August 18, 1912, pp. 6-7.

[28] Wu Ching-lien, chairman of the Peking Provisional Parliament, was
from Liao-ning.

major political role. Yet the party was reluctant to merge unconditionally with the T'ung Meng Hui. Its terms were unex-
pectedly stiff: the name T'ung Meng Hui should be abandoned
and a new designation be given the union of the two political
parties; the T'ung Meng Hui's principles of people's livelihood
should be discarded; there should be an internal reorganization.[29] To abandon the party's name and its cherished social
principle could not be decided without consulting the two
most respected national leaders. Sun Yat-sen and Huang Hsing
both gave their approval,[30] but in other quarters the acceptance
of the conditions was bitterly resented.[31]

A third political group, the Kuo-min Kung-tang (National
Public Party), expressed its desire to join with the other two
to form a new political party.[32] Representatives of the three
parties, meeting on August 5, discussed first the issue of the
new party's designation. The name Min-chu Tang (Democratic Party) was proposed and rejected. The parties finally
decided upon the title Kuomintang (Kuo-min Tang, National
People's Party). Chang Yao-ts'eng, a member of the T'ung
Meng Hui, submitted a political program, but the T'ung-i
Kung-ho Tang and the Kuo-min Kung-tang objected to the use
of the term *min-sheng* (people's livelihood) in the new party's
statement of purpose. The declaration read: "The aim of the
party is to secure the Republic and nourish people's livelihood." They felt that the term had too narrow a meaning and
also that it would be confused with the T'ung Meng Hui's
principle of people's livelihood. Instead, the following was
proposed: "The aim of the party is to secure the Republic and
to effectuate democracy [politics of the people]." The T'ung

---

[29] *Min-li Pao*, August 18, 1912, p. 6-7.

[30] *Ibid.*, August 12, 1912, p. 3.

[31] Resentment at Sung Chiao-jen was especially bitter. Writing some
eighteen years later, Feng Tzu-yu still could not forgive Sung for abandoning the principle of people's livelihood. Feng Tzu-yu, *She-hui chu-i yu
Chung-kuo* (Hong Kong, 1920), p. 6.

[32] *Min-li Pao*, August 18, 1912, pp. 6-7.

Meng Hui representatives insisted on the retention of the term *min-sheng*, explaining that otherwise the merger could not gain the acceptance of the party. After heated debate, a compromise was reached, and the term *min-sheng* was included in the new party's five-point political program: the promotion of political unification, the development of a local self-government, the abolition of racial discrimination, the adoption of a social policy (*min-sheng*), and the maintenance of international peace.

Seven elected directors would select from among their number a director-general. Seven names were proposed at the meeting: Sun Yat-sen, Huang Hsing, Sung Chiao-jen, and Chang Feng-hui, representing the T'ung Meng Hui; Wu Ching-lien, Ts'ai O, representing the T'ung-i Kung-ho Tang; and Ch'en Ch'un-hsuan, representing the Kuo-min Kung-tang.

A second meeting was convened on August 11.[33] Present at the meeting were two additional minor political groups desiring to join with the other three: the Kuo-min Kung-chin Hui (Joint Citizens' Progress Society) and the Kung-ho Kung-chin Hui (Progressive Republican Society). The delegates were: Sung Chiao-jen, for the T'ung Meng Hui; Hsu Lien, for the Kung-ho Kung-chin Hui; Ku Chung-hsiu, for the T'ung-i Kung-ho Tang; Yu Chao-cheng, for the Kuo-min Kung-tang; and Hsu Ch'ien, for the Kuo-min Kung-chin Hui. Sung Chiao-jen served as chairman of the conference. Hsu Ch'ien requested clarification of the term *min-sheng*. A satisfactory explanation must have been offered, for no further questions were raised. Sung Chiao-jen's proposal to create a secretary-general responsible to the directors to manage party affairs was rejected on the ground that it would concentrate too much power in one person. Instead, five separate departments were established: general affairs, secretariat, political affairs, social, and finance. Sung Chiao-jen, no doubt bearing in mind the parliamentary elections, argued the need for a separate department to manage

---

[33] *Ibid.*

elections. But according to Ku Chung-hsiu, China's traditional distaste for political contests made the founding of a separate department unwise. He proposed that elections be managed by the political affairs department.[34]

The Kuomintang manifesto, issued on August 12,[35] stressed the importance of political parties in a republic. Unlike a monarchical system, where authority was vested in one individual, the center of power in a constitutional republic rested with the people. But as not everyone could participate in the government, working machinery was necessary. The function of political parties was to provide legislative and governmental leadership. The idea of a two-party system was emphasized. The multiparty system was condemned, since numerous parties contributed to political instability. The manifesto cited China's experience with the multiparty system as evidence of its unworthiness, and emphasized the superiority of the cabinet system: "In a nation which adopts a responsible cabinet system, the president occupies a nonpolitical position. Therefore, political parties need not compete over the presidency. They need

---

[34] Other rules and regulations published later included the following: (1) Membership was open to all Chinese citizens who shared the principles of the party. Prospective members were to be introduced by two party members. A one-*yuan* entrance fee was charged. Members were not to belong to another party concurrently. (2) Headquarters were to be at the nation's capitol. Directly under its jurisdiction were the communications departments, at important commercial capitals, and local subbranches. Overseas, any important center which had a Chinese population in excess of 1,000 could establish a branch. (3) Nine directors, elected for a two-year term, would elect from their own number a director-general. Directors managed party affairs in general. Thirty counselors, elected for two-year terms, would advise on important matters. Three finance officers were elected for a year's term. Seven auditors each served a one-year term. An unspecified number of secretaries were elected for a one-year term to head the five departments. A policy committee was also established. (4) A national congress was to be held yearly at headquarters. In a state of emergency, the national congress could be convened by the directors.

[35] *Min-li Pao*, August 14, 1912, p. 3. The full text of the Kuomintang manifesto may be found also in Tsou Lu's *Chung-kuo Kuo-min Tang shih-kao*, (Chungking, 1944), I, 126-128.

only concentrate on organizing a cabinet." The manifesto concluded with a restatement of the five-point political program of the Kuomintang.

Basic agreement had been reached on the institution of a new political party. The national T'ung Meng Hui was nearing a long-sought goal. However, while an accord had been achieved with the other four parties, approval had yet to be obtained from the membership. Even within the national T'ung Meng Hui there was opposition to the proposed merger.[36] However, the group favoring merger predominated, and the measure was sanctioned. The provincial and local branches remained ominously silent. Only the Shanghai branch reportedly gave full support to the new political party.[37]

T'ung Meng Hui members had two principal objections to the proposed new political party: the change of party designation and the compromised political program. The older members felt a sentimental attachment to the T'ung Meng Hui appellation. It was under the T'ung Meng Hui banner that the struggle to overthrow the Ch'ing dynasty had been waged, that many comrades had given their lives, and the Chinese Republic had been attained. The name held symbolic significance. Wang Ching-wei declared that the designation must be kept to remind T'ung Meng Hui members of their responsibilities,[38] and Ts'ai Yuan-p'ei also argued against discarding the name.[39] Perhaps Wei Ch'en-tsu's remarks best illustrated the party's problem.[40] First, since the T'ung Meng Hui had been organized as an antidynastic secret society, once its goal was achieved and a Republic founded there was no further reason to support or join it. Second, the society's upper class refrained from participating in the T'ung Meng Hui, now at the height of its power,

---

[36] *Min-li Pao*, August 12, 1912, p. 3.

[37] *Ibid.*

[38] *Ibid.*, April 7, 1912, p. 10.

[39] "Speech of Mr. Ts'ai Yuan-p'ei," *Chung-kuo T'ung Meng Hui Yueh Chih-pu Tsa-chih*, No. 7 (September 1, 1912), pp. 4-5 (individual pagination).

[40] "Speech of Mr. Wei Ch'en-tsu," *ibid.*, pp. 1-4 (individual pagination).

so as not to convey an impression that they sought favors. Third, there was opposition to the party. A change in name was not absolutely necessary to overcome these obstacles, but the retention of the T'ung Meng Hui designation would obstruct the party's struggle for power. Hence the issue of whether to retain the title T'ung Meng Hui or adopt the title Kuomintang was a matter of political survival.

If the T'ung Meng Hui name was recalled with fond remembrance by its members, its political program was regarded with reverence. Homage, however, did not imply conviction. T'ung Meng Hui members paid tribute to the principle of people's livelihood, but made no attempt to carry it out. In the first years of the Republic, Sun Yat-sen was the only T'ung Meng Hui leader to promote the principle. Yet other members continued to accept it as the party's goal.[41] The T'ung Meng Hui's insistence upon the retention of the principle in the new party's platform was perhaps due more to a sense of history than to faith in its attainment. The principle of people's livelihood had become synonymous with the T'ung Meng Hui. Both represented the goal of overthrowing the Ch'ing dynasty and founding a Republic.

Most of the T'ung Meng Hui platform provisions, formulated in March, 1912, were easily dispensed with. The Kuomintang platform did not mention compulsory education, nor was obligatory military service included. And T'ung Meng Hui's phrase "to strive for international equality" became "the maintenance of international peace" in the Kuomintang platform. However, one provision caused difficulty—the program calling for the equality of men and women, a radical advocacy in China in 1912 which no other party tolerated. When Sung Chiao-jen was questioned on the elimination of the equality provision[42] at a meeting on August 13, two women created a

---

[41] See Wei Ch'en-tsu's speech before the T'ung Meng Hui summer quarterly meeting, *ibid.*

[42] *Min-li Pao*, August 18, 1912, p. 7.

disturbance. Later, at the same meeting, Sung Chiao-jen was bodily attacked by a male member for eliminating the equality provision from the Kuomintang platform. The issue was resolved only after Chang Chi pleaded with the members to exercise restraint, and to await the arrival of Sun Yat-sen to render judgment.

Sun arrived in Peking on August 24, his first journey north since the founding of the Republic. On August 25 the T'ung Meng Hui met for the last time.[43] The occasion served as both a farewell meeting and a welcome to Sun. In his speech Sun emphasized the distinction between the past and the present role of the party. Whereas the past constituted a period in which old institutions were destroyed, the republican era was a time for construction. He urged T'ung Meng Hui members to forget old wounds and join with others in a spirit of mutual love to build the Republic. With Sun's speech the T'ung Meng Hui passed into history.

The inauguration of the Kuomintang was held on August 25, 1912. Before events began, Sung Chiao-jen was again bodily attacked for eliminating the equality provisions in the Kuomintang platform. After order was restored, a resolution restoring the equality provision in the party's platform was defeated. A few members objected to the Kuomintang title, and Min-chu Tang (Democratic Party) was offered in its place. This proposal was also defeated. Election of the seven directors followed. When a protest was lodged against the preselection of candidates, it was decided that the seven members who received the largest number of votes should be declared the directors. The following were elected: Sun Yat-sen, Huang Hsing, Sung Chiao-jen, Wang Ch'ung-hui, Wang Jen-wen, Wang Chih-hsiang, Wu Ching-lien, Chang Feng-hui, and Kung-sang-no-erh-pu (Prince Kalaching of Inner Mongolia).

---

[43] The following account of the passing of the T'ung Meng Hui and the birth of the Kuomintang is taken primarily from the August 26, 27, and 31, 1912, issues of the *Min-li Pao*, pp. 3 and 6.

Officiating at the birth of the new party, Sun stressed the necessity of putting country above party.[44] Other political parties
should be treated as brothers, for the Republic required the
support of all. He also touched upon the delicate issue of
equality of men and women. Personal goals should be placed
second to national interests. He therefore ruled that the equality issue should be postponed until the Republic had been
stabilized. Sun's appeal to patriotism satisfied both the men and
the women. Sun assured his audience that they need not fear
military interference in government. The military, too, cherished the Republic and had the national interests at heart.

Sun equated the social policy provision of the Kuomintang
platform with the principle of people's livelihood. Again he
sought to dispel the notion that it was designed to "seize the
wealth of the rich." Instead, he declared, it was intended to
prevent the "oppression of the poor by capitalists." Sun's ut-
terance must have caused concern among those who earlier had
demanded the removal of this principle from the Kuomintang
program, but his statement passed unchallenged.

The formation of the Kuomintang in 1912 must be seen in
terms of the introduction of Western democratic institutions
into China and, specifically, the attempt to create a true political party. The reorganized T'ung Meng Hui had proved inadequate, for it had remained an assemblage of old-time revolutionists who engaged in self-praise, glorifying their role in the
revolution of 1911. The party had failed to expand beyond its
traditional areas of influence in central and southern China. Its
political program, especially the people's livelihood principles,
was little understood. Yet to capture power in the new parliament the party required a majority, which depended upon its
acceptance by the electorate nationally. The reorganization of
the T'ung Meng Hui into the Kuomintang was the answer
to these and other problems. The T'ung Meng Hui, through
its merger with other political groups, expanded its base and

---

[44] *Ibid.*, August 31, 1912, p. 6. For the full text of Sun's speech see *Kuo-
fu ch'uan-chi*, III, 51-53.

acquired new vitality. The Kuomintang represented a mile-
stone in China's political tradition: a political party based
upon the Western model was unconditionally accepted as the
method of attaining power. Unfortunately for the Kuomintang, China was not prepared for Western-style political parties.

The Kuomintang became the leading political party and,
more important, won a resounding victory in the parliamentary
elections. But success, in a sense, led to its downfall. The party's
faith in the new democratic institutions and its readiness to
work with these handicapped it in the struggle with entrenched
traditional forces.

The tragedy which subsequently befell the Kuomintang was
not apparent to its leaders in 1912. Writing in the *Min-li Pao*,
Hsu Hsu-erh hailed the Kuomintang as a symbol of political
progress.[45] Sun Yat-sen remarked that the strength of the Kuomintang, resulting from the amalgamation of five parties,
greatly contributed to the nation's political progress.[46] Kuomintang membership increased by leaps and bounds. As the well-
known correspondent Huang Yuan-yung recorded, the Kuomintang had an overwhelming political magnetism in recruiting
members.[47]

The party's greatest achievement, however, lay in the parliamentary elections of December, 1912, and January, 1913. Out
of 596 seats in the House of Representatives, the party captured
269.[48] In the Senate the party captured 123 out of 274 seats. In
both houses the Kuomintang occupied about 45 percent of the
membership.

The Kuomintang was organized primarily with the intent of

---

[45] Hsu Hsu-erh, "Our Paper's Words of Congratulations on the Founding of the Kuomintang," *Min-li Pao*, September 2, 1912, p. 2.

[46] Speech of Sun Yat-sen on August 25, 1912, in *Kuo-fu ch'uan-chi*, III,
51-53.

[47] Huang Yuan-yung, *Yuan-sheng i-chu* (Shanghai, 1927), II, 156.

[48] Owing to the practice of members' belonging to more than one party
concurrently, it is difficult to estimate the number of seats held by the
Kuomintang in Parliament. The figures cited are from Tsou Lu, *op. cit.*,
I, 144.

neutralizing the powers of the chief executive, Yuan Shih-k'ai. However, party members differed in their attitude toward Yuan. Sun Yat-sen, who was elected *tsung-li* (director-general) of the party, expressed his uncompromising support of Yuan. At a banquet given by Yuan in his honor, Sun lavishly praised his host.[49] Sun declared that he had heard numerous complaints about the Republic, but people failed to realize that a tradition of absolutism of several thousand years could not be transformed overnight. "According to my private views, ten years will be required to effectuate the true republic. It is indeed the good fortune of China that today we have President Yuan, rich in political experience, to manage the affairs of state."[50] He especially admired Yuan for his role as a military trainer, for the young Republic required the military to protect its independence. Sun advised him to train an army of five million during his ten-year term of office, for only thus could China secure international equality.[51] While Yuan led the nation toward stability, Sun would concentrate on the country's railway development. Within the ten-year period he planned to build 200,000 *li* of railway financed by foreign loans, which he intended to obtain abroad. He would resign from his position as Kuomintang *tsung-li* to devote himself to the social reconstruction of the nation.[52]

Sun Yat-sen, perhaps realizing his own position and the Kuomintang's in relation to the traditional forces represented by Yuan Shih-k'ai, may have sought to increase Yuan's awareness of his responsibilities. Sun's optimistic prediction of a stabilized Chinese Republic within a ten-year period was a close approximation of the T'ung Meng Hui's revolutionary program, which provided for a nine-year period of tutelage

---

[49] *Min-li Pao*, August 30, 1912, p. 3. For the text of Sun's speech see *Kuo-fu ch'uan chi*, III, 53-54.

[50] *Kuo-fu ch'uan chi*, III, 53-54.

[51] *Min-li Pao*, August 31, 1912, p. 3.

[52] Speech of Sun Yat-sen on September 4, 1912, in *Kuo-fu ch'uan-chi*, III, 67-69.

designed to introduce China to constitutional democracy. Sun's subsequent withdrawal from both party and government to concentrate on social reforms lends weight to the supposition that Sun saw in Yuan a substitution for the originally intended party tutelage. Sun chose to give Yuan a free hand in governing the infant Republic. After a grand tour of northern China, Sun retired to Shanghai and began to make plans for China's railways. His attitude toward Yuan was perhaps best summarized by the remark, "Yuan is capable of doing good; do not compel him to do evil."[53]

Sun's personal view of Yuan was in no sense that of the Kuomintang. The party was widely divided. The Sung Chiao-jen faction of the Kuomintang perhaps came closest to sharing Sun's opinion. Between August, 1912, the month which witnessed the birth of the Kuomintang, and February, 1913, two months before China's first Parliament convened, the Sung faction cooperated with Yuan fully. Even Yuan's execution of Chang Chen-wu, a revolutionary military hero, failed to arouse the Sung faction against Yuan personally. This toleration of the Ch'ing military lord-turned-republican was violently opposed by the old T'ung Meng Hui left-wing faction of the party—the same group which had previously sought the military unification of the country without compromising with the monarchical camp. It had opposed the renovation of the T'ung Meng Hui in March, 1912, and had been slow to accept the formation of the Kuomintang.[54] It charged Sung Chiao-jen and his followers with opportunism.[55] It claimed that they refrained from attacking Yuan because of their desire for official posts and because they had been bribed. The Sung faction cited

---

[53] Yu Yu-jen, "Answer to a Certain Person," *Min-li Pao*, September 13, 1912, p. 2. This statement is attributed to Sun by Yu.

[54] The Kwangtung branch of the Kuomintang did not change its designation until January 26, 1913. Tsou Lu, *op. cit.*, I, 124.

[55] Yu Yu-jen, "Answer to a Certain Person," *Min-li Pao*, September 13, 1912, p. 2; September 14, 1912, p. 2; September 15, 1912, p. 2.

Sun Yat-sen's position in its defense.[56] Had not Sun extended full support to Yuan?

The Kuomintang's remarkable victory at the polls produced an interval of party unity. Contention faded into the background while the party prepared to assume management of the Republic. Sung Chiao-jen was appointed acting *tsung-li* of the Kuomintang. Again the destiny of the party lay with the faction that had advocated a broadening of its base.

Sung Chiao-jen had masterminded the T'ung Meng Hui's reorganization and the merger with other parties to form the Kuomintang. While he had made compromises in the process of enlarging the T'ung Meng Hui's base, he had been successful in securing a responsible party cabinet system. With the Kuomintang's victory in the parliamentary elections, the leaders assumed it was merely a question of time until the party accepted the mandate of the people and took its rightful position as the guardian of the Republic. In preparation for the transfer of power, Sung Chiao-jen, as the Kuomintang's *tsung-li*, sought to present to the people the course which his party intended to pursue.

One reason for the abatement of the seemingly eternal conflict between the Sung faction and the old T'ung Meng Hui left-wing faction may have been the change in Sung's attitude toward the Peking administration of Yuan Shih-k'ai. After the election, with control of the government assured, Sung became a fearless critic of the government. In February, 1913, he revised his earlier views of Yuan and levied a series of criticisms against the Peking government. Sung began his task in Hankow before a Kuomintang meeting.[57] He warned that both the people and the Republic were in serious trouble. Internally, China suffered from financial chaos, but the government had no plans for financial reorganization, and depended solely upon foreign loans for survival. Externally, the government had done noth-

---

[56] *Min-li Pao*, September 14, 1912, p. 2.

[57] "Bold Words of Sun Tun-ch'u [Sung Chiao-jen]," *ibid.*, February 13, 1913, p. 7.

ing in regard to Russia's recognition of Mongolian independence. Sung stated that he had warned Yuan Shih-k'ai of the seriousness of the Mongolian situation, but no steps had been taken to alleviate the crisis. Sung thus set the stage for the Kuomintang's march to Peking.

China's first Parliament was nearing its opening date, April 8, 1913. Kuomintang members from southern and central China were preparing to converge on the nation's capital to discuss party strategy. During his trip down the Yantze River from Hankow, Sung Chiao-jen stopped to address party comrades, and at every port renewed his charges against the government. However, he had reserved his crowning attack upon Yuan and the Peking government for the Kuomintang meeting in Shanghai.[58]

Sung told the members that the 1911 revolution had succeeded in one aspect only—the overthrow of the Manchus; but the original goal of the political revolution—a truly republican system of government—had yet to be attained. This could be realized through the constitution, which is "the guarantor of the republican system." He advocated a cabinet system because it could easily be changed if necessary. Under a presidential system, that would be impossible, for a president served for a fixed term. He charged the government with endangering national survival. The loss of Mongolia could lead to an upsetting of the balance of power among the foreign nations in China. The domination of one would lead to China's extinction. The nation, therefore, could ill afford to allow the Russians to set a dangerous precedent. The government was leading the country toward financial disaster. The complete dependence upon foreign loans would also expose the country to foreign domination. Under Yuan's administration, China appeared to be at the end of her road.

More than a hundred Kuomintang members of Parliament

---

[58] *Ibid.*, February 20, 1913, p. 11. Sung's speech, delivered on February 19, 1913, was recorded by *Min-li Pao* correspondent Hsu Hsu-erh.

had gathered in Shanghai to formulate a program and discuss strategy. In the absence of Sun Yat-sen, who had left on February 11 for a forty-day tour of Japan,[59] the Shanghai meeting was dominated by Sung Chiao-jen. Huang Hsing assisted in entertaining the delegates. According to Tsou Lu, elected to Parliament from the third district in Kwangtung, the Shanghai conference failed to agree upon a specific directive.[60] However, there was agreement on three general issues: (1) the provincial assemblies were to serve as the bodies through which the president would be elected; (2) the national government would be organized as a parliamentary system under which the prime minister would be elected by the House of Representatives and appointed by the president; the prime minister in turn would appoint his cabinet members, who would require the president's approval; and (3) the provincial system would be maintained and the governors elected by the provincial assemblies. The Kuomintang members of Parliament nominated Sung Chiao-jen parliamentary party leader.[61]

Sung drafted a political program to serve as the party's guide. The program presented directives on two levels: the structure of government, and governmental policy.[62] For the structure of government, Sung outlined five conditions: (1) a unitary state; (2) a responsible cabinet system; (3) provincial governors initially elected locally, but eventually appointed by the national government; (4) provinces to be self-governing bodies, with legislative powers; (5) the prime minister to be elected by the House of Representatives.

A ten-point prospectus was also formulated: (1) military

---

[59] *Ibid.*, February 11, 1913, p. 10. The *Min-li Pao* reported that Sun intended "to investigate Japan's industry, commerce, and railways."

[60] Tsou Lu in *Chung-kuo chin-tai shih lun-ts'ung*, ed. by Pao Tsun-p'eng *et al.* (Taipei, 1957), I, No. 8, pp. 81-95 (hereafter cited as Chung-kuo *chin-tai shih lun-ts'ung*).

[61] *Ibid.*

[62] *Min-li Pao*, April 2, 1913, p. 2; April 3, 1913, p. 3; April 4, 1913, p. 2; April 5, 1913, p. 3; April 6, 1913, p. 3; April 7, 1913, p. 3. Sung's political program was published after his death.

reorganization; (2) the creation of two governmental units below the national government: provincial and local administrative units, with the province serving as the chief self-governing entity; (3) provincial officers to be appointed by the national government; (4) financial reform; (5) development of natural resources; (6) promotion of local self-government; (7) a state-owned communication industry; (8) promotion of education; (9) judicial unification; (10) acquisition of foreign allies and attainment of a *status quo* regarding foreign interest in China.

Sung declared that if the proposed political program were carried out according to plans, the country could expect to achieve a degree of stability within ten years.[63] Sung and the Kuomintang were thus prepared to assume the responsibilities of managing the nation. Had not the party received its mandate in the parliamentary elections? As the majority party, was not the Kuomintang entitled to form the government? Indeed, according to the democratic process, Sung and the party were the rightful claimants to power. China could look forward to a period of construction, and the Kuomintang as a political party would guide the nation toward stability.

The hopes and aspirations of the Kuomintang were shattered on March 20, 1913, when Sung Chiao-jen was assassinated at the Shanghai railway station,[64] where he was awaiting a train to Peking to attend the opening of Parliament. Investigation revealed that Prime Minister Chao Ping-chun and Yuan Shih-k'ai were responsible for Sung's murder. The Kuomintang now faced an internal crisis. The party was confronted with the choice of continuing its goals through parliamentary means, thereby seeking justice for Sung's death through legal channels, or of obtaining revenge in a forceful manner by overthrowing the existing government.

The decision of an overwhelming majority to adopt a peace-

---

[63] *Ibid.*, March 23, 1913, p. 3. Sung's remarks were made two days before his death.

[64] *Ibid.*, March 21, 1913, p. 10.

ful answer to Sung's violent death may be attributed to several factors. In spite of Sung's death, the party still occupied a majority in Parliament and thus had the strength to organize the government. The nation could ill afford a civil war, which would shake the foundation of the infant Republic.[65] Perhaps the primary reason, according to a report by *Min-li Pao* correspondent, was the fact that the country had no desire for a renewal of conflict.[66] Thus the Kuomintang sought to protect its dominant parliamentary position.

If the Kuomintang had been overly confident before Sung Chiao-jen's assassination, it became increasingly disillusioned after the opening of Parliament. Instead of solidifying and presenting a united front, the Kuomintang began to disintegrate, and countless groups of Kuomintang members suddenly emerged.[67] Tsou Lu attributed the breakup of the party primarily to Yuan Shih-k'ai's bribery. Yuan operated on two fronts: financial assistance to the Kuomintang opponents and monetary inducements to Kuomintang members. Parliamentary membership was divided among four political parties.[68] The

---

[65] Tsou Lu, *Hui-i lu* (Taipei, 1915), I, 58-59.

[66] *Min-li Pao*, June 1, 1913, p. 2.

[67] Tsou Lu in *Chung-kuo chin-tai shih lun-tzu*.

[68] The standard breakdown of the political complexion of China's first Parliament is as follows:

Party	House	Senate
Kuomintang	269	123
Kung-ho Tang	120	55
T'ung-i Tang	18	6
Min-chu Tang	16	8
Independent	26	44
Members belonging to more than one party	147	38

See Tsou Lu, *Chung-kuo Kuo-min Tang shih-kao*, I, 144; Yang Yu-chun, *op. cit.*, p. 61; and Hsieh Pin, *Min-kuo cheng-tang shih* (Shanghai, 1928), pp. 51-52. The Min-chu Tang mentioned here, incidentally, is not to be confused with the rejected Min-chu Tang designation proposed for the Kuomintang during the latter's reorganization in August, 1912. The Min-chu Tang mentioned here was a minor party organized by Liang Ch'i-ch'ao

Kuomintang, with 45 percent of the membership in each house, constituted the majority party. Yuan Shih-k'ai first provided each non-Kuomintang member of Parliament with a monthly allowance of two hundred *yuan*; the parties themselves were also provided with generous gifts.[69] However, even the support of the minor parties proved insufficient. Yuan therefore proceeded to subvert the Kuomintang. Parliamentary members, upon the promise of financial rewards, were induced to declare their separation from the party. There were methods by which Kuomintang parliamentary members did not even need to withdraw from the party, and yet could still receive monetary "gifts." They were promised specific sums if they voted as instructed, or if they refrained from voting; even nonattendance was rewarded. Perhaps even more effective was the monetary encouragement extended to Kuomintang members to form their own parties. Tsou Lu records that he rejected an offer of 400,000 *yuan* from the government to organize a new party. But other Kuomintang members succumbed to temptation, and before long half a dozen parties composed of former Kuomintang members had emerged.[70] As a result the strength of the Kuomintang was seriously diminished.

In the organization of Parliament, the Kuomintang managed to secure the election of its nominees only to the presidency and vice-presidency of the Senate.[71] The House elected T'ang Hua-lung of the Min-chu Tang as its speaker and Ch'en Kuo-hsiang of the Kung-ho Tang as deputy-speaker. With control of the House in the hands of the other parties, the Kuomintang's

in 1912; it subsequently merged with the Kung-ho Tang and the T'ung-i Tang to form the Chin-pu Tang (Progressive Party) in 1913.

[69] Tsou Lu in *Chung-kuo chin-tai shih lun-ts'ung.*

[70] The new parties included the Hsiang-yu Hui (Society of Mutual Friends), led by Liu K'uei-i; the Cheng-yu Hui (Society of Political Friends), led by Ching Yao-yueh; the Ch'ao-jen She (Impartial Society), led by Kuo Jen-chang; the Chi-i She (Society for Mutual Welfare), led by Chu Chao-hsin; and the Kuei-ch'ou T'ung-chih Hui (Society of the Comrades of 1913), led by Ch'en Chia-ting. The parties ranged in size from about twenty to seventy. Yang Yu-chun, *op. cit.*, p. 69-70.

[71] Chang Chi was elected president, and Wang Chen-t'ing vice-president.

dream of dominating Parliament and organizing a cabinet
suffered its first rebuff. In May, 1913 the Kuomintang faced a
new rival in the party organized through the merging of the
three minor parties in Parliament. The Chin-pu Tang (Progressive Party) became the Kuomintang's archrival for political
power.[72] Theoretically, the two-party system had come of age.

The emergence of a single major opposition party failed to
bring about a change in the power relationship. In the famous
Quintuple Loan affair,[73] the Chin-pu Tang consistently supported Yuan Shih-k'ai's position, and the Kuomintang was increasingly relegated to a secondary position. The victory in the
parliamentary elections had by now proved ephemeral. The
Chin-pu Tang, not the Kuomintang, second to Yuan Shih-k'ai,
now occupied the seat of power. What had caused the Kuomintang to fall from the height of influence to the depth of despair
within six months? The tragedy of Sung Chiao-jen's untimely
death and Yuan Shih-k'ai's financial manipulations both played
a part in its downfall. The Kuomintang's blind faith in democratic institutions and techniques also contributed to its collapse. But the final determinant of its fall from power must be
laid to the party itself. The Kuomintang had neither an effective organization nor dedicated leadership. In its concentration

---

[72] The Chin-pu Tang was formed by the amalgamation of the Kung-ho
Tang, the T'ung-i Tang, and the Min-chu Tang. Among its leaders were
Liang Ch'i-ch'ao, archrival of the Kuomintang from the T'ung Meng Hui
days.

[73] See Li Chien-nung, *The Political History of China, 1840-1928*, ed.
and trans. by Ssu-yu Teng and Jeremy Ingalls (New York, 1956), pp. 288-
293. The Quintuple Loan (also known as the Reorganization Loan) affair
centered around the £25,000,000 loan extended to the Yuan Shih-k'ai
government in April, 1913, by the Five Power Consortium (representing
England, France, Germany, Japan, and Russia). The loan was declared to
meet immediate administrative needs and to effect a general administrative reorganization. The loan, however, was secured without the formal
approval of Parliament. Already angered by the March Sung Chiao-jen incident, elements of the Kuomintang in and out of Parliament attacked
Yuan for his illegal handling of the loan.

upon capturing a parliamentary majority, the party had neglected the building of an organizational structure.

While the parliamentary Kuomintang party and others sought a legal solution to Sung's assassination, another faction within the party supported a more direct policy, namely, a military expedition against Yuan and the Peking government. Sun Yat-sen, who was in Japan at the time of Sung Chiao-jen's death, had returned to Shanghai on March 25, 1913. Many years later Sun declared that party comrades had sought his advice on the proper action to be taken with respect to Sung's death, and that he had urged immediate armed revolt, since he did not believe the issue could be solved legally.[74] Ch'en Ch'i-mei's open letter in 1914 to Huang Hsing also stressed Sun's early insistence upon military action against Yuan Shih-k'ai, which he said was rejected by party members.[75] This may have been true. However, Sun's behavior immediately after his return from Japan does not bear out his version of these developments.

When Sun was interviewed by the English-language *China Republican*, edited by his former English secretary, Ma Soo,[76] he made no mention of the Sung case, but spoke of the need for the establishment of cordial relations between China and Japan. The *Min-li Pao* reported Sun's visit to Huang Hsing and stated that Sun also favored a legal solution to Sung's murder.[77] Perhaps Sun was awaiting the results of the investigation then under way. The outcome of the inquiry was made known on April 26 in a public wire from Governor Ch'eng Te-ch'uan of Kiangsu to Yuan Shih-k'ai.[78] Both Prime Minister

---

[74] Speech of Sun in Canton, November 25, 1923, in *Kuo-fu ch'uan-chi*, III, 281-290.

[75] For the text of Ch'en's letter see Tsou Lu, *Chung-kuo Kuo-min Tang shih-kao*, pp. 266-271.

[76] *China Republican*, March 28, 1913, p. 13.

[77] *Min-li Pao*, March 26, 1913, p. 10.

[78] *Ibid.*, April 27, 1913, p. 2. For a partial English translation of the document see Li Chien-nung, *op. cit.*, pp. 286-287.

Chao Ping-chun and Yuan Shih-k'ai were implicitly, if not explicitly, involved. Meanwhile, the Kuomintang members who favored meeting force with force were urging Sun to assert his leadership. An editorial in the *China Republican* appealed to Sun "to exert every effort in his power to take up the task which he has set himself to accomplish and carry it to its logical conclusion. . . . He should take up his work where he had left off in February of last year. . . . The nation expects him to save the situation. How much longer can he withhold his services from the nation which is in need of them?"[79] On April 26 Sun and Huang Hsing dispatched a joint wire to the provincial assemblies urging them to investigate the Sung case and bring the guilty parties to trial.[80] In the midst of the Sung affair, Sun left Shanghai on June 17 for Macao to see his daughter, who was dying from Bright's disease. He returned to Shanghai on June 29, four days after her death. While in the south, Sun was interviewed by a correspondent of the Hong Kong *Central China Post*.[81] The reporter found Sun "very depressed in mind over the illness of his daughter," and reluctant "to talk of the affairs in China." Questioned about his views of the Sung murder, Sun remarked, "I have finished with politics now, and therefore I cannot tell you anything about what is going on." However, the correspondent obtained the following comments from Sun:

I have worked hard for President Yuan in the past. I have always said he was the best man for the presidency, and have worked for him not only in China but in all parts of the world. But this Sung murder has upset all that, and you may say that I am disgusted at the whole affair. The idea that the government should be implicated in the murder has outraged my sense of justice. I do not say that the President is himself concerned in it, but it was his premier, his own secretary, and he must have known something about it. . . . the whole thing has disgusted me and made me sick at heart.

Sun appeared indecisive. However, events were moving

---

[79] *China Republican*, April 4, 1913, p. 21.
[80] For the full text see *Kuo-fu ch'uan-chi*, IV, 183-184.
[81] The report was printed in the June 24, 1913, edition of the *Central*

rapidly. Yuan Shih-k'ai had dismissed the Kuomintang governors of Kiangsi and Kwangtung,[82] and relieved the governor
of Anhwei of his office.[83] The dismissal of the Kuomintang
governors touched off a military uprising against Yuan and
the Peking government. The war, or the "second revolution" as
it is known today, began on July 12. The Kuomintang, like
the T'ung Meng Hui before it, was ill-prepared. Huang Hsing,
Ch'en Ch'i-mei, Li Lieh-chun, and other Kuomintang military
leaders were no match for Yuan Shih-k'ai's military machine.
By September, 1913, the second revolution had almost col-
lasped, and the rebels were forced into hiding.[84]

Even while the Kuomintang in the south engaged in bitter
conflict with Yuan Shih-k'ai's forces, the Kuomintang parliamentary party continued to sit in both houses, and Kuomintang
members of Parliament sought to impeach Yuan in the belief
that he could be overcome through constitutional restraints.[85]
Once Yuan was elected president and the constitution established, they argued, he would be subject to its provisions. But
Yuan struck first. On November 4, 1913, after his election to
the presidency, he ordered the Kuomintang dissolved.

The Kuomintang thus vanished from China as quickly as it

China Post. The *China Republican* (July 18, 1913, p. 4) reprinted the full
interview.

[82] Li Lieh-chun, governor of Kiangsi, was dismissed on June 9, and Hu
Han-min, governor of Kwangtung, on June 14.

[83] Governor Po Wen-wei was dismissed on June 30, 1913.

[84] Sun left Shanghai on August 7, 1913 (*China Republican*, August 8,
1913, p. 8). He is reported to have arrived in Japan about August 9.
(*Japan Weekly Mail*, August 16, 1913, p. 196).

[85] At a party meeting on July 10, Kuomintang members discussed cabinet
reorganization, impeachment of the government, and nomination of cabinet members (*Min-li Pao*, July 14, 1913, p. 2). Even some of the Peking
Kuomintang members became discouraged with the government's conduct.
Chang Chi, Kuomintang president of the Senate, finally left Peking and
joined up with the south. Chang declared in a manifesto: " . . . We are
not altogether blameless for this [Yuan's] tyranny. It was foolish confidence
in trust which allowed such a state of affairs to come to pass . . ." (*China
Republican*, July 18, 1913, p. 20). Tsou Lu also left Peking about mid-July.
(Tsou Lu, *Hui-i Lu*, p. 68). But the majority of the Kuomintang parliamentary party stayed.

had appeared. The attempt to establish Western democratic institutions had failed. In the annals of the Kuomintang the period between January, 1912, and November, 1913, was a forgotten and discredited era because it constituted a clear departure from the party's sacred principles. The renovated T'ung Meng Hui of March, 1912, and the Kuomintang both forsook the three-stage policy of the party's 1905 manifesto, and the Kuomintang abandoned also the cherished principle of the people's livelihood. Sung Chiao-jen, as the prime instigator of both the republican T'ung Meng Hui and the parliamentary Kuomintang, must be held responsible for these actions.

Yet the years from 1911 to 1914 represented a great experiment. It was inevitable that an effort should have been made to build a democratic state based upon Western political concepts, for the Ch'ing dynasty had not been overthrown by the revolutionary forces merely to be replaced by another absolute state. It was believed that political parties were the chosen instruments for the building of a constitutional democratic system. The republican T'ung Meng Hui and the parliamentary Kuomintang represented this "wave of the future." But the political traditions of China placed strong limitations upon Western-modeled institutions, including political parties. The hopes for democracy failed to materialize, and a period of reaction followed.

V THE SECRET SOCIETY MODEL:
THE CHUNG-HUA KEMINTANG

IF THE KUOMINTANG years represented a venture into modernity, the succeeding period constituted a retreat into traditionalism. When his attempt to transplant Western democratic institutions ended in failure, the Kuomintang succumbed to the forces of tradition. With the outlawing of the Kuomintang in November, 1913, the era of open democratic political parties of the Western model came to a dramatic end.

The failure of the second revolution in 1913 produced an exodus of Kuomintang adherents from China. Some departed for Southeast Asia, Europe, or the Americas, but the majority escaped to Japan, which offered a natural sanctuary for the defeated Kuomintang members. Japanese public opinion was sympathetic toward the rebellious forces.[1] Sun Yat-sen fled to Japan in August, 1913, and Huang Hsing soon followed.[2] Be-

---

[1] For an account of Japanese interest in the 1913 revolution see Marius B. Jansen, *The Japanese and Sun Yat-sen* (Cambridge, 1954), pp. 162-167.

[2] Huang Hsing reportedly arrived in Japan under the disguised name of Imamura Chozo about August 11. *Japan Weekly Mail*, August 16, 1913, p. 196.

fore long hundreds of Kuomintang rebels had arrived in Japan.[3] Japan again became the center of a Chinese revolutionary movement.

The failure of the Kuomintang forced Sun out of political retirement. In his customary optimistic and determined manner, he set out immediately to build a new party to replace the discredited Kuomintang and to overthrow Yuan Shih-k'ai. In an interview on his arrival in Japan, Sun declared that " . . . China will never witness a real restoration of peace and order until President Yuan surrenders to the South. The Revolutionists are quite confident as to their final victory."[4] A month later, Sun restated his expectation: "The recent attempt at a counter revolution has certainly failed, as anyone can see. Its supporters have been for the time scattered, and are apparently suppressed. But this attempt to overthrow the rule of Yuan Shih-k'ai, though unsuccessful, will be made again, and indeed must be again attempted. . . . Moreover, I have no hesitation as to the ultimate results. The new Revolutionary Party will be successful before they are satisfied. . . ."[5]

Sun regarded the Kuomintang as a total failure and later spoke of it with considerable bitterness. In 1923 he charged the Kuomintang with failing to effectuate the three people's principles and the five-power constitution; he also accused Huang Hsing, Sung Chiao-jen, and others of forsaking the secret society "old revolutionary party" by organizing the Kuomintang as a Western-style political party.[6] The chief factors which had con-

---

[3] No exact figures are available. Feng Tzu-yu put the number at "several thousands." See Feng Tzu-yu in *Ke-min wen-hsien*, ed. by Lo Chia-lun (Taipei, 1953), V, 59 (hereafter cited as *Ke-min wen-hsien*). However, a more realistic number appears to have been hundreds. In April, 1914, Sun claimed only 400 to 500 followers, and complained of the small number who had gone to Japan. See Sun's letter to Teng Tse-ju, *ibid.*, V, 579-580.

[4] *Japan Weekly Mail*, August 16, 1913, p. 197.

[5] Sun's interview, in the Hong Kong *China Mail*, was reprinted in the *China Republican*, September 12, 1913, p. 20.

[6] Speech of Sun Yat-sen in Canton, November 25, 1923, in Kuomintang, *Kuo-fu ch'uan-chi* (Taipei, 1957), III, 281-290. Hereafter cited as *Kuo-fu ch'uan-chi*.

tributed to the bankruptcy of the Kuomintang were the prevalence of factionalism and disobedience to the leader. Writing to a comrade on the Kuomintang years, Sun spoke of disagreements within the party and the refusal of members to submit to his guidance.[7] He complained of being a mere figurehead during his brief term as president of the provincial government in Nanking in 1912. On another occasion Sun attributed the failure of the T'ung Meng Hui and the Kuomintang to their emphasis upon principles, to the neglect of the character of the membership.[8]

Sun's remedy for these and other party ills consisted in the creation of a centralized and disciplined party which demanded the personal and undivided loyalty of the members to him as leader. Each must take an oath[9] to sacrifice his life and freedom for the cause of saving China and rescuing the people; he was "to follow obediently Mr. Sun Chung-shan [Sun Yat-sen]," to raise again the banner of revolution; he was also to strive for the success of the principles of democracy and people's livelihood and the realization of the five-power constitution. The adherents of the new party agreed to accomplish the aims prescribed, obey orders, fulfill their duty, observe strict secrecy, and swear to live and die together. To seal the oath the adherent was required to affix his fingerprint to the declaration.[10] In effect, Sun's process constituted a personal endeavor to regenerate a disintegrated party.

But Sun encountered strong opposition. Even under the shadow of obliteration, the Kuomintang remained divided. A group including Huang Hsing, Chang Chi, and Li Lieh-chun

---

[7] See Sun's letter of April 8, 1914, to Teng Tse-ju, in *Ke-min wen-hsien*, V, 579-580.

[8] See Sun's letter of June 15, 1914, to Ch'en Hsin-chen, *ibid.*, V, 583-584.

[9] For the full text of the oath see Tsou Lu, *Chung-kuo Kuo-min Tang shih-kao* (Chungking, 1944), I, 159-160.

[10] Whereas Tsou Lu merely includes the fingerprint requirement, according to Yeh Hsia-sheng each new member had to affix the print of his right forefinger to the declaration. Yeh Hsia-sheng, *Kuo-fu min-ch'u ke-min chi-lioh* (Taipei, 1960), p. 82.

protested the inclusion in the oath of the provision to follow
Sun. They argued that in a revolutionary movement one should
give allegiance to a set of principles, not to an individual. To
agree "to follow obediently Mr. Sun Chung-shan" was tantamount to following one man and assisting him to engage in a
personal revolution, which was contrary to the spirit of republicanism and democracy. They objected to the fingerprinting of new members as an insulting procedure befitting crim-
inals only.[11]

According to Chu Cheng, who was also in Japan, Sun considered it essential that a revolutionary party function under
the absolute control of one leader.[12] He asked his critics not to
interpret the oath as a call to personal allegiance. Rather, they
should regard it as a summons to overthrow absolutism and to
establish republicanism. Sun declared that he was indispensable
to the revolutionary movement because of his long experience,
which gave him special insight; his positive plans for revolutionary strategy were also valuable.

Sun's critics proposed that the oath be eliminated, that
former members of the T'ung Meng Hui who had previously
taken an oath be required only to express their desire to the
tsung-li for membership in the new party. However, Sun's
critics were willing to retain the oath if certain changes were
made. They proposed that the term *fu-ts'ung*, to follow obediently (connoting personal allegiance), be changed to *fu-ts'ung*,
to obey (suggesting an impersonal loyalty). They demanded
that the clause "to follow obediently Mr. Sun Chung-shan," be
modified to read "to obey the *tsung-li*." Sun accepted the first
recommendation; however, the provision "to follow obediently
Mr. Sun Chung-shan" remained.

Sun was equally firm regarding the fingerprinting procedure,
which was intended to impress the sanctity of his oath upon the

---

[11] Chu Cheng, *Chu Chio-sheng hsien-sheng ch'uan-chi* (Taipei, n. d.), I,
153; Shao Yuan-chung, *Hsuan-pu i-shu* (Taipei, 1954), II, 606; Yeh Hsia-
sheng, *op. cit.*, pp. 83-84; Chang Chi, *Chang P'u-ch'uan hsien-sheng ch'uan-
chi* (Taipei, 1951), p. 240.

[12] Chu Cheng, *op. cit.*, I, 153-154.

adherent. The act of fingerprinting constituted a means through which the new revolutionary party could overcome the "face" problem, encourage sacrifice, and build unity. Thus, despite the severe criticism of his proposals, Sun maintained his determination to build a disciplined and centralized party.

In September, 1913, Sun began recruiting a core of adherents personally loyal to him.[13] In April, 1914, Sun reported that four or five hundred followers in Japan had taken the oath, signifying their willingness to join the new party.[14] Subsequently, a political training center and a military school for Sun's adherents were established.[15] A party organ, the *Min-kuo* (The Republic), was also published. According to Chu Cheng (subsequently director of the party affairs bureau of the Chung-hua Kemintang), the majority of Sun's followers came from the provinces of Hupeh, Hunan, Anhwei, and Kiangsi. A number came also from Chekiang, Kwangtung, Szechwan, Fuchien, and Kiangsu.[16] Some of the more prominent included Ch'en Ch'i-mei, Chu Cheng, Feng Tzu-yu, Wu T'ieh-ch'eng, Liao Chung-k'ai, Hu Han-min, and Tai Chi-t'ao. Concurrently, Sun sought to reenlist the support of the overseas Chinese. The proven formula of financial support by the overseas Chinese to a core group of revolutionists engaging in direct action was again applied.

Sun's insistence upon personal allegiance, party discipline, and centralized structure did little to smooth the path of the proposed new party. Huang Hsing and Chang Chi were equally firm in their opposition to Sun's return to the secret-society type of party. With neither side willing to compromise, a schism

---

[13] According to one source, Sun's first follower was Wang Tung, a former naval officer, who took the new oath. Feng Tzu-yu in *Ke-min wen-hsien*, V, 628.

[14] See Sun's letter of April 8, 1914, to Teng Tse-ju, *ibid.*, pp. 579-580. According to other sources, by the spring of 1914 less than 200 had joined forces with Sun. See Chu Cheng, *op. cit.*, I, 155; and Feng Tzu-yu in *Ke-min wen-hsien*, V, 628.

[15] Tsou Lu, *op. cit.*, I, 271.

[16] Chu Cheng, *op. cit.*, I, 155.

resulted among the exiled revolutionaries. Instead of unifying the Kuomintang, as Sun intended, his plan created further disunity. Huang Hsing, Chang Chi, Li Lieh-chun, and others openly broke with Sun and departed for the Americas and Europe.[17] The intraparty rupture in 1913 probably contributed to the long delay in the formation of the new party, for Sun had been in Japan nearly a year before the party was formally inaugurated.[18]

A preliminary meeting of the new party, the Chung-hua Kemintang (Chinese Revolutionary Party) was held in Tokyo on June 22, 1914, but it was not until July 8 that the party was formally established. The manifesto[19] of the Chung-hua Kemintang, issued on September 1, 1914, opened with the statement that since the 1911 revolution the T'ung Meng Hui and the Kuomintang had taken upon themselves the responsibilities of securing the Republic and realizing the principles of democracy and people's livelihood. However, the assassination of Sung Chiao-jen and the Quintuple Loan affair produced the second revolution. Unfortunately, the party's spirit weakened and a series of defeats ensued. Exile to Japan followed.

The manifesto described the division among the exiles: ". . . Some opposed engaging in a revolution; others spoke in terms of ten years hence. All are discouraged. The revolutionary spirit and organization of twenty years are almost down to its last breath. . . ." The manifesto declared that Sun advocated moving forward rapidly to continue the revolution. He thus initiated the Chung-hua Kemintang. The manifesto reported on Sun's election as *tsung-li* of the new party at a meeting in June, attended by representatives of eight provinces.

---

[17] Huang left Japan in July, 1914; Chang and Li also departed sometime in 1914, Huang for the United States, the other two for France.

[18] Other rebels subsequently followed. In 1915 a group of exiled Kuomintang members in Japan who refused to join Sun established a separate organization, the Ou-shih Yen-chiu Hui (Association for the Discussion of European Affairs). According to one source, the majority of the members were followers of Huang Hsing. Chang Chi, *op. cit.*, p. 241.

[19] For the full text of the manifesto see Tsou Lu, *op. cit.*, I, 18.

The manifesto served notice on the comrades in China and abroad that, with the founding of the Chung-hua Kemintang, the Kuomintang was officially dissolved. Henceforth all branches were to be organized under the new party's designation and regulations. Only those who took the oath were recognized as members. The new party was a secret organization, different in character from a political party; overseas party branches could retain the Kuomintang appellation if they were organized internally according to the new regulations. All party members were called upon to strive for the third revolution. The purpose of the new regulations was to clear bureaucrats and false members out of the party. This was to prevent the corruption of the party by unsympathetic forces, as had happened after the first revolution. The manifesto noted that the war in Europe precluded the foreign powers from actively intervening in China's domestic affairs. The war also served to exclude foreign financial assistance to Yuan Shih-k'ai. The members were to utilize these opportunities and move forward.

The characteristics wherein the Chung-hua Kemintang differed from a political party are revealed in its constitution,[20] which began with a declaration of purpose and a statement of goals. The new party sought the fulfillment of the principles of democracy and people's livelihood, the obliteration of the forces of political absolutism, and the construction of a true republic. Except for the exclusion of the principle of nationalism, which was considered attained with the 1911 revolution, the Chung-hua Kemintang continued the democratic socialistic tradition. The three-stage process, first presented in the T'ung Meng Hui manifesto of 1905, reappeared in modified form as the revolutionary program in 1914. Government by military rule constituted the first stage, during which military power would be utilized to overcome all obstacles and to lay a republican foundation. The second stage would be government through tutelage, whereby the people would be trained in the administration of local government institutions. Government by a

---

[20] For the full text of the constitution see *ibid.*, pp. 161-167.

constitution represented the third stage, the successful conclusion of the revolution. The Chung-hua Kemintang constitution stipulated that the period between the rise of the Revolutionary Army and the constitutional stage would be known as
the revolutionary period. Within this period, all military and
civil affairs were to be undertaken only by Chung-hua Kemintang members. Although the new party adopted the three-stage
process of the T'ung Meng Hui, the Chung-hua Kemintang
plan differed from the 1905 model. Under the T'ung Meng
Hui revolutionary program the three stages were known, respectively, as government by military law, government by provisional constitution, and government by constitution. Under
the Chung-hua Kemintang program the three stages were designated government by military rule, government by tutelage,
and government via constitution. According to the T'ung Hui
revolutionary program, a nine-year period was stipulated between the first and third stages—a definite schedule for leading
the people toward constitutional democracy. However, the new
party in 1914 refrained from establishing a time limit for the
three stages. Presumably it would depend upon the readiness
of the people.

Another novelty of the Chung-hua Kemintang was the concept of party rule throughout the revolutionary period. The
T'ung Meng Hui manifesto had left open the question of the
role of the party after the revolution. It provided neither for
party dictatorship nor excluded other parties from participating
in government. Rather, during the first and second stages (of
government by military law and provisional constitution) the
military government would rule supreme. The Chung-hua
Kemintang, however, introduced the concept of party tutelage.
Until the declaration of the constitution, the nation would be
guided toward democracy by the party. Formerly the chief
function of the party had been conceived in terms of a nega-
tive, destructive role. Beginning with the Chung-hua Kemintang the party assumed the positive function of guiding the
nation through the three-stage process toward constitutional
government.

The concept of the three-stage process, although introduced in the T'ung Meng Hui platform as early as 1905, had remained incomprehensible to the majority of the party members. This was shown by its prompt abandonment after the 1911 revolution. Sun Yat-sen considered the discard of the three-stage process as one of the chief factors contributing to the failure of the first revolution.[21] Sun's misgivings were echoed by some of his followers, who had been convinced by the experience of the 1911 revolution and the failure of the second revolution that the masses were politically unawakened and needed guidance.[22] The three-stage process, therefore, was reintroduced into the Chung-kuo Kemintang program in 1914.

The three-stage process was still little understood. Its reinstatement brought forth cries that Sun was attempting to restore absolutism.[23] The critics reluctantly accepted the first and third stages of military rule and constitutional government. The first stage constituted a necessary evil; the last stage represented a common goal. However, they were firmly opposed to the second stage of political tutelage. Sun's critics expressed faith in the ability of the Chinese masses to govern themselves, and charged that political tutelage pertained to the absolutist rule of emperors. The revolutionary party had no right to act as guardians of the people.

If Sun Yat-sen displayed a self-righteous attitude in insisting on a pledge from Chung-hua Kemintang members, he was equally persistent regarding the adoption of the three-stage process.[24] Indeed, he told his critics, the failure of the Republic could be attributed to the nonfulfillment of the T'ung Meng

---

21 Shao Yuan-chung, *op. cit.*, II, 603-707; Chu Cheng, *op. cit.*, I, 165-166.

22 See Chu-fei (Hu Han-min), "Opening Statement," *Min-kuo* (The Republic), No. 1 (May 10, 1914), 1-3; Szu-ch'iu Lou Wu (pseud.), "A Limited Knowledge," *ibid.*, pp. 181-189; Szu-ch'iu (Tai Chi-t'ao), "On the Chinese Revolution," *ibid.*, No. 2 (June 10, 1914), 1-23; and Ch'ien-chin (Chu Chih-hsin), "Revolution and Psychology," *ibid.*, No. 4 (August 10, 1914), 1-21.

23 Shao Yuan-chung, *op. cit.*; Chu Cheng, *op. cit.*

24 Chu Cheng, *op. cit.*

Hui's revolutionary program. To insure its success, the third revolution must have a firm foundation, which the three-stage process would provide. The success or failure of the revolution depended upon the success or failure of the second stage of political tutelage. From the Chinese classic, *Shang-shu* (Book of History),[25] he cited the guidance of the youthful Shang Emperor Tai-chia by his minister Ying-ying as an example of tutelage. Sun compared the Chinese people to the emperor and the Chung-hua Kemintang to the minister. Since the people were immature and could not personally govern, the Chung-hua Kemintang must act as their protector. And through such tutelage a secure republican foundation would eventually be established.

Sun Yat-sen is usually referred to as the great transmitter of Westernism into China. It was Sun who introduced *avant-garde* Western teachings (e.g., socialism) into the T'ung Meng Hui, and constantly cited Western writers and theories as his authorities. Even in 1913 and 1914 he had quoted Robert Michels in order to justify his endeavor to centralize the Chung-hua Kemintang.[26] At a moment in history during which the Chinese were searching for the "new learning" of the West, Sun's West-

---

[25] *Ibid.* Sun is usually accused of exaggerating his inheritance from Chinese orthodox tradition. This may be correct. Since Sun received primarily a Western education, he could not have been entirely familiar with Chinese tradition. However, his formal Western education does not preclude his self-study of Chinese classics and history. If Sun could absorb Western learning, no doubt he could also read Chinese classics. There is some evidence that Sun began to read the Chinese classics in his later years. In a speech delivered in 1916, Sun remarked that as a child he had been taught to read the Four Books (*Ta-hsueh, Lun-yu, Chung-yung,* and *Mencius*) and the Five Canons (*I-ching, Shu-ching, Shih-ching, Li-chi,* and *Ch'un-ch'iu*), but that he had forgotten most of what he had learned. Years later, Sun continued, he reread the Four Books and the Five Canons in their Western (English) translations. See speech of Sun in Shanghai, July 15, 1916, in *Kuo-fu ch'uan-chi,* III, 135-138. I have no intention of minimizing the Western influence upon Sun; however, my feeling is that Sun derived many of his ideas from Chinese orthodox tradition.

[26] See Sun's letter to Ch'en Hsin-cheng in *Ke-min wen-hsien,* V, 583-

ern background provided the link between the old and the new. Yet in 1914 Sun turned increasingly to the sages of the ancient East. Although Sun remained committed to a democratic goal, China's initial experience at republicanism had shaken his faith in the free application of Western institutions. The political chaos between 1911 and 1913 convinced Sun of China's unpreparedness. By refraining from imposing a definite schedule upon the new three-stage process and insisting upon the retention of the political tutelage stage, he expressed his attitude toward the vicissitudes of the gigantic task of making China a democracy. Hence Sun's emphasis upon political tutelage—an undemocratic method directed at a democratic goal.

The Chung-hua Kemintang set rigorous standards for its members. They were required to take an oath to sacrifice life and freedom for the revolutionary cause. An entrance fee of ten *yuan* was charged, and members were to contribute one *yuan* yearly to headquarters. Each member must introduce new members into the party. However, if a member violated the party's regulation, both he and his sponsor would be punished.

There were three classifications of membership, depending upon the date of entry into the party. Persons joining the party before the rise of the Revolutionary Army were designated founding members. During the revolutionary period, founding members could participate in both the legislative and executive branches of government. Associate members, the second classification, were those who entered the party after the rise of the Revolutionary Army but before the establishment of the revolutionary government. Associate members could vote and hold office. General members, the lowest category, were given rights of suffrage only. Members in all three classifications enjoyed the status of citizenship. Interestingly, the Chung-hua Kemintang constitution included a provision relating to nonmembers: dur-

584; and to comrades in Singapore, etc., *ibid.*, V, 585. Sun, of course, was citing Robert Michels' famous work, *Political Parties* (New York, 1959), first published in 1915. According to Sun, using Michels as his authority, even the most democratic of parties requires obedience to the leader.

ing the revolutionary period nonmembers were excluded from citizenship. Only upon the declaration of the constitution were equal rights to be granted party and nonparty members alike. The Chung-hua Kemintang, therefore, assured for itself a complete monopoly of political power. Until the party chose to declare the constitution, control of the nation rested fully within its dominion.

The membership provisions of the Chung-hua Kemintang were designed to correct past blunders and prevent future carelessness. However, while the oath requirement served primarily as an elimination process, the membership regulations served as a preventive measure. The membership classification scheme sought to forestall the entrance of opportunists into the party upon its seizure of power. Sun Yat-sen justified the undemocratic characteristics of the new party's membership provisions by pointing to the degeneration of the party after the 1911 revolution which had resulted from the infiltration of nonrevolutionary groups.

The party's constitution provided for the election of a *tsung-li* and an associate *tsung-li*. The *tsung-li* had full powers to organize party headquarters as the command post of the Revolutionary Army. Five bureaus were created at headquarters: general affairs, party affairs, finance, military, and political. The *tsung-li* appointed all bureau heads and officers. In preparation for the future administration of the nation, four councils—legislative, judicial, control, and examination—were established to train members. Together with the party's five bureaus, regarded as the executive department, preparations were made for the realization of the five-power constitution. The constitution also provided for the establishment of branches. Domestic branches engaged in military uprisings and other activities related to the attainment of power; overseas branches were to secure financial support. Political or patriotic organizations having a membership of 10,000 or more could upon acceptance of the Chung-hua Kemintang's constitution, become branches of the revolutionary party.

A new revolutionary party was thus launched with members dedicated to leader, party, and country. Sun Yat-sen became the undisputed head, at least among those who took the prescribed oath. Other pillars of the Chung-hua Kemintang included Ch'en Ch'i-mei, head of the general affairs bureau; Chu Cheng, head of the party affairs bureau; Hu Han-min, head of the political bureau; Hsu Ch'ung-chih, head of the military bureau; and Liao Chung-k'ai, head of the finance bureau.[27] The position of associate *tsung-li* was never filled. The post was reportedly offered to Huang Hsing, but after Huang's break with Sun it was kept vacant either in anticipation of their reconciliation or because no one of equal prestige could be induced to occupy it.

If the new party represented but one element from the old party, its membership was also greatly restricted. Although it included a cross section of China, members from central and southern China predominated. The Chung-hua Kemintang marked the reentrance of Hu Han-min and other southerners into the party's inner councils, but there were no leaders from northern China. Members of the parties which had amalgamated with the T'ung Meng Hui to found the Kuomintang were conspicuously absent. The Chung-hua Kemintang was thus composed primarily of members who had participated in the pre-1912 antidynastic movement and who were personally loyal to Sun Yat-sen.

The failure of the 1911 revolution and the Kuomintang as an open political party delivered a death blow to democracy in China for the immediate future. The Chung-hua Kemintang represented a violent reaction against the optimism which had prevailed during the initial years of the Republic—a rejection of Western democratic principles and institutions in favor of accepted traditional techniques and institutions. However, al-

---

[27] Sun had a difficult time filling the post of the head of the finance bureau. At one time he offered it to Teng Tse-ju, on another occasion to Chang Jen-chieh, but both declined it.

though it leaned toward dictatorship internally, the basic goal of republicanism remained. The Chung-hua Kemintang thus constituted a return to the T'ung Meng Hui pattern and a repudiation of the Kuomintang model. The new party also witnessed the reemergence of Sun Yat-sen. It was Sun, the Western-educated innovator of things Occidental, who initiated the withdrawal into traditionalism. However, Sun was responsible also for the three-stage process of the T'ung Meng Hui. The search for new institutions and ideology had thus gone full circle.

Ironically, many of the vicissitudes of the party derived from Sun's attempt to regenerate the revolutionary organization and spirit. Instead of unifying the old party, however, the Chung-hua Kemintang only served to create a division within the revolutionary ranks. Numerous factions emerged, all seeking to realize the common goal of overthrowing Yuan Shih-k'ai. No single political group had sufficient human and material resources to gain power.

At its beginning and throughout its existence the Chung-hua Kemintang was engaged in factional contentions. The two major issues in the conflict with other groups from the defunct Kuomintang were the difference in strategy with regard to Yuan Shih-k'ai and the obtaining of funds from overseas Chinese. The large Chinese population residing abroad, especially in southeast Asia and the Americas, had made possible the continuance of the drive to overthrow the Ch'ing dynasty, and both the Hsing Chung Hui and the T'ing Meng Hui as parties in exile had depended heavily upon their financial support. For a time the overseas Chinese had been neglected,[28] but, after the failure of the second revolution in 1913 and the exile of the defunct Kuomintang members, Sun Yat-sen and the anti-Yuan Shih-k'ai groups again turned to them for material assistance.

The majority of the revolutionists arrived in Japan penniless

---

[28] This "neglect" on more than one occasion turned into hatred. See the contemptuous account of Sun by Huang San-te, *Hung-meng ke-min shih* (n. p., 1936).

and spiritually dejected. Writing to a comrade in Southeast Asia in April, 1914, Sun spoke of their financial difficulties.[29] Sun himself lived under trying conditions.[30] He and his followers subsisted primarily on piecemeal contributions from the overseas Chinese.[31]

During these difficult days Sun wrote his famous letter to Count Okuma Shigenobu, the Japanese prime minister, appealing for assistance in overthrowing Yuan Shih-k'ai and capturing power.[32] In return, economic privileges were offered to Japan: "China will open her markets for the benefit of Japan's industry and commerce."[33] A customs union with Japan was also proposed. For Sun realized that "if the revolutionists do not enjoy the support from a powerful nation, it will be extremely difficult to realize the revolutionary objective."[34] But Great Britain, France, and the other powers all seemed to favor Yuan Shih-k'ai and approved granting the much-publicized Quintuple Loan to the Peking government. Although Japan had assisted the revolutionists during the antidynastic movement, and seemed to be the sole and logical means by which Sun might recapture the Mandate of Heaven, in 1914 Japan turned a deaf ear to his pleas.[35] Japan's refusal to support the anti-Yuan movement destroyed his hope for a quick victory. With the door of foreign assistance closed, Sun and the Chung-hua Kemintang turned to other sources of support.

---

[29] See Sun's letter of April 18, 1914, to Li Ken-yuan in *Ke-min wen-hsien*, V, 582.

[30] Shao Yuan-chung, *op. cit.*, II, 602-603.

[31] According to Shao, all the revolutionists in exile turned to Sun for financial assistance. Sun in turn would wire his supporters among the overseas Chinese to raise the urgently needed funds. From several hundred to 20,000 *yuan* arrived at irregular intervals. *Ibid.*

[32] See Sun's letter of May 11, 1914, to Okuma: "A Proposal for a Sino-Japanese Alliance," *The Vital Problem of China* (Taipei, 1953), pp. 135-142.

[33] *Ibid.*

[34] *Ibid.*

[35] For an account of Japanese reaction to Sun's letter see Jansen, *op. cit.*, pp. 188-189.

Again the overseas Chinese became the basis of the revolutionary movement. Even before Sun's appeal to Japan in May,
1914, contact had been renewed with old followers abroad. Indeed, among the very first measures adopted after Sun's arrival
in Japan was the deputation of representatives to reorganize the
overseas branches of the Kuomintang. In effect, Sun and the
Chung-hua Kemingtang sought to reestablish the pre-1912 pattern of financing the revolution through the contributions of
the overseas Chinese.

The Chung-hua Kemintang's efforts to obtain the support
of the overseas Chinese did not go unchallenged. Whereas in
the pre-1912 contest Sun and the K'ang-Liang forces each represented a completely different goal, that of republicanism
versus constitutional monarchism, in 1914 the forces of protest
shared one purpose, the overthrow of Yuan Shih-k'ai. Therefore, the choice in 1914 for the overseas Chinese was not whether
to preserve monarchism or accept republicanism, but which
element from the defunct Kuomintang they would assist against
Yuan Shih-k'ai. The situation was complicated by the emergence of a number of secondary national leaders after the 1911
revolution. Sun Yat-sen no longer dominated the arena of
leadership. Huang Hsing, Li Lieh-chun, Po Wen-wei, and
others had emerged as national leaders during the brief republican years of power. After the failure of the second revolution,
each sought to utilize his prestige among the overseas Chinese
to obtain their support.

The struggle for survival among the anti-Yuan factions centered in Southeast Asia and in the Americas. In the United
States, Sun Yat-sen competed with Huang Hsing for the moral
and financial support of the Chinese Americans. Sun was the
first to reestablish contacts with the Chinese in the United
States. When Hsieh Ying-p'ai and Lin Shen passed through
Japan toward the end of 1913 and took Sun's prescribed oath,
they were appointed to reorganize the Kuomintang in Hawaii
and in the United States.[36] Subsequently, Wu T'ieh-ch'eng,

---

[36] See Feng Tzu-yu in *Ke-min wen-hsien*, V, 60.

Feng Tzu-yu, Sun Fo (Sun's son), and others were designated
as representatives of the Chung-hua Kemintang upon their departure for the Western Hemisphere.[37] Hsieh Ying-p'ai was
elected head of the Kuomintang (known as the Chinese Nationalist League) in the Americas upon his arrival in San Francisco,
site of the Kuomintang headquarters in the Americas.[38] However, Hsieh soon resigned the post in favor of Feng Tzu-yu, who
became acting head of the party. In the winter of 1914, at the
general meeting of the American Kuomintang, Lin Shen was
elected chairman and Feng vice-chairman of the party in the
Americas.[39] Their chief mission was to raise funds to finance
revolutionary uprisings in China. Feng reported that until
Yuan Shih-k'ai's death in 1916, the Republican Preservation
Society in the United States raised about 1,200,000 Japanese
yen, which was sent to Sun in Tokyo.[40] However, Huang Hsing's
arrival in the United States introduced a new element into the
survival struggle.

After breaking with Sun Yat-sen, Huang Hsing left Japan on
July 2, 1914. After a brief stay in Honolulu, Huang arrived in
San Francisco on July 15, 1914,[41] and was warmly welcomed by
the San Francisco Chinese, who presented him with a gold
medal.[42] Huang declared that the purpose of his trip was to
raise funds to overthrow Yuan Shih-k'ai,[43] who, he charged, was
"a dictator of 'more vicious tactics than former President Huerta
of Mexico.' "[44] The fact that Huang had refused to join the

---

[37] *Ibid.*; Wu T'ieh-ch'eng, *Wu T'ieh-ch'eng hsien-sheng hui-i lu* (Taipei,
1957[?]), p. 37b.

[38] See Feng Tzu-yu in *Ke-min wen-hsien*, V, 62.

[39] *Ibid.*

[40] *Ibid.*, V, 65.

[41] *Chung-sai Yat-Po*, July 16, 1914, p. 2. Traveling with Huang Hsing
were Teng Chia-yen, Li Shu-ch'eng, Shih Tao-ch'uan, and Hsu Hsin-pai.

[42] *San Francisco Chronicle*, July 31, 1914, p. 20.

[43] *Chung-sai Yat-po*, July 27, 1914, p. 3.

[44] *San Francisco Chronicle*, July 31, 1914, p. 20. American reaction to
the arrival of Chinese revolutionists who began raising funds among the
American Chinese is illustrated by the following editorial. " . . . as for the
merits of the [Chinese] revolutionary movement, they do not concern us

Chung-hua Kemintang and had openly broken with Sun Yat-sen did not seem to affect his popularity among the Chinese Americans. Even Feng Tzu-yu reports that Huang was enthusiastically greeted in San Francisco, causing a sudden increase in the local Kuomintang membership.[45]

Huang's presence in the United States, where he remained until 1916, posed a dilemma for those in the American Kuomintang who were loyal to Sun. Dissension within the anti-Yuan ranks might cause the Chinese in America to withhold their contributions from either faction. Huang's prominence as a revolutionary hero, second only to Sun in prestige, and a founder of the Republic precluded any attempt to discredit him before the Chinese in America. On the other hand, to surrender to Huang would be to betray Sun. Feng Tzu-yu and many of the Chinese in America had known Sun personally since the pre-1912 era. Moreover, Sun was from Kwangtung, whence most of the Chinese in America had come, and this must have further strengthened the ties. Moreover, Sun's son, Sun Fo, was in the United States in 1914. The American Kuomintang, therefore, could neither reject Sun nor accept Huang.

The predicament was resolved through the inclusion of Huang's followers in the American Kuomintang and, more importantly, by giving the Huang faction a share of the contributions collected in the United States. Teng Chia-yen, a member of Huang's entourage, was brought into the American Kuomintang organization and was elected to one of the fund-raising groups to tour the United States.[46] Although Huang Hsing and Sun Yat-sen may have differed over the organization of the

---

beyond the hope that good hard-earned American gold will not be used to foment strife in a friendly country. Let China settle her own troubles in China." *Ibid.*, July 29, 1914, p. 6.

[45] See Feng Tzu-yu in *Ke-min wen-hsien*, V, 64.

[46] *Ibid.* Teng played a very active role in the American Kuomintang convention held from July 25 to August 3, 1915, in San Francisco. He was also made editor of the convention's journal. See Teng Chia-yen, ed., *Chung-kuo Kuo-min Tang k'en-ch'in ta-hui shih-mo chi* (San Francisco, 1915).

Chung-hua Kemintang, they were realistic enough to cooperate externally. Both factions gained from the partnership. As Feng Tzu-yu subsequently wrote, during the anti-Yuan campaign the American Kuomintang exceeded all other party branches in the amount of funds raised.[47]

Whereas Sun Yat-sen had conspicuously refrained from personally directing party affairs in the Americas, he actively guided the Chung-hua Kemintang in Southeast Asia. Sun's chief representative in Southeast Asia, Teng Tse-ju, directed the local party units. In April, 1914, Sun authorized Teng to reorganize the party on the basis of the new regulations formulated in Tokyo.[48] Whether as a reward or as an encouragement, Sun appointed Teng head of the finance bureau of the Chung-hua Kemintang in October, 1914, and asked him to manage fund-raising campaigns in the British and Dutch colonies in Southeast Asia.[49] Teng's activities on behalf of Sun and the Chung-hua Kemintang encountered strong competition from other anti-Yuan groups.

Numerous factions emerged to contend for the moral and financial support of the Chinese communities in Southeast Asia, especially in Singapore and Malaysia. The battle was chiefly between Sun's Chung-hua Kemintang and a group led by former provincial governors who had been removed from office by Yuan Shih-k'ai in 1913. Among the leaders of the latter group were Ch'en Chiung-ming, onetime governor of Kwangtung, Po Wen-wei, past governor of Anhwei, and Li Lieh-chun, former governor of Kiangsi.[50] Together they formed an organization known as the Shui-li Kung-szu (Conservancy Company) which favored retaining the name Kuomintang. It argued that Yuan Shih-k'ai had outlawed the Kuomintang only in China. Foreign governments did not interfere with overseas branches; hence there was no reason to organize a new party. Sun's opponents

---

[47] See Feng Tzu-yu in *Ke-min wen-hsien*, V, 640.

[48] See Sun's letter to Teng Tse-ju, *ibid.*, V, 579-580.

[49] See Sun's letter of October 20, 1914, *ibid.*, V, 587.

[50] See Teng Tse-ju's letter to Sun, *ibid.*, V, 593-595; Yeh Hsia-sheng, *op. cit.*, p. 87.

favored independent action by the various factions against
Yuan. However, Sun would be invited to join in governing the
country after the attainment of their common goal. The Shui-
li Kung-szu group thus not only opposed the organization of a
centralized party, as demanded by Sun, but also challenged
Sun's leadership within the anti-Yuan movement. The Shui-li
Kung-szu group thus constituted a basic threat to Sun Yat-sen's
role in the Chinese revolutionary movement.

The factional contention in Southeast Asia was not limited
to formally established opposition groups. Sun's efforts to organize the Chinese in Southeast Asia were hindered by schism
within the ranks. The intraparty conflict was due primarily to
Sun's appointment of more than one director of party affairs
and fund-raising campaigns in Southeast Asia. When Teng
Tse-ju took charge of party and financial affairs in April, 1914,
he soon found his authority and his effectiveness seriously challenged by Lu Wen-hui, who had also received a commission
from Sun, on October 8, 1914, to raise funds and reorganize the
local Kuomintang.[51] Sun had apparently assumed that Teng
and Lu would jointly manage the party's financial dealings.
However, instead of cooperating, the two began to compete for
the privilege of representing Sun in Southeast Asia. Lu is reported to have accused Teng of supporting a rival anti-Yuan
group and not forwarding the money to Sun in Japan.[52] The
contest between Teng and Lu was detrimental to party activities, and shook the confidence of the local Chinese, who withheld their financial contributions.[53]

Sun rightly perceived that if his opponents were deprived of
the material backing of the Chinese abroad their power and influence would be sharply curtailed. The problem of factional
contention would be resolved, and he, Sun, would emerge as
the unchallenged leader of the anti-Yuan forces. The Chung-
hua Kemintang in turn would become the sole body through

---

[51] See Sun's letter of April 18, 1914, to Li Ken-yuan in *Ke-min wen-hsien*,
V, 582.
[52] See Teng Tse-ju's letter to Sun, *ibid.*, V, 593-595.
[53] *Ibid.*

which the anti-Yuan movement could rally. Sun thus repeatedly instructed his representatives to forward all the funds collected directly to Japan, where he would distribute the money according to need. In a letter to Teng Tse-ju, Sun pleaded with him to send the contributions from the overseas Chinese directly to Tokyo.[54] Indeed, Sun was determined to undermine the financial support of his opponents even at a sacrifice. If the Chinese in Southeast Asia were unwilling to support the Chung-hua Kemintang, he preferred that they withhold their contributions altogether. In spite of all he could do, however, the overseas Chinese continued their indiscriminate support of all the anti-Yuan factions, including Sun's Chung-hua Kemintang. The seriousness of the division within the anti-Yuan movement caused Sun to remark that success in the campaign against Yuan would depend less upon exterminating the enemy than upon overcoming factional differences.[55] Yet the divisions remained, partly as a consequence of the tactics and policy pursued by Sun.

The heterogeneity of the anti-Yuan movement was further manifested in the division over strategy. The Chung-hua Kemintang manifesto publicly admitted the wide differences of opinion concerning the action to be taken against Yuan Shih-k'ai. The division ranged from those who advocated postponing indefinitely any attempt to overthrow Yuan, to those who demanded immediate action to regain power. The latter group, though divided internally, predominated. And it was this group, exemplified by the Chung-hua Kemintang, which worked among the overseas Chinese to secure financial support for uprisings in China. The majority of the revolutionists in exile felt a personal animosity toward Yuan Shih-k'ai because he had deprived them of the fruits of victory.

Japan's presentation of her infamous Twenty-one Demands to China in January, 1915, introduced a new element into the anti-Yuan movement. Overnight Yuan Shih-k'ai became the symbol of China's fight against Japanese aggression. Instead of

---

[54] See Sun's letter of October 20, 1914, to Teng Tse-ju, *ibid.*, V, 587-589.
[55] *Ibid.*

a usurper of power, he was looked upon as the defender of the Republic. Yuan was a Han (Chinese), not a so-called alien Manchu. Therefore, when the Japanese imposed their demands, Chinese everywhere went to his assistance, since the Japanese, like the Manchus, represented external aggression. The national crisis cast its shadow on the anti-Yuan forces. An immediate re-action was the founding of the Ou-shih Yen-chiu Hui (Associa-tion for the Discussion of European Affairs) by a group of former Kuomintang members, including Li Ken-yuan, Chang Hsin-yen, and Niu Yung-chien, exiled in Japan. This group ap-pealed for national unity above party differences,[56] for China's very existence was threatened by the Japanese demands. Civil conflict between Yuan and his antagonists greatly weakened China's position. The Ou-shih Yen-chiu Hui therefore called upon the anti-Yuan groups to put aside their petty hatreds and cease revolutionary activities. All Chinese were urged to join in a national front to resist Japanese aggression.

The appeal to patriotism soon engulfed the Chung-hua Ke-mintang in a bitter intraparty conflict. Huang Hsing, Li Lieh-chun, Po Wen-wei, Ch'en Chiung-ming, and Niu Yung-chien circulated a telegram expressing their willingness to cease revo-lutionary activities and join in a common front against Japan.[57] The Chung-hua Kemintang continued, however, in its steadfast opposition to Yuan Shih-k'ai. Yet even within Sun's party there were rumbles of discontent. A group of Chung-hua Kemintang members, including Lin Shen (the party's head in the Amer-icas) and Hsieh Ying-p'ai (former head of the party in the Amer-icas) wired Sun in Japan asking him to agree to the cessation of revolutionary activities.[58] They expressed concern that the party's antinationalist attitude would make a bad impression on their fellow countrymen. But Sun, blinded by his enmity toward Yuan, and convinced of the correctness of his own position, flatly rejected his comrades' plea.[59] Yuan Shih-k'ai, wrote Sun,

---

[56] See Feng Tzu-yu, *ibid.*, V, 640.
[57] *Ibid.*
[58] *Ibid.*
[59] *Ibid.*, V, 641.

proposed to sell the country; only through his defeat could China be preserved. Sun called upon the party to continue the revolutionary movement to overthrow Yuan.

Sun not only stubbornly maintained his opposition to Yuan, he still clung to the dream of a Sino-Japanese alliance. In March, 1915, he again attempted to obtain Japanese assistance by promising in exchange liberal political, economic, and military concessions, which Japan rejected.[60] Sun's continued silence in regard to Japan's Twenty-one Demands placed the party in a very difficult position. Sentiment against Japan was on the rise; yet the Chung-hua Kemintang persisted in calling Yuan Shih-k'ai the national enemy. In San Francisco the party was confronted with open revolt.[61] The local Chinese wired the national government in Peking extending their support against the Twenty-one Demands, and accused the Chung-hua Kemintang of aiding the Japanese. To placate the dissidents, the party hastily organized an overseas Chinese "Dare-to-Die" corps, which would return to China to defend the homeland. Sun's persistence cost the party dear, and none was more aware of its increasing isolation than the party's representatives abroad.

The Chung-hua Kemintang sought to rectify its unpopular stand, regain a position of leadership for the party, and bring together the diverse elements from the defunct Kuomintang. Motivated by the national crisis produced by Japan's Twenty-one Demands and the rising tide of nationalism among the overseas Chinese, a group of party leaders abroad sought to modify the party's extreme position.[62] It also aspired to establish a common front among the revolutionists in exile. The party

[60] On March 14, 1915, Sun submitted an eleven-point "sample treaty" to the Japanese Foreign Office renewing his earlier plea for assistance to overthrow Yuan. Sun promised, among other things, that China would depend upon Japan to equip her armed forces, employ Japanese military and political advisers, establish a Sino-Japanese bank to facilitate economic cooperation, and seek Japanese capital to develop China's railroads, coastal trade, etc. See Jansen, *op. cit.*, pp. 192-193.

[61] See Feng Tzu-yu in *Ke-min wen-hsien*, V, 641-642.

[62] *Ibid.*

members in America felt that a division within the revolutionary ranks endangered China. There was an urgent demand for unity among the various former Kuomintang elements. Feng Tzu-yu was therefore appointed by the party in the United States to convey its message to Sun in Japan.

When Feng Tzu-yu arrived in Japan in July, 1915, he was warmly welcomed by Sun Yet-sen, who fully agreed with him on the need for unity. Indeed, Feng was informed that talks were already under way between Sun's group, Chang Hsin-yen, and other representatives of the Ou-shih Yen-chiu Hui. Feng participated in a meeting between the two groups, and met separately with Li Ken-yuan and members of the Ou-shih Yen-chiu Hui. But the talks were suddenly terminated, and Sun dispatched Feng to raise funds for the anti-Yuan movement in the Philippine Islands. It is evident that Sun's persistence in continuing the anti-Yuan movement was a chief factor in the failure of the peace talks. Sun had agreed on the need for unity, but had not consented to cease opposing Yuan Shih-k'ai, whom he could not forgive for betraying the Republic. In spite of Japan's Twenty-one Demands, Sun still considered Yuan a far greater evil than the Japanese. Pan-Asianism was also close to Sun's heart, so he could not join with Yuan in opposing Japan. Ironically, Sun Yat-sen, who had inspired China in the movement to overthrow the alien Manchus, became increasingly withdrawn from the main stream of the national current.

If Sun had blundered in underestimating the rising tide of nationalism among his fellow countrymen, Yuan Shih-k'ai erred still more. Thinking that the initial failure of the Republic justified its rejection, Yuan promoted a movement to restore the monarchy which culminated in his acceptance of the throne on December 12, 1915. Yuan's mistake was Sun's salvation, for open revolt against the monarchical movement followed.

After nearly three years of exile, Sun and the party returned to Shanghai.[63] Two military expeditions were organized, one in Kwangtung and the other in Shangtung.[64] However, the Chung-

---

[63] Sun Yat-sen returned to Shanghai on March 27, 1916.

[64] The expeditionary forces in Kwangtung were led by Chu Chih-hsin and those in Shangtung by Chu Cheng.

hua Kemintang's expeditionary armies constituted a very minor
segment of the anti-Yuan forces. The major challenge to Yuan's
dream was the rise of the National Protection Army in southwest China.[65] Soon the antimonarchical movement spread to
other provinces. Yuan's abandonment of the plan to restore the
monarchical system and his subsequent withdrawal from power
were due rather to national indignation. The situation in 1916
was very similar to that in 1911. Just as the overthrow of the
Ch'ing dynasty was not won by the military force of the T'ung
Meng Hui, so Yuan's final downfall was not the result of military victories of the Chung-hua Kemintang. In both instances,
the parties had been carried along by the actions of other dis-
contented elements. Thus Sun Yat-sen and the Chung-hua Kemintang, like the T'ung Meng Hui in 1911, represented only
one of the elements which contributed to the new order.

If the overthrow of the regimes in 1911 and in 1916 had basic
similarities, they also had vast differences. The 1911 revolution
represented a victory against an alien dynasty. The introduction
of the republican form of government symbolized China's entrance into a new era. To a degree, Yuan's ascendancy after the
establishment of the Republic represented increasing disillusionment with republican institutions. Yet disillusionment did
not represent outright rejection or a desire to retreat to the past.
In 1911, although the empire was crumbling, the Manchus still
represented the sole center of government. The revolutionists,
despite their factionalism, were united against a common ad-
versary. In the intervening years, however, a host of centrifugal forces—militarists—were unleashed. Yuan's withdrawal
from power heightened the process of division. Therefore, unlike the T'ung Meng Hui, which could concentrate its strength
externally, the Chung-hua Kemintang was involved with a multitude of divergent political and military powers. In 1916 Sun

---

[65] The National Protection Army had its beginning in Yunnan. Several
groups had a hand in promoting the revolt against Yuan. Liang Ch'i-ch'ao
is most prominently mentioned, together with other elements from the
Chin-pu Tang. However, Li Lieh-chun, Li Ken-yuan, and other members
from the old Kuomintang also played a part in the antimonarchical uprising. Together they raised the banner of revolt on December 25, 1915.

Yat-sen and the Chung-hua Kemintang had to do battle on many fronts, provincial and national, political and military.

Yuan Shih-k'ai's unexpected (but natural) death on June 6, 1916, brought to an end the political force which had dominated China, and ushered in a period of direct struggle for power by the Chung-hua Kemintang. Immediately the various groups began jockeying for position to gain control of the government. From 1916 until the unification of China by the Kuomintang armies in 1928, the Peking government was little more than the plaything of the militarists. The rest of the country was divided into numerous semiautonomous areas, each governed by a military lord. During this period, the political groups attached themselves to one or another of the militarists. Lacking a military machine of their own, the political groups could not hope to attain power. The militarists also needed the political groups, which gave them a sense of legitimacy and a chance to staff the bureaucracy. The year 1916 initiated what is commonly referred to as the war-lord era.

The Chung-hua Kemintang began the war-lord era with full faith in the democratic process. In separate orders to the party's armies in Kwangtung and Shangtung in June, 1916, Sun Yat-sen directed them to cease fire immediately.[66] Yuan Shih-k'ai's death, asserted Sun, had completely changed the situation. The country should now await the resumption of constitutional government by the new president, Li Yuan-hung. In a telegram to Huang Hsing, who was returning to China after an extended stay in the United States, Sun recalled the aims of the expeditionary armies:[67] to remove Yuan, restore the provisional constitution, and reconvene Parliament. Since Yuan was now dead, Li Yuan-hung's accomplishment of the latter two goals would reunite China, which could then embark upon a period of reconstruction. Sun had not lost faith in the application of Western constitutional government in China, for he approved

---

[66] See text of telegrams of June 9, 1916, to Chu Cheng, and of June 10, 1916, to Chu Chih-hsin in *Kuo-fu ch'uan-chi*, IV, 262.

[67] Telegram to Huang Hsing on June 13, 1916, *ibid.*, IV, 263.

China's direct entrance into the constitutional stage of government in 1916.

Sun Yat-sen's behavior in 1916 was directly contrary to the
revolutionary strategy which he had formulated in 1914. Sun
had attributed the Kuomintang fiasco in 1913 to the party's
failure to adopt the three-stage process, and had therefore reintroduced the concept into the Chung-hua Kemintang. He had
given the party the responsibility of guiding the country during
the three stages. Sun's Chung-hua Kemintang was expected to
seek the military unification of China, followed by a period of
political tutelage. The explanation for Sun's abrupt reversal
can perhaps be found within the Chung-hua Kemintang. The
party had neither the military force to achieve its goal nor the
organization and disciplined membership to carry out its program. In short, Sun Yat-sen lacked the means to implement his
1914 policy in 1916.

When Parliament was reconvened on August 1, 1916, in
Peking, the Chung-hua Kemintang, along with other political
groups, prepared to continue China's introduction to republicanism which had been interrupted by Yuan Shih-k'ai. The
earlier experience, however, had left its mark, especially with regard to the behavior of political parties. Sentiment was strongly
against the reintroduction of political parties and party politics.[68] Consequently, political parties were forbidden in the new
parliament. In their place, however, numerous cliques and factions arose. This affected the Chung-hua Kemintang very little,
for, as a secret-society type of organization, it could not openly
enter the political arena. But this did not prevent its members
from participating in Parliament.

The 1916 Parliament was divided between the followers of
the two archrivals of the 1913 Parliament: the former Kuomintang and the former Chin-pu Tang. Each faction, however, was
badly split internally. The former Chin-pu Tang split into two

---

[68] Tsou Lu, *Hui-i lu* (Taipei, 1951), I, 80; Chang Chi, *Chang P'u-ch'uan
hsien-sheng ch'uan-chi*, p. 241.

groups: the Hsien-fa T'ao-lun Hui (Constitution Discussion Society), headed by T'ang Hua-lung, and the Hsien-fa Yen-chiu
Hui (Constitution Research Association), led by Liang Ch'i-
ch'ao. The two groups occupied about one hundred fifty seats
in Parliament.[69]

The four hundred former Kuomintang members constituted
by far the largest single bloc in the 1916 Parliament. Supposedly
gathered under the common banner of the Hsien-cheng Shang-
chueh Hui (Society for the Discussion of Constitutional Government),[70] they were actually divided into numerous groups
representing the various political shades in the party. Initially,
there were three major factions. The largest was the Ko-lu
(Temporary Resident), with a membership of about two hundred fifty, led by Chang Chi, Ku Chung-hsiu, Wu Ching-lien,
and Chang Yao-ts'eng, all prominent members of the 1913 Parliament who had been instrumental in the formation of the
Kuomintang. Subsequently, the Ko-lu group underwent a division into two separate groups: the Cheng-hsueh Hui (Political
Study Group), which included among its members Ku Chung-
hsiu and Chang Yao-ts'eng; and the I-yu She (Beneficial Friends
Group), led by Chang Chi and Wu Ching-lien.

The Chung-hua Kemintang was represented by some fifty
members in Parliament, known as the Ping-ch'en Chu-lo Pu
(Political Club of 1916). Among its members were Lin Shen,
Chu Cheng, T'ien T'ung, and others who had remained loyal
to Sun Yat-sen. The third major political group, the Tao-yuan
(Tao Gardens) a mixture of former Kuomintang and Chin-pu
Tang members, had a parliamentary membership of about fifty.
Among its leaders were Sun Hung-i and Yeh Hsia-shang. The
latter group subsequently merged with the Ping-ch'en Chu-lo
Pu to form the Min-yu She (People's Friend Society).

The factional composition of the 1916 Parliament did not
contribute to legislative harmony. The two major factions, one
consisting of members from the former Chin-pu Tang and the

---

[69] Yang Yu-chun, *Chung-kuo cheng-tang shih* (Shanghai, 1937), pp. 91-
92; Hsieh Pin, *Min-kuo cheng-tang shih* (Shanghai, 1928), p. 68.

[70] Yang Yu-chun, *op. cit.*, pp. 89-91; Hsieh Pin, *op. cit.*, pp. 66-68.

other of members from the defunct Kuomintang, were soon
locked in bitter combat. The struggle reached its climax in the
discussion of the provincial system in conjunction with the work
of constitution-framing, which had been dropped in 1913. The
former Kuomintang elements favored a provincial system freed
from the control of Peking, and sought to make the provinces
self-governing political units, with the governors elected by the
people. The former Chin-pu Tang groups demanded that the
provinces be subject to the direct control of the national government. The contention dating from the pre-1912 era between
the Chin-pu Tang and the Kuomintang was thus resumed in
1916.

However, the "party" line between the former Chin-pu Tang
and Kuomintang factions was not always so clearly differen-
tiated. More often than not, the line-up in Parliament was determined by the opportunities available to each group for
gaining power or merely holding office. Within the Kuomintang, the Ko-lu group was the most insistent in seeking governmental positions. Its members sought to organize a separate
"party," complaining that the existing factional structure prevented them from holding office.[71] At one time they even suggested replacing Sun Yat-sen with Ch'en Ch'un-hsuan as the
"party's" leader.

In domestic party activities the Chung-hua Kemintang seems
to have remained aloof. Sun and the party did maintain contact
with Chung-hua Kemintang and former Kuomintang members
of Parliament, but exercised little influence over them.[72] In the
dispute over China's declaration of war against Germany in
1917, the old Kuomintang elements in Parliament were badly
divided. Chang Chi, Chang Yao-ts'eng, and Ku Chung-hsiu
favored China's entrance into the war,[73] but Sun objected to

---

[71] Tsou Lu, Hui-i Lu, I, 80-82.

[72] Lo Chia-lun, ed., Kuo-fu nien-p'u ch'u-kao (Taipei, 1958), II, 417-418.
Although Sun called upon branches of the former Kuomintang to change
their designation to the Chung-hua Kemintang, few took the trouble to do
so. Overseas branches continued to use the Kuomintang designation.

[73] Yang Yu-chun, op. cit., p. 95.

this policy.[74] According to Tsou Lu, Sun favored using the opportunity presented by the Powers' preoccupation with the war to initiate internal reforms.[75] China did not have the strength, anyway, Sun is reported to have said. And if China did partake in the venture, he saw nothing to China's advantage. His advice went unnoticed, however.

Parliament was now confronted with the strong extraparliamentary force of the militarists. The two met head-on over the matter of China's participation in the war against Germany.[76] Again, as in 1913, the introduction of constitutional government received a setback in China. Under pressure from the militarists, President Li Yuan-hung dissolved the Parliament on June 13, 1917.

The year 1917 marked the beginning of another eventful episode in China's political development. In that year China became divided between the north and the south, and was not reunified until 1928. In the north, the Peking government was dominated by the militarists, with the support of Liang Ch'i-ch'ao and the former Chin-pu Tang. In the south, Sun Yat-sen and elements from the old Kuomintang gathered. After Chang Hsun's attempt to restore the Ch'ing dynasty in July, 1917, Sun led a group of more than a hundred former Kuomintang members of Parliament to Canton, Kwangtung, where he held a special conference of the Parliament and proceeded to organize a military government.[77] On September 1, 1917, Sun was elected grand marshal of the Canton government, established to oppose Peking.[78]

The Canton members of Parliament were as divided as they had been in Peking. Factional strife continued, and the local

---

[74] See Sun's telegram of May 16, 1917, in *Kuo-fu ch'uan-chi*, IV 275-276.

[75] Tsou Lu, *Hui-i lu*, I, 89. According to Tsou, he was called from Peking to Shanghai for Sun's message and instructed to deliver the message to other members of Parliament.

[76] See Harley F. MacNair, *China in Revolution* (Chicago, 1931).

[77] Shao Yuan-chung, *op. cit.*, II, 615, 637.

[78] For a personal account of the power struggle during Sun's brief stay in Canton, 1917-1918, see *ibid.*, II, 615-637.

war lords also challenged the Canton government. Sun was freed from this impossible position in April, 1918, when the local militarists, after an almost continuous feud with him for supremacy, forced a reorganization of the military government. Sun as grand marshal was replaced by a seven-member committee, most of whom were local militarists. He subsequently resigned his committee post and returned to Shanghai. Thus concluded the first direct attempt of Sun and the Chung-hua Kemintang to seize power since 1914. Toward the end of 1918 the possibility of regaining control seemed remote. The Chung-hua Kemintang had also failed to emerge as a unified and disciplined revolutionary party.

Since the Chung-hua Kemintang could claim success neither before Yuan Shih-k'ai's death nor after, what function did the party serve? The idea that the party constituted an integrating force must be ruled out, for it further divided the anti-Yuan movement. The concept that the Chung-hua Kemintang and Sun Yat-sen stood in the forefront of the Chinese nationalist movement must also be rejected. By refusing to condemn Japan's aggression in the Twenty-one Demands, Sun and the party had compromised their principles. Personal revenge took the place of national interest.

However, there was a positive phase to the Chung-hua Kemintang era. Whereas in years past Sun Yat-sen had concerned himself chiefly with revolutionary strategy, between 1913 and 1919 he turned to the organizing of the party, and drew up a well-defined plan for its functioning, once it came into power again. Reaching back to the T'ung Meng Hui, he reintroduced the famous three-stage process, but in the Chung-hua Kemintang constitution he added a provision for tutelage by the party. Thus by 1914 Sun had formulated the first theory of party government: the proper role of a party in an emerging society was to guide the masses toward democracy. Sun Yat-sen, however, had not realized this goal. He had yet to build an effective organization based upon the ideas set forth in 1914.

VI REBIRTH: PRELUDE
TO REORGANIZATION

By 1918 IT WAS CLEAR that the Chung-hua Kemintang had failed to capture power and attain the goal of a centralized revolutionary party. The cleavage within the old party ranks remained. Yet after 1918 the internal political climate of China and the impact of the Russian Revolution combined to transform the Chung-hua Kemintang into a totally new revolutionary organization.

The Chinese revolutionary movement led by Sun Yat-sen had, by 1918, lost the dedicated spirit of the anti-Ch'ing period. Yuan Shih-k'ai's removal had not brought Sun and his followers to power. And Sun's most recent attempt to regain control in Kwangtung had ended in failure. Sun and his party could point neither to a glorious past nor to a promising future.

It is to Sun Yat-sen's credit that failure rarely discouraged him. As a political activist, he would begin almost immediately to initiate new undertakings. The organization of the Chung-hua Kemintang on the eve of the Kuomintang's defeat was a prime example of Sun's tireless determination. Yet his firmness of purpose was not always shared by his followers. And without a following, Sun became but another voice crying in the wilderness. After Japan's Twenty-one Demands, Sun remained without power except for a brief period in Kwangtung. The Chunghua Kemintang, with no visible rewards in sight, became a small elite of unrelenting fighters. After 1915 it was merely a group of Sun's personal followers.

On the verge of collapse, the Kuomintang was resurrected through a series of reorganizations beginning in 1919. The party and its leadership began to awaken to the fundamental social, economic, and political changes taking place in China, and the new international political climate.[1] The party reorganization took place against the background of a rising tide of nationalism, frustration in the implementation of Western liberal institutions, and the division of the country by war lords. These and other indignities were vividly brought to the forefront by the May Fourth incident of 1919.[2] Again, as with the anti-Manchu movement, a national awakening had taken place. But, whereas the 1911 revolution was primarily "racial" in character, the May Fourth Movement (as this massive upheaval has become known) encompassed far greater changes, for it represented a social, cultural, ideological, and political revolution.

After the May Fourth incident there was a sudden proliferation of newspapers and periodicals in the vernacular, publicizing modern Western ideas. Sun and his party hastened to join the nation's literary "renaissance." Since the termination of

---

[1] We shall return to the subject of the new international political climate and the Chinese revolutionary movement later.

[2] The May Fourth incident (May 4, 1919) refers to the student demonstration of that date in Peking. The cause of the incident was anti-foreign feeling, especially against Japan. Subsequently, the May Fourth incident has come to signify the beginning of a new era in China, with the whole traditional system coming under increasing attack. The immediate importance of the incident was the emergence of Chinese nationalism. For an account of the May Fourth incident and its impact upon China, see Chou Tse-tung, *The May Fourth Movement* (Cambridge, 1960).

the *Min-kuo* in Tokyo in 1914, the Chung-hua Kemintang had engaged in limited propaganda efforts,[3] and party organization had been badly neglected.

The May Fourth Movement transformed the party, projecting it once again into the national limelight. In August, 1919, the party began publishing the famous journal *Chien-she* (The Construction), to whose pages Sun Yat-sen, Hu Han-min, Liao Chung-k'ai, Chu Chih-hsin, Wang Ching-wei, Tai Chi-t'ao, and others of the party contributed. Sun wrote the opening declaration.[4] Surveying the Republic since its establishment in 1912, he charged that it had brought neither international recognition nor internal peace to China, because the revolution had not been followed by a period of constructive work. The *Chien-she* would propagate constructive ideas to make the principles of the party better known and accepted. Sun's *Chien- kuo fang-lueh* (Plans for National Reconstruction) in which he stressed the need for material rehabilitation and psychological change, was run serially beginning with the first issue.

The pages of the *Chien-she* reflected also the controversy over socialist thought in China. The party under Sun's guidance had long before propagated socialist ideas. However, the *Chien-she's* attitude was one of apprehension over aspects of the "new culture" rather than of encouragement. Some of the *Chien-she* writers accepted the materialistic concept of history,[5] as did Hu Han-min. But Hu did not accept Marxist conclusions. Perhaps the *Chien-she's* position was best represented in the famous exchange between Hu Han-min, Liao Chung-k'ai, Chu Chih-hsin, and Hu Shih over the existence of the well-field system

---

[3] This did not apply to individual party members. The Shanghai *Min-kuo Jih-pao* (Republican Daily), edited by Yeh Ch'u-ts'ang and Shao Li-tzu, was for many years the party's unofficial organ.

[4] *Chien-she*, I, No. 1 (August 1, 1919), pp. unnumbered (first two leaves). For an English translation see Sun Yat-sen, *Fundamentals of National Reconstruction* (Taipei, 1953), pp. 207-208.

[5] See Hu Han-min, "A Materialistic Study of the History of Chinese Philosophy," *Chien-she*, I, No. 3 (October 1, 1919), 513-543; and No. 4 (November 1, 1919), 655-691.

in ancient China.[6] Whatever the merits of the controversy, it did establish the *Chien-she* writers, and thus the party, as equal to the most progressive advocates of the new culture. Indeed, Sun and the party were trying hard to capture the leadership of the newly-awakened nation.

The *Chien-she* printed a large number of translations of Western writings. A translation of Delos F. Wilcox's *Government by All the People; or The Initiative, the Referendum, and the Recall as Instruments of Democracy* ran through many issues of the journal.[7] Karl Kautsky's *Karl Marx's Oekonomische Lehren* was translated,[8] and selections from A. L. Lowell's *Public Opinion and Popular Government* also appeared.[9] Sun and the party thereby attempted to identify themselves with antitraditional, progressive elements.

An intensive long-range propaganda campaign was planned, with the publication of numerous journals and booklets to spread the party's principles; an English-language newspaper was also contemplated. To insure the success of the venture, a printing press was purchased through the contributions of party comrades in China and abroad, and a publishing house was established in Shanghai.[10] Sun and the party took on an increasingly active revolutionary role.

Though Sun Yat-sen and the Chung-hua Kemintang may

---

[6] For an excellent summary of this controversy, see Joseph R. Levenson, "Ill Wind in the Well-Field: The Erosion of the Confucian Ground of Controversy," *The Confucian Persuasion*, ed. by Arthur F. Wright (Stanford, 1960), pp. 268-287.

[7] Delos F. Wilcox, "Government by All the People . . . ," trans. by Liao Chung-k'ai, began in *Chien-she*, I, No. I (August 1, 1919), and continued through II, No. 4 (May 1, 1920).

[8] Karl Kautsky, "Karl Marx's Oekonomische Lehren," trans. by Tai Chi-t'ao, began in *ibid.*, I, No. 4 (November 1, 1919), and continued in II, No. 2 (February 1, 1920), through No. 5 (June 1, 1920).

[9] A. L. Lowell, "Public Opinion and Popular Government," trans. by Sun Fo, *ibid.*, I, No. 3 (October 1, 1919), 545-554; No. 4 (November 1, 1919) 743-753.

[10] Tsou Lu, *Chung-kuo Kuo-min Tang shih-kao* (Chungking, 1944), II, 572-573.

have identified themselves with the national political current, the party was still far from a coherent body. And without an effective organization it was extremely difficult to mobilize the people. The Chinese revolutionary movement, beginning with the Hsing Chung Hui, had been driven underground, and there had been little opportunity to build a genuine party and discipline its members.[11] By 1919 Sun was still without power, and the party was reduced to a mere cluster of followers personally loyal to Sun. Yet the rebuilding of the party could be achieved only by the capture of power. This may explain in part Sun's stubborn determination to establish a foothold in Kwangtung, for, without a territorial base, the party would remain an illegal body.

On October 10, 1919, the Chung-hua Kemintang was officially reorganized as the Chung-kuo Kuomintang.[12] The reorganization, however, was concerned primarily with the party overseas. Since the outlawing of the old Kuomintang in 1913, its successor, the Chung-hua Kemintang, had never been able to operate openly in China. Between 1913 and 1919, therefore, only the branches in Southeast Asia, the Americas, and other foreign lands comprised integral units of the revolutionary organization. In 1919 it was this overseas party which was reorganized.

The overseas branches had always occupied a special position in relation to the party in general. In the Americas, for example, free from governmental suppression, the parties had always enjoyed freedom of action.[13] Thus the Chung-hua Kemintang

---

[11] The Russian Communist Party may be one of the world's most disciplined political "parties" today, but in the pre-1917 era it was struggling with the problem of organizational unity. Not until after the seizure of power in 1917, with definite assurance to all "revolutionists" of visible rewards, was an efficient, disciplined Communist Party made possible. For an account of the Russian Communist Party before 1917, see Leonard Schapiro, *The Communist Party of the Soviet Union* (New York, 1960), pp. 36 ff.

[12] Tsou Lu, *op. cit.*, I, 287. The words "Chung-kuo" (China) were added to distinguish the new party from the Kuomintang of 1913.

[13] In 1915, while the "mother" party was outlawed in China and was in

took on a peculiar dual character: it was both an open and a closed party, legal and illegal simultaneously. And because of the loose structure of the parties, the fortunes of one segment did not necessarily affect the destiny of the others. Indeed, it may even be argued, aside from Sun Yat-sen's leadership and the political turn of events, that the party's dual character saved it from complete destruction in 1913. However, the presence of two more or less separate and independent entities within a single organization had its detrimental aspects.

There is no indication that overseas members endorsed the Chung-hua Kemintang's attempt to organize the party into a centralized structure. The majority of the overseas branches had retained the Kuomintang designation. Considering the fact that by 1919 the overseas party constituted the sole basis of the mother party in China, it is understandable that Sun should begin the party reorganization overseas, for the financial support of the Chinese abroad was needed to implement the party's program.[14]

Article 1 of the new party's regulations[15] declared the purpose of the new Kuomintang to be "the strengthening of the Republic, and the effectuation of the San Min Chu I." Article 2 opened membership to all adult Chinese upon the recommendation of two members. Article 4 granted members of the Chung-hua

---

exile and in underground status in Japan, the overseas party in America was operating openly, and was reported to have over 100 branches with a membership exceeding 10,000. It even held a national convention from July 24 to August 3, 1915, in San Francisco. See *Chung-kuo Kuo-min Tang ch'uan-t'i ken-ch'in ta-hui* (Program of the National Convention of the Chinese Nationalist League of America) and Teng Chia-Yen, ed., *Chung-kuo Kuo-min Tang ken-ch'in ta-hui shih-mo chi* (San Francisco, 1915).

14 Sun was forced to reject appeals for financial assistance in 1919, explaining that he "was in a very difficult (financial) position at the moment." Kuomintang, *Kuo-fu ch'uan-chi* (Taipei, 1957), 373-394 (hereafter cited as *Kuo-fu ch'uan-chi*). In January, 1920, Sun asked the overseas comrades to raise $500,000 to publish an English-language party journal and operate a printing press in Shanghai. See Sun's letter, *ibid.*, V, 384-389.

15 For the complete text see Lo Chia-tun, ed., *Ke-min wen-hsien* (Taipei, 1953), VIII, 1009-1013. Hereafter cited as *Ke-min wen-hsien*.

Kemintang the privilege of exchanging their membership from the old party to the new. Article 5 required members of the new Kuomintang to adhere to the party's principles; Article 8 prohibited them from concurrently joining other political groups. Article 12 provided for the office of *tsung-li* to represent the party and serve as its director. Article 13 created three departments—general affairs, party affairs, and finance—with provision for the establishment of others as the need arose. Article 19 provided that the post of *tsung-li* was to be elected by the party congress, which article 21 stipulated was to be held annually. Article 20 provided that department heads were to be appointed by the *tsung-li* for a two-year term. Article 22 provided an elaborate system to govern voting rights at the party congress: branches with less than 500 members were given one vote; those over 500, two votes; those less than 2,000, three votes; and those between 2,000 and 3,000, four votes. Each additional thousand members were entitled to one extra vote, but no branch was entitled to more than ten votes. According to article 24, the party was to derive its support from membership entrance fees, annual dues, special assessments, and loans. In addition to the constitution, the new Kuomintang formulated detailed regulations on the organization of overseas branches.[16]

Viewed as a whole, the 1919 reorganization was seemingly a retreat from the rigid party organization and revolutionary strategy conceived in 1914. Gone was the oath requirement, and the provision demanding sacrifice of life and liberty of members. Another feature contributing to the liberalization of the new Kuomintang was the abolishment of the threefold membership classification. In the new party all members were equal and enjoyed the same privileges. Also missing was the three-stage process, that sacred formula intended to lead China to full democracy. Thus the nondemocratic characteristics of the Chung-hua Kemintang were abandoned. However, the 1919 reorganization was concerned explicitly with the party abroad, which occupied a unique position within the party and served

---

[16] *Ibid.*, VIII, 1013-1022.

the specific function of raising funds. Given these and other considerations, the new Kuomintang was merely acknowledging the differences which distinguished the overseas party from the mother party in China.

With the overseas party reorganized, Sun Yat-sen and his followers began the reorganization of the domestic Kuomintang in 1920. The drive to revitalize the party in China presented far greater problems, for, unlike the party members abroad, those in China were forever confronted with the political realities of gaining and holding power, and were identified with the party's future.

The major challenge confronting Sun Yat-sen and his diminutive band of loyal followers was the rebuilding of the dormant party. Sun's task was to reunite the various political groups, the majority of which were composed of political opportunists without mass support, in one coherent political body, much as he had brought together the Hsing Chung Hui, the Kuang Fu Hui, and other factions to form the T'ung Meng Hui.

Sun began by publicly retreating from the authoritarian organization of the Chung-hua Kemintang and by revising the revolutionary strategy. The new principles and strategy were incorporated in the new constitution of November 9, 1920.[17] The implementation of the San Min Chu I (article 1) and the establishment of the five-power constitution (article 2) were reiterated. Membership in the party was open to all adult Chinese men and women (article 5). Members were required to take an oath to observe forever the party's principles (article 6). Organizationally, besides the traditional general affairs, party affairs, and finance departments, a propaganda department was created (article 8). Officers included the *tsung-li*, empowered with absolute authority over the party (article 10), and departmental heads and other workers, appointed by the *tsung-li* (article 11).

Perhaps the outstanding feature of the November 9, 1920, constitution was the reincorporation of Sun's three-stage pro-

---

[17] For the full text see *ibid.*, VIII, 1022-1024.

cess, now disguised in the form of what may be called a two-
stage process. Article 3 outlined the new program. The first
stage would be rule by military government. During this period,
all obstacles would be removed by force. Concurrently, this
stage would serve also as a period of political tutelage, to guide
the people in the practice of local self-government. The second
and final stage would be rule by constitutional government.
Upon the successful attainment of local self-government, a committee to draft the constitution would be elected by the people
to found a government based upon the principles of the five-
power constitution. The idea of one-party government, first
introduced in 1914, was again put forth. Article 4 stipulated
that the interval between the beginning of the revolution and
the declaration of the constitution would be known as the
revolutionary period, during which all military and civil affairs
would be the sole responsibility of party members. On November 19 Sun further revised the party's regulations.[18] He had
wisely abandoned or modified the main points of contention of
the Chung-hua Kemintang: division of membership into different levels, requirement of an oath of personal loyalty to Sun,
and emphasis upon the stage of political tutelage.

While Sun made outward concessions, these did not reflect
a change in his thinking. This was clearly shown in a series of
addresses he made at the party's Shanghai headquarters just
before the 1920 reorganization. On November 14, 1920, Sun
explained his conception of loyalty.[19] Because of the need to
realize its principles, a party emphasized the concept of personal rule, so that there would be unity of action. Sun defended
the provision that had required members to declare their loyalty to him personally. Principles, religions, theories, and national policies could all be represented by an individual: thus
one speaks of Confucius' teaching, the religion of Jesus, the
Darwinian theory of evolution, and even the Monroe Doctrine.
"My San Min Chu I and five-power constitution can also be

[18] See *ibid.*, VIII, 1024-1027, for the text of the revised regulations.
[19] *Kuo-fu ch'uan-chi*, III, 180-184.

known as Sun Wen's revolutionary [principles]. Therefore, to obey me is to submit to the revolution which I advocate. And if one follows my revolution, naturally one should [also] obey me." Here was reaffirmation of Sun's 1914 position on the eve of the 1920 reorganization.

Sun was equally persistent concerning the idea of political tutelage. Though relegating the period of tutelage to the background in the constitution, he was bold enough to deliver a speech before the party emphasizing the importance of the tutelage stage on the very day the new constitution was declared.[20] He admitted the seemingly contradictory aspect of tutelage—the monopolization of political power by the party when in fact political sovereignty rested with the people. However, Sun argued, the idea of tutelage was really not contradictory, since the purpose of the party in carrying out the revolution was to seize political power. Furthermore, tutelage was a necessity. The Republic had failed because the people did not comprehend the true meaning of republicanism. Thus the need for another revolution. Sun declared he intended to use the revolution not only to sweep aside corrupt government, but to adopt revolutionary methods, namely, political tutelage, to engage in national reconstruction. After several thousand years of slavery, the people were not accustomed to the exercise of sovereignty. Hence the party had to adopt forceful methods to instruct them in self-government. It was obvious that Sun had not retreated one inch on the importance of political tutelage in the revolutionary strategy. Indeed, the failure of the 1911 revolution to usher in a full-fledged republic only strengthened his conviction of the necessity for a period of guardianship of the people.

The reorganization of 1920 took on new meaning with the almost concurrent recapture of Canton by the pro-Sun forces led by Ch'en Chiung-ming on November 1, 1920.[21] The revolu-

---

[20] *Ibid.*, III, 184-185.

[21] Ch'en Chiung-ming, who had organized a separate movement to oppose Yuan Shih-k'ai, had rejoined Sun's camp, and in 1917 commanded a twenty-battalion force in Canton. To prevent the Kwangsi militarists

tionary center shifted from Shanghai to Canton. The party was liberated from the secretive, hostile environment of the Shanghai foreign settlement to the open, friendly environment in Canton. Moreover, it offered the party an opportunity to implement the new constitution.

Unfortunately, the 1920 version of the Kuomintang was never given an opportunity to develop. Sun returned to Canton on November 29 to engage in the problem of organizing a new southern government, of which he became president.[22] Subsequently he was occupied with the Northern Expedition of 1921, which he directed personally from Kwangsi. The party followed Sun, concentrating its energies on the political stabilization of the south and the military reunification of China. Wang Ching-wei became involved in the administration of Kwangtung's educational program;[23] Hu Han-min was appointed minister of political affairs in the Canton government;[24] Liao Chung-k'ai was in charge of fiscal affairs;[25] Tsou Lu was appointed salt commissioner of Kwangtung and Kwangsi prov-

---

from absorbing the twenty battalions, then the only military force considered belonging to the party, Ch'en was ordered to lead his troops to southern Fuchien. When Sun was ejected from Canton, the Kwangsi militarists took control of Kwangtung, but Ch'en and his twenty battalions were safe in Fuchien. In time he built up his force until he controlled some twenty-six *hsien* in southern Fuchien, with headquarters at Chang-chou. Ch'en maintained contact with Sun, and soon numerous party leaders converged on Chang-chou. Chang-chou, not Shanghai (where Sun was residing), became the revolutionary center. In 1920 Ch'en led his troops against the Kwangsi militarists and recaptured Canton. Tsou Lu, *Hui-i lu* (Taipei, 1951), I, 102 ff.; Wu T'ieh-ch'eng, *Wu T'ieh-ch'eng hsien-sheng hui-i lu* (Taipei, 1957 [?]), pp. 50b-58a; Liang Ping-hsien (pseud. Hai-yu Ku-k'e), "Special Memoirs of the Liberation," *Tzu-yu Ien*, Nos. 73-86 (November 14-December 29, 1951); Ch'en Ching-ts'un, *Ch'en Chiung-ming hsien-sheng nien-p'u* (Hong Kong, n.d.).

[22] Sun was elected by the Canton Parliament on April 7, 1921.

[23] "News from South China," *Millards Review of the Far East*, March 12, 1921, pp. 107-108.

[24] Lo Chia-lun, ed., *Kuo-fu nien-p'u ch'u-kao* (Taipei, 1958), II, 506, hereafter cited as *Kuo-fu nien-p'u ch'u-kao*.

[25] *Ibid.*, p. 505.

inces.[26] The party, however, was neglected, and its headquarters remained in Shanghai.[27] A business office of the Kuomintang was eventually established in Canton on February 12, 1921,[28] only to be closed a year later.[29] Thus, even with the acquisition of a territorial base, the new Kuomintang remained dormant as a party. One of the immediate consequences of their neglect of the party was their forceful ejection by Ch'en Chiung-ming from Canton and southern China in June, 1922.[30] Thus even by 1922 the new Kuomintang, in spite of Sun's attempts at reorganization, had yet to develop into an effective revolutionary party.

While the party's 1913 debacle can be attributed to the external environment, its failure in 1922 must be laid primarily to internal deficiencies. The 1920 reorganization was a beginning toward party harmony and reunification. However, the new party was never given the opportunity for development. Instead of consolidating the party with the acquisition of a territorial base the party was preoccupied with the routine of government and the military unification of the country. Without the party, Sun was forced to rely upon the whims of the militarists. And without an effective, well-organized party, Sun had no power upon which to call for assistance. Between 1920 and 1922, the

---

26 Tsou Lu, *Hui-i lu*, I, 108-113; "News from South China," *Millards Review of the Far East*, December 11, 1920, p. 104. According to Tsou Lu, revenue from the salt tax constituted the sole source of income of the Canton government. Provisions for the 1921 northern expeditionary forces were also supplied from the salt-tax revenue.

27 Tsou Lu, *Chung-kuo Kuo-min Tang shih-kao*, I, 302-303; Chu Cheng, *Chu Chio-sheng hsien-sheng ch'uan-chi* (Taipei, n.d.), I, 55.

28 "News from South China," *Millards Review of the Far East*, March 5, 1921, p. 53. Kuomintang sources give no dates for the establishment of the party's Canton business office. All agree, however, that it was in early 1921.

29 Tsou Lu, *Chung-kuo Kuo-min Tang shih-kao*, I, 303.

30 In accounts of the final split between Ch'en Chiung-ming and Sun Yat-sen, Ch'en is always blamed for his ungrateful revolt against Sun. This may be true. But Sun's reliance upon Ch'en must also be questioned. Ch'en had expressed hesitancy in regard to the 1921 Northern Expedition. At any rate, Ch'en's turnabout caught Sun by surprise and forced him to flee to Shanghai.

new Kuomintang was still primarily an institution of Sun's personal power and a grouping of his personal followers.

The year 1923 may be considered the dividing line in the Chinese revolutionary movement led by the new Kuomintang and its predecessors. In that year plans were formulated for a totally reorganized party. The turning point in Sun's long and frustrating career and the realization of an effective party came with the arrival of the Russian Communists.

Since its inception in 1894 the revolutionary movement led by Sun had always sought foreign assistance. As late as 1921, Sun had endeavored to obtain help from America,[31] and had appointed Ma Soo as a special representative to Washington for that purpose.[32] But the United States and other Western countries turned a deaf ear to Sun's requests. It was therefore a relief when Russia extended the hand of friendship to Sun and the Kuomintang. Just as Sun and the party had freely accepted Japanese assistance in their attempts to overthrow the Ch'ing dynasty, so they welcomed Russian aid to reorganize the party and reconstruct China.

In comparison to Great Britain, France, Japan, and other powers, Soviet Russia made a late entry into the crowded and chaotic Chinese political scene, after Lenin's "discovery" of Asian nationalism as an ally in the world struggle for power. On August 1, 1918, the Canton government received a message from Chicherin, Soviet commissar for foreign affairs,[33] in which he praised Sun for his determination in the struggle between democracy and militarism and imperialism. Chicherin called

---

[31] In 1921 Sun appealed to President Harding of the United States to help China by recognizing the Canton government. See U. S. Department of State, *Papers Relating to the Foreign Relations of the United States, 1921* (Washington, D. C., 1936), I, 336.

[32] "News from the South," *Millards Review of the Far East*, July 7, 1921, p. 312. According to this report, Ma Soo was in Washington attempting to influence the Congress on behalf of Canton. The U. S. Secretary of State was said to have received Sun's appeal for recognition of the Canton government.

[33] *Kuo-fu nien-p'u ch'u-kao*, II, 454-455; Jane Degras, *Soviet Documents on Foreign Policy* (London, 1951), I, 92-93.

upon his Chinese brothers to join in the struggle against imperialism, declaring that "our [Soviet Russia's] victory is your
[China's] victory. Our defeat is your defeat."[34] Sun had already
left Canton for Shanghai in June, after the reorganization of
the Canton government. However, Chicherin's message must
have reached him, for Sun replied with a telegram congratulat-
ing Soviet Russia on the success of her revolution.[35]

In 1918 and 1919, Soviet Russia, in attempts to influence
the domestic and foreign policies of China, had repudiated the
unequal treaties concluded by the tsarist government. In contrast to the Versailles Peace Conference, which aroused only
anger, the Soviet promises created a residue of good will.[36] The
1917 Russian Revolution interested the Chinese as a living example of a successful revolution which they might emulate. In
1918 a society for the study of Marxism was formed in Peking
under the leadership of Li Ta-chao, a professor at Peking University.[37]

Sun's first direct contact with a Soviet representative took
place in November, 1920,[38] the month in which pro-party forces
had recaptured Canton. Sun was a confident man, with a newly
reorganized party, and certain of military victory. Thus at the
first meeting with the Soviet Union's representative, Gregory
Voitinsky, head of the Eastern department of the Communist
International, Sun led from strength.[39] He told Voitinsky of
military movements in the south and his plans to carry the
revolutionary movement into central and northern China (the

---

[34] Degras, *op. cit.*

[35] *Kuo-fu nien-p'u ch'u-kao*, II, 456.

[36] This was illustrated upon the arrival of Adolph A. Joffe in Peking
in August, 1922. He was welcomed by local students and other social
groups, but the Peking government gave him a cool reception. See Chou
Tse-tsung, *op. cit.*, p. 214.

[37] Wang Shih *et al.*, *Chung-kuo Kung-ch'ang Tang li-shih chien-pien*
(Shanghai, 1958), p. 15.

[38] Xenia Joukoff Eudin, and Robert C. North, *Soviet Russia and the
East* (Stanford, 1957), pp. 218-219. Kuomintang sources do not record this
encounter.

[39] *Ibid.*

Northern Expedition). Sun showed interest in the Bolshevik
Revolution and in conditions in Russia, but he did not seem
anxious to secure Russian assistance. He did, however, propose
that the Soviets build a radio station in Vladivostok to com-
municate with Canton. The meeting ended with no binding
commitments made on either side.

Sun's next encounter with the Soviet Union occurred in
March, 1921, when Sun and the party were preparing for the
Northern Expedition. While still in Canton, Sun talked with
Alexleff, correspondent of the Russian Rosta News Agency, but
there is no account of their conversations.[40]

The Northern Expedition was formally launched on November 18, 1921. On December 4, Sun, Hu Han-min, Li Lieh-chun,
and others arrived in Kweilin, Kwangsi, to establish the Northern Expedition headquarters, and prepare for the offensive into
Hunan in the coming spring. It was while Sun awaited the
passing of winter in Kweilin that he received the third emissary
from the Soviet Union. Maring (or Sneevlite), the Soviet representative, arrived in Kweilin in December, 1921. Earlier he
had conferred with Wu P'ei-fu, the war lord in central China;
he had also attended, as Comintern delegate, the first congress
of the Chinese Communist Party, July, 1921.[41] Thus, unlike
previous Soviet representatives in China, he had some knowledge of the complex Chinese political scene. Accompanied by
Chang Chi and an interpreter, Chang Tai-lei, Maring traveled
to Canton. Ch'en Kung-po, who served as a delegate from
Kwangtung to the first congress of the Chinese Communist
Party, has left a brief account of Maring's stay in Canton.[42]
Ch'en was invited to meet Maring by Chang Chi, and they had
an informal discussion of the problem of uniting the Kuomintang and the infant Chinese Communist Party. According to
Ch'en, Chang was in favor of the union, for the Kuomintang

---

[40] Tsui Shu-chin, *Sun Chung-shan yu Kung-ch'ang chu-i* (Hong-Kong,
1956), p. 21.

[41] For an account of Maring's many activities see Conrad Brandt, *Stalin's
Failure in China, 1924-1927* (Cambridge, 1958), p. 24 ff.

[42] Ch'en Kung-po, *Han-feng chi* (Shanghai, 1944), pp. 191-267.

was getting old and needed new blood. In terms of principles, there was little difference between the San Min Chu I and communism. Lenin's New Economic Policy was, in fact, equivalent to the principles of people's livelihood. Since both the Kuomintang and the Chinese Communist Party were revolutionary parties there would be no conflict between them. Before meeting with Sun, Maring talked with other local leaders, including Wang Ching-wei, and delivered a lecture on conditions in Russia since the revolution.[43]

During a three-day stay in Kweilin, Maring conferred twice with Sun.[44] Others who attended these historic meetings included Hu Han-min, Hsu Ch'ung-chih, Ch'en Shao-pai, Sun Fo, Lin Yun-kai, Ts'ao Ya-pe, Chu Chou-wen, Li Lu-ch'ao, Teng Chia-yen, Huang Chang-ku, and Chang Tai-lei. Maring presented three basic proposals: (1) reorganize the Kuomintang to include other social elements, especially peasants and workers; (2) establish a military academy to create an armed revolutionary foundation; and (3) cooperate with the Chinese Communist Party. He emphasized the Soviet Union's desire to form an alliance with the Kuomintang.

If Voitinsky's meeting with Sun had produced no results because of its inopportune timing, Maring had arrived at an even worse moment, for Sun and the party were at the height of power. Canton had been recaptured, and the Northern Expedition was about to begin. The accounts of the Maring-Sun meetings partially verify the sense of optimism and self-confidence which prevailed. Sun ignored Maring's proposals, no doubt feeling that the party's recent success spoke for itself. Sun was noncommittal in regard to an alliance with the Russian Communist Party. While the problems and goals of revolutionary

---

[43] *Ibid.*

[44] The following account is taken from Teng Chia-yen in *Ke-min wen-hsien*, IX, 1409-1411; Huang Chang-ku, *Kuo-fu shih-szu ch'ien wu-nien chih Chung-kuo ke-min shih-liao* (Taipei, 1957); *Kuo-fu nien-p'u ch'u-kao*, II, 518-520; and Su Te-yung, "On the Correction of the Time and Place of Maring's Visit with Tsung-li," *San Min Chu I Pan-yueh K'an*, No. 35 (October 1, 1954), 45-50.

parties were similar, their revolutionary principles differed. But for Sun there was an even more important reason why the alliance was not feasible. He was about to embark upon the military unification of China, liberating first the Yangtse River region under the domination of the war lord Wu P'ei-fu. However, that region was also a British sphere of interest. If the party concluded an alliance with the Soviet Union, the British would surely be aroused and attempt to sabotage his plans. Sun thus proposed, in the place of an alliance between the Soviet Union and the Kuomintang, a "moral fellowship."[45]

Maring's brief encounter with Sun Yat-Sen was not a total failure, however. Both came away with a better understanding of the other's position. Although the Soviet representative had received nothing more than a vague promise, he was able to assess the strength and weakness of the Kuomintang and to examine the situation in the south.[46] Maring was greatly disturbed about the military and political situation in Kwangtung, the Kuomintang's territorial base. The party was overly dependent upon the local militarists. (The untenable nature of the situation was subsequently verified when Sun and the Kuomintang were again expelled from Kwangtung in August, 1922). Maring was concerned also about the party's weakness in organization and neglect of propaganda. Indeed, he questioned whether the Kuomintang could shoulder the revolutionary responsibilities of capturing power and reconstructing China.

For his part, Sun had received valuable information about Russia.[47] He was especially interested to learn that communism was not being practiced in Russia, a country which he had long considered economically unprepared for such a doctrine. Maring told Sun that Russia had since introduced the New Economic Policy, which Sun regarded as similar to his own industrial plan. Sun's new understanding of the Soviet Union undoubtedly lessened the distance, in Sun's mind, between Lenin

[45] Teng Chia-yen, *Ke-min wen-hsien, op. cit.*

[46] Tsou Lu, *Chung-kuo Kuo-min Tang shih-kao*, I, 304.

[47] Wang Ching-wei, *Wang Ching-wei hsien-sheng ti wen-chi* (Shanghai, n.d.), III, 127-156.

and himself, thereby paving the way for subsequent cooperation between the two parties.

The decision to form an alliance with the Soviet Union had its origin in the events of August, 1922. Sun returned to Shanghai on August 14, 1922, after the revolt of Ch'en Chiung-ming. By August 25 he was conducting negotiations with a representative of the Soviet emissary, Adolph A. Joffe; meetings with other Soviet representatives followed.[48] Sun and the party were in a sorry predicament. Ch'en Chiung-ming had scattered their plans for the military unification of the country; the party returned to an underground secret society type of organization; and both Sun and the party were again "exiled." As Sun remarked in his report to the party, "No failure has ever been so grievous as this recent one."[49] It was the Soviet Union's turn to call the tune, and it pushed for a quick agreement. The Soviet representative at first demanded a two-party alliance, but Sun rejected this proposal. By the end of August an agreement had been reached permitting Chinese Communist Party members to join the Kuomintang individually, but to retain membership in the Communist International as well.[50] Li Ta-chao, who was introduced by Kuomintang member Chang Chi, became the first to implement the new agreement;[51] other Chinese Communists followed.

The implementation of the new alliance and the admission of the Chinese Communists into the Kuomintang necessitated a change in the party. On September 4 Sun Yat-sen called a meeting of provincial party representatives in Shanghai,[52] which was attended by fifty-three members. It is known only that the discussion centered on the new alliance with the Soviet Union. The party membership was in no position to question the Soviet's intentions, but was forced to accept an immediate alliance. Acceptance would bring changes. Primarily, it meant the

---

[48] *Kuo-fu nien-p'u ch'u-kao*, II, 557-558.

[49] *Kuo-fu wen-chi*, V, 458-466.

[50] Wang Ching-wei, *op. cit.*

[51] *Ibid.*

[52] *Ke-min wen-hsien*, VIII, 1039-1040.

transformation of a tightly knit group of dedicated men around Sun into a broader-based party. One of the conditions of Soviet assistance was the admission of Chinese Communists into the party; another was the reorganization of the party itself. To the old hands, the very foundation of the party was threatened. (This is perhaps why, just before the formalization of the party's reorganization in 1924, a group of Kuomintang members protested against the influence of the "new" members in the party.[53]) But on September 4, 1922, the proposed Soviet alliance, the admittance of Chinese Communists into the party, and the complete reorganization of the party had to be accepted. On September 6, Sun appointed a committee of nine consisting of both Kuomintang and Chinese Communist members to draft plans for the party's reorganization.[54] To all appearances, the Kuomintang was about to enter a new stage in its long history.

Events, however, soon added another dimension to the party's future. While the Kuomintang was negotiating with the Soviet Union, the party undertook independent measures to capture power. While the party was undergoing reorganization in Shanghai, representatives of the Kuomintang and the northern war lord Chang Tso-lin were negotiating an alliance. On September 22, Sun even dispatched Wang Ching-wei to conduct personally the talks with Chang Tso-lin in Manchuria.[55]

After their ouster from Canton, many of the Kuomintang members of Parliament had returned to Peking, where, with the backing of the northern war lords, Li Yuan-hung had reconvened the old Parliament of 1917. Tsou Lu, one of the Kuomintang members of Parliament, reported that he found great enthusiasm among Peking students.[56] He personally recruited scores of them into the Kuomintang and secretly organized student party units.

The center of action, however, was in the south, where Sun

---

[53] See pages 173-174.

[54] See Chu Cheng in *Ke-min wen-hsien*, VIII, 1040-1043. The Communist representative was Ch'en Tu-hsiu.

[55] *Kuo-fu nien-p'u ch'u-kao*, II, 559.

[56] Tsou Lu, *Hui-i lu*, I, 128-129.

was determined to oust Ch'en Chiung-ming from Canton. Indeed, so great was Sun's hatred of Ch'en that all other party activities were relegated to a secondary role. It was reported that war lord Chang Tso-lin had advised Sun to forget about the south and concentrate on seizing central China first,[57] but Sun insisted that Ch'en had to be driven out before central China would fall. Thus most of the party's strength was devoted to the recapture of Canton. This was achieved on January 26, 1923, through the cooperation of other southern militarists. Overnight, therefore, Sun and the Kuomintang found themselves in a stronger position, which influenced the subsequent course of the Kuomintang-Soviet alliance.

The Kuomintang, despite the capture of Canton and other recent successes pointing to a resurgence, still faced many obstacles. The party was disorganized. Ch'en Chiung-ming, although expelled from Canton, remained a constant threat in Kwangtung. Canton was not China, which had still to be liberated. Moreover, no other government had joined the Soviet Union in offering assistance to the party. Yet without external assistance the party was no match for the strongly-entrenched war lords. Thus, while the Kuomintang had gained a victory, the problem of winning China remained. It was within this context that the historic Sun-Joffe agreement was concluded.

The Sun-Joffe joint declaration of January 26, 1923, formalized what had hitherto been an informal working agreement between the Soviet Union and the Kuomintang.[58] Four major issues were agreed upon: (1) conditions in China did not exist "for the successful establishment of either Communism or Sovietism"; instead, the achievement of national unification and of full national independence were recognized as China's chief goals; (2) Joffe reiterated the Soviet Union's position regarding the renunciation "of all the treaties and exactions which tsardom had imposed in China . . ."; (3) the question of the Chinese Eastern Railway "can be satisfactorily settled only at a

---

[57] *Ibid.*, I, 130.

[58] For the full text of the declaration see *The China Year Book* (Tientsin, 1928) p. 1318.

competent Russo-Chinese Conference"; (4) Joffe "categorically declared" that the Soviet Union did not intend "to pursue an imperialistic policy in Outer Mongolia or to cause it to secede from China"; Sun agreed to the stationing of Russian troops in Mongolia for the time being. Thus the Kuomintang-Soviet entente was born.

The dominant reason for the alliance, from the Kuomintang's viewpoint, was the party's desire to strengthen itself, thus enabling it to capture power. However, the alliance must also be seen from another perspective. Since the success of the Russian Revolution of 1917, Sun and the party had shown increasing interest in the Russian venture. The Kuomintang and the Russian Communist Party had both begun as parties in exile, and both were struggling against internal disorder and foreign opposition. Moreover, the two held similar views on issues such as Lenin's theory of the "vanguard" and Sun's idea of political tutelage. Thus the alliance was based upon certain common experiences and beliefs in addition to the immediate needs of the two participants.

In the meantime the Kuomintang was moving rapidly toward a basic structural reorganization. On November 15, 1922, the committee of nine appointed by Sun had completed the draft of the party's new platform and regulations.[59] Hu Han-min and Wang Ching-wei submitted a draft declaration of the party's reorganization to a meeting attended by sixty-five party representatives on December 16. After some revisions, the declaration was adopted and, together with the earlier drafted constitution and regulations, became the basis for the reorganized party. On December 16 the old party officially came to an end with the resignation of department heads. It was soon to be replaced by a new party, as one product of the Kuomintang-Soviet Union alliance.

The year 1923 was important in the annals of the Kuomintang, for during that year the basic foundation was laid for the total transformation of its organization and ideology. The dec-

---

[59] See Chu Cheng in *Ke-min wen-hsien* VIII, 1040-1043.

laration of the Kuomintang, issued on January 1, 1923, illustrated the doctrinal change.[60] Hitherto, the San Min Chu I had been defined in a very narrow sense, based primarily upon conditions before the 1911 revolution. *Min-tsu chu-i* (the principle of nationalism) was now defined both in terms of integrating all the people on an equal basis within China, and revising the unequal treaties in order to restore China's freedom and equality within the family of nations. *Min-ch'uan chu-i* (the principle of democracy) was interpreted in terms of direct democracy, with the people exercising the rights of initiative, recall, and referendum. The meaning of *min-sheng chu-i* (the principle of people's livelihood) was extended to include, among other items, land taxation, national ownership of major industries and commerce, fiscal reform, improved working conditions, equality of men and women, and rural reform.

On January 2, party members gathered in Shanghai to give their final approval to the party's platform and regulations. The platform consisted of a restatement of the party's San Min Chu I and the five-power constitution.[61] The only change was the specific inclusion of Sun's favorite "equalization of land rights" policy along with nationalization of industries and fiscal reform as part of the *min-sheng chu-i*. Article 1 of the party's new regulations[62] stipulated that all adult Chinese men and women who supported the party's platform and were willing to adhere to its rules would be admitted as members upon the recommendation of two members. In the organization of the party, the outstanding feature was the expansion in the number of departments. Besides the general affairs, party affairs, fiscal affairs, and propaganda departments, a number of committees were added: political, military, peasants and workers, and women's committees. Each was given the function of investigating the domestic

[60] *Ibid.*, VIII, 1044-1047. For an English translation of the declaration see Li Chien-nung, *The Political History of China, 1840-1928* (New York, 1956), pp. 446-450.

[61] For the full text of the platform see *Ke-min wen-hsien*, VIII, 1047-1049.

[62] For the full text of the regulations see *ibid.*, VIII, 1049-1052.

and foreign (possibly the Soviet Union) conditions in their respective fields, and of drawing up plans for reform in China. The department heads and committee chairmen were to be elected by the party congress, and appointed by the party's *tsung-li*, who ruled over the whole party.

The new regulations called for an annual party congress, with provision for special meetings in the event of emergencies. Between congresses the party would be governed by a central cadre council (Chung-yang Kan-pu Hui-i), composed of department heads, committee chairmen, and other officials, meeting monthly. Both the party congress and the council were to be called into session by the party's *tsung-li*, who would preside over both meetings. Another novel feature of the new regulations was the provision relating to party discipline. In the past, party discipline had been outlined in rather vague terms, but the 1923 regulations specified conditions under which a member could be expelled. According to article 22, members faced ejection from the party for (1) belonging to another party concurrently, (2) publicly revolting against the party, (3) disclosing party secrets, and (4) conducting themselves in a manner that endangered the party's reputation. Article 23 stipulated that expelled members desiring to reenter the party must present evidence of their loyalty and obtain the personal approval of the party's *tsung-li*. While the provisions on party discipline contained many flaws, they were a great improvement over past endeavors to maintain party discipline. It is clear that outside influences were at work. The creation of a peasants and workers committee must be attributed to Soviet influence. Also of interest was the addition of the central cadre council. Until now the party had been governed by Sun Yat-sen personally. This change, based on the concept of institutional rather than personal leadership, was an important step in the party's reorganization. No evidence is available, but there is little doubt that this change too can be traced to Soviet demands. Sun was granted the post of party leader, *tsung-li*, although "collective leadership," Kuomintang and Communist, took the place of

Sun's personal rule. Yet the 1923 party reorganization was still far from a duplication of the Soviet Communist Party.

Sun's speech at the party conference in Shanghai, January 2, 1923, reflected the significant changes in party policy.[63] Sun, emphasizing the role of the party in the road toward revolution, dismissed both the parliamentary political approach and sole reliance upon military action as ineffective means toward that end. Both had proved undependable. The party remained as the only instrument for the achievement of victory. And only the party had grown progressively stronger despite its neglect by the leadership and the decline in revolutionary spirit. The most important task was that of propaganda to win converts to the party cause. The revolution would succeed if and when the party successfully converted the people of China. Sun then went on to attribute the success of the Russian Revolution to propaganda. Party reorganization was the key to party progress. This speech reveals that Sun Yat-sen had finally decided that the proper role of the party was to direct political and military activities, but not to subordinate the party to them. There was a new emphasis on the technique of winning the masses by presenting a challenging ideology (redefined in the light of changing conditions). Both the supremacy of the party and the emphasis on propaganda activities became realities in 1924. However, in 1923 they were still in process of being formulated, though Sun was already giving clear evidence of the course to be taken.

While the 1923 reorganization and the Kuomintang-Soviet Union talks were in progress, pro-party forces recaptured Canton. When Sun returned in triumph to Canton on February 21, 1923, the party was again occupied with the problems of government,[64] and the pressing issue of dealing with the many local militarists. The plans previously formulated for the reorganization of the party were forgotten or relegated to secondary im-

---

[63] *Kuo-fu ch'uan-chi,* III, 235-238.

[64] Upon his arrival in Canton, Sun proceeded to organize a military government, which was founded March 2.

portance. Party headquarters and the central cadre council remained in Shanghai; Sun even designated another member to direct the headquarters.[65] A branch of the Kuomintang opened in Canton on March 1, but the problems of government and survival continued to dominate Sun and the party leaders. Between March and November, 1923, Canton was repeatedly threatened by the surrounding militarists, and once Ch'en Chiung-ming almost retook Canton. Throughout this period Sun remained in the south to direct the struggle for survival. Canton was saved, but the party had returned to its previous state of disorganization.

Again an external force came to the party's rescue. The first Soviet assistance, in the person of Michael Borodin, arrived in Canton in August, 1923. By October, he had convinced Sun and the party leaders in Canton that party reforms must be undertaken immediately.[66] On October 24, Sun instructed Liao Chung-k'ai and Teng Tse-ju to call a special meeting to discuss a new party reorganization.[67] According to Tsou Lu, Sun, with a sense of melancholy at the breakup of the traditional personal relationship between leader and follower, consented to the full adoption of the impersonal pattern of the Soviet Communist Party.[68] On October 25 Sun appointed a provisional central executive committee of nine to draft plans on party reorganization.[69] The committee included Teng Tse-ju, Lin Shen, Liao Chung-k'ai, Ch'en Shu-jen, Sun Fo, Hsu Tsung-ching, Hsieh Ying-p'ai, Yang Shu-k'an, and the Chinese Communist T'an P'ing-shan. Borodin was invited to sit with the committee as adviser. Between October 28, 1923, and January 19, 1924, the eve of the first party congress, the provisional central executive

---

[65] *Kuo-fu nien-p'u ch'u-kao*, II, 590. Hsia Ch'ih, head of the party affairs department, was appointed to take charge of the Shanghai headquarters.

[66] Martin C. Wilbur and Julie Lien-ying How, *Documents on Communism, Nationalism, and Soviet Advisers in China, 1918-1927* (New York, 1956), p. 144.

[67] *Kuo-fu nien-p'u ch'u-kao*, II, 621-622.

[68] Tsou Lu, *Chung-kuo Kuo-min Tang shih-kao*, I, 315.

[69] *Ke-min wen-hsien*, VIII, 1077-1079.

committee met for the twenty-eight sessions. Among the important decisions made at these meetings were to hold the first party congress on January 20, 1924; to draft the party's manifesto, platform, and regulations; to register party members in Canton; to investigate the conditions of peasants, workers, and the middle class; to unify the party's propaganda organizations; to restrict the right of members to express their views on the party publicly; to organize the Canton party branch into districts and subdistricts; to establish a school to train executive committee members of the branches and districts.

Under Borodin's guidance the Kuomintang was quickly rebuilt, using the Soviet Communist Party as a model. The completeness of the transformation, and no doubt the haste, aroused the opposition of a group of Kuomintang members. Led by Teng Tse-ju, a member of the provisional central executive committee, eleven members of the party presented a petition[70] to Sun on November 29, charging that, while Borodin had drafted the party's plans for reorganization, Ch'en Tu-hsiu (secretary-general of the Chinese Communist Party) was the actual author of the party's political program, and that the Communists were seeking to use the Kuomintang for their own purposes. The fear was expressed that Ch'en Tu-hsiu would be elected the party's *tsung-li* after five years, thereby completely absorbing the Kuomintang. Ch'en and the Communists were charged also with attempting to isolate the Kuomintang internationally, through their anti-imperialism policy, and domestically, through their antimilitarists attitude. Sun, however, assured his followers that Ch'en Tu-hsiu had no part in drafting the program, which Sun identified with his own. Reprimanding the accusers, he declared that the reason the Russian Revolution had succeeded and the Chinese Revolution had not was that the party members did not understand the San Min

---

[70] For the full text of the petition with Sun's marginal comments, see Kuomintang, *T'an-ho Kung-ch'ang Tang liang ta-ya-an* (Nanking, 1927), pp. 1-11. For an English translation of Sun's comments see Conrad Brandt et al., *A Documentary History of Chinese Communism* (Cambridge, 1952), pp. 72-73.

Chu I. Sun reaffirmed his faith in Soviet friendship, declaring
that the Western powers had often sided with the enemies of
the party. He cautioned his followers to distinguish between
the Soviet Union and Ch'en Tu-hsiu, and not to suspect the
former because of the latter.

With Sun Yat-sen's full backing, the party reorganization
under Borodin's direction moved to a climax, the first party
congress of January 20, 1924. Plans for the reorganization, however, had been carried out by the provisional central executive
committee in Canton. The party's highest body, the central
cadre council in Shanghai, had not been consulted, but a report
of the proposed changes was made to them on December 9, 1923
by Liao Chung-k'ai.[71] He attributed past failures to the party's
dependence upon the military. But a more important cause of
past defeats was to be found within the party itself, which, Liao
asserted, had lacked an effective organization since the T'ung
Meng Hui era. In fact, the party had consisted of "a few officials
without members." This topheavy structure had repeatedly contributed to the party's weakness. To rectify past mistakes two
steps had been decided upon: to begin organizing the party
from the bottom up, and to build a party army.[72] The central
cadre council then gave its approval to the coming party reform.
The long struggle to build a centralized, disciplined party was
at last nearing reality. All that remained was formal ratification
by the congress.

On January 20, 1924, the first party congress of the Kuomintang opened in Canton. During the next ten days, representatives gave their approval to the total reorganization of the party.
At its conclusion on January 30 a new party had been born,
destined to unify the country and capture political power. Sun
told the congress ". . . in the past thirteen years, we have gained

[71] *Ke-min wen-hsien*, VIII, 1084-1087.

[72] *Ibid.* Liao reported that Canton had been divided into twelve districts for party registration. Each district was administered by an executive
committee of three members, who met weekly. District members met every
other week. The district party branch would serve as the party's basic unit.
A military force of six hundred men was being trained.

a variety of political experiences and discover numerous new methods. . . . However, during the past thirty years the Revolutionary Party was driven chiefly by will power . . . and knew not by which method to reconstruct the country. Only now have we secured the method. . . ."[73] Indeed, with the reorganization of 1924 based upon the Russian "method" the Kuomintang as a true revolutionary party became a reality.

Sun had never permitted the party to develop its own chain of command, its own bureaucracy. Instead, he was the source of all decisions; he *was* the party. This very personal manner of rule was never more clearly evident than in the decision leading to the 1924 reorganization. The reorganization of 1923 had created a central cadre council as the party's highest governing body. But that body was not even informed of the party's plans to remodel until almost the eve of the reorganization. Ignoring the council, Sun personally had decided upon the change. Sun's complete domination of the party must, therefore, be cited as a factor in the repeated failures of attempts to reorganize the party. While Sun at times reached towering heights, the party remained weak and disorganized, an instrument for personal rule rather than a public body. The 1924 reorganization brought this situation to an end: Sun remained the party's leader, but he became the party's captive instead of the party itself.

[73] *Ibid.*, VIII, 1105-1109.

VII THE KUOMINTANG:
A PROFILE

THE KUOMINTANG is essentially a product of the Western impact upon China. Its birth in the form of the Hsing Chung Hui (Revive China Society) in 1894 was in part a reaction against China's repeated humiliations at the hands of the Western powers. The party began as an antidynastic movement, seeking to overthrow the discredited Ch'ing ruling house. It was organized on the model of the traditional closed secret society. However, the Hsing Chung Hui differed from the traditional antigovernment groups. Because it was a consequence of the Western impact, the first of the predecessors of the Kuomintang adopted a Western goal, that of republicanism. The Hsing Chung Hui had broken the traditional dynastic cycle. If the Hsing Chung Hui was a radical departure from custom, its successor, the T'ung Meng Hui (Common Alliance Society), founded in 1905, departed even farther from the accepted norm. The T'ung Meng Hui's three people's principles (nationalism, democracy, and people's livelihood) constituted an even more extreme injection of Western concepts into China. The impact of Western liberalism reached a climax with the overthrow of the Ch'ing dynasty in 1911. With the establishment of the Republic in 1912, Western-style institutions were introduced en masse.

The T'ung Meng Hui, reorganized as the Kuomintang, was to take its place among the Western-influenced institutions after the founding of the Republic. Overnight the party was transformed from a closed secret society into an open democratic political party. To the revolutionists who had dedicated their lives to the political development of China, their country had finally come of age in 1912. China, it was thought, by overthrowing the Ch'ing dynasty and becoming a republic, had shaken off the ties of traditions and joined the modern world.

China's brief flirtation with republicanism and liberalism came to an abrupt end in 1914. In that year the dream of a new China based upon a liberal Western model was shattered. Yuan Shih-k'ai, the Ch'ing militarist turned republican who had been given the presidency of the infant Republic, dissolved Parliament and proceeded to restore the monarchical system. Political parties such as the Kuomintang, which had emerged immediately after the overthrow of the Ch'ing dynasty, were crushed. From the new frontier of Westernism, China retreated into the world of traditionalism. The Kuomintang in the form of the Chung-hua Kemintang (Chinese Revolutionary Party), founded in 1914, returned to the time-tested secret society model. This marked the end of China's experiment with institutions based wholly upon the Western model. The 1924 reorganization of the Kuomintang combined Chinese traditional concepts with Western methods. By that time the Western impact, though still influential, had given place to a new appreciation of things traditional.

Between 1894 and 1924 the party underwent two major stages. The first, dominated by liberal Western concepts, included the entire anti-Ch'ing period and the first years of the Republic—a period of intense nationalism. During this period the principal characteristic of the party, though overshadowed by racialism, and organized on the traditional secret society model, was its Western orientation. The first stage reached its climax in 1912, when the Kuomintang became an open political party on the liberal Western model.

The later stage of the Kuomintang lasted from 1914 to 1924. This phase constituted a return to traditionalism. The secret society model was restored, and the traditional concept of tutelage was formally incorporated into the party as a means of guiding the nation. In the end, the Kuomintang was reorganized on the basis of both the Western model and traditionalism.

The interaction between the forces of the modern West and the indigenous political culture of China thus constituted an important factor in the development of the Kuomintang. This was even more clearly demonstrated within the party itself. Notwithstanding its basic goal of a Western-modeled republican form of government, the party remained for the most part traditionalistic. After 1913 it emphasized loyalty of the members to the leader, which typified the dominance of the old elements, and drew upon the traditional concept of tutelage. Thus, while the party sought to develop China according to the Western image, the Kuomintang itself retained the traditional model until 1924. The West had provided the inspiration, but both the form and the substance remained Chinese.

For most of its life between 1894 and 1924, the Kuomintang was a party in exile. The Hsing Chung Hui in 1894 began as an overseas party in Hawaii, and its successor, the T'ung Meng Hui, continued to operate from abroad, chiefly in Japan and Southeast Asia. Only with the successful overthrow of the Ch'ing dynasty in 1912 did the party triumphantly appear openly in China. However, the victory was short-lived. Less than two years after China was declared a republic, the party was again forced into exile, and remained only in the Americas, Japan, and Southeast Asia until 1916. But even upon returning to China, except for brief moments of power, the party was confined chiefly to the foreign settlement in Shanghai, hence still in "exile." Not until 1923, with the permanent capture of Canton by pro-party groups, was the Kuomintang in possession of a territorial base. Only then did the party begin to sink roots in China.

More than one revolutionary group in exile has passed into oblivion because of prolonged exile. And even among those which survive, the chances of remaining intact as an effective unit decrease with the years. The success of the Russian revolutionists before November, 1917, for example, was by no means certain. They, too, constituted a movement in exile, primarily in Western Europe, and they, too, were plagued with factionalism. Nearly thirty years elapsed before they finally captured power. Even the Bolsheviks, the faction within the larger group which achieved supremacy and political power, suffered from dissension among themselves.

Another problem of an exiled revolutionary party has been to meet the demands of its members. Except for a few dedicated revolutionists, the majority need some visible reward. This has meant in China, as in the Russian experience, a state of fluidity among the general membership and a concentration of power in a select few. The emphasis upon a "vanguard," therefore, made sense especially for an exiled party. It required the devotion of the dedicated to carry on the movement and direct the party, lest both disintegrate.

The Kuomintang's nearly thirty years of continuous exile profoundly influenced the nature of the party. Factionalism remained a serious threat to its existence up to 1924. Beginning as a loose alliance of antidynastic groups, the precursors of the Kuomintang soon disintegrated into a broad revolutionary movement—little more than a coalition of warring factions. Divisions multiplied with each revolutionary failure. The successful overthrow of the Ch'ing dynasty in 1912 did not bring reunification; instead, several factions became independent political parties. Perhaps the worst period of factional contention developed after 1913, during the Chung-hua Kemintang era, when the party almost disintegrated. While the pre-1912 factions had maintained a semblance of unity, the factions which emerged after 1913 recognized no single authority. The Chung-hua Kemintang represented but one element from the old party, the group personally loyal to Sun Yat-sen.

Much of the factional contention throughout the party's history derived from its almost continual struggle for power in exile. During the antidynastic revolutionary period, while the main body of the T'ung Meng Hui concentrated on establishing a foothold in southern China, another group within the party consistently advocated striking at Peking, the Ch'ing capital. But contention over strategy constituted only one of the many differences within the Kuomintang. The major split within the party after 1913 grew out of Sun Yat-sen's proposal to reorganize the party on a centralized basis. Also in dispute was the matter of strategy, namely, how to oppose Yuan Shih-k'ai, who had just defeated the party. Other factional squabbles arose from personality differences and petty jealousies.

There is a recurrent charge that factionalism within the party was based primarily upon provincial or regional divisions. This may have been true in the early pre-Republican stage of the party. However, in its post-1912 development the party and its factions cut across provincial and regional differences. For example, Sun Yat-sen's faction included adherents from central as well as south China (e.g., Hu Han-min, Chu Cheng, Ch'en Ch'i-mei[1]). And among his opponents were men from central and north China (e.g., Huang Hsing and Chang Chi[2]) and Sun's native province of Kwangtung (e.g., Ch'en Chiung-ming).

When the party was in power (or nearing the capture of power), as it was in 1912 and 1913, factionalism was at a minimum. But during the party's struggle for power, nearly always in exile, the Kuomintang suffered from factional contention, especially during the Chung-hua Kemintang era. The divisions were based upon a difference of opinion regarding strategy, against the common enemy and directed toward the party itself.

The majority of exiled parties, such as the pre-1917 Russian group, were responsible to no one but themselves. Rarely could they draw upon active mass support: the conspirators lived in a foreign world, surrounded by foreign nationals. The Kuomintang, however, differed radically from the usual pattern in being

---

[1] Hu was from Kwangtung, Chu from Hupeh, and Ch'en from Chekiang.
[2] Huang was from Hunan and Chang from Hupeh.

responsible to a constituency, the overseas Chinese. In return for their financial support, the party had to satisfy their demands. It was perhaps no mere coincidence that the party should have raised the banner of revolt in the southern coastal provinces, and in particular Kwangtung, for the great majority of the Chinese abroad had come from that region. Of the nine major uprisings directly or indirectly initiated by the T'ung Meng Hui between 1906 and 1911, five were planned in Kwangtung province, including the famous April 27, 1911, uprising in Canton, and one each in the provinces of Kwangsi and Yunnan. This pattern of concentrating the party's attention in southern China was repeated between 1916 and 1924. The party has argued that the southern provinces were farthest from the center of power, Peking, and therefore represented the most vulnerable areas of the government. There is some truth to this argument. But the party may have felt obligated also to cater to the demands of its constituency. Thus the Kuomintang as an exiled party derived both advantages and disadvantages from its mass support. The party's zealous effort directed at one particular area was one price it paid for the assistance of the overseas Chinese. But without the support of the Chinese abroad, the Kuomintang might have passed unnoticed into history, like many other parties in exile.

Closely related to the Kuomintang's status as a party in exile has been its dual character, as a domestic and an overseas party simultaneously. This is somewhat analogous to the relationship between the Communist International and the Communist parties throughout the world. Each has its own precise function. In the Communist experience, the "overseas" Communist parties in each country have served as the battle troops. The Communist International's role is to guide the national parties and render assistance, both moral and material. However, the similarity between the Kuomintang and the Communists extends only as far as their dual character. The role and function of the domestic and the overseas parties of the Kuomintang were just the reverse of that of the Communists. In the Kuomintang experience, the overseas party, while able to influence the party's course through its financial contributions, served primarily as a supporting unit, and was never directly involved in the struggle to seize power. Neither were its members dependent upon the success or failure of the party for their livelihood. The domestic party constituted the active unit, which planned, directed, and led the party on the battlefields. It was the domestic party which was daily confronted with the political reality of gaining and holding power. In turn, its members were totally dependent upon the party.

In general, this dual character worked well for the Kuomintang. Notwithstanding its long exile and repeated failures, the party's longevity and final success owe much to this duality. The eventual resurrection of the Kuomintang undoubtedly would have been more difficult had it not enjoyed a twofold structure.

A salient characteristic of the Kuomintang was the oligarchical nature of its leadership structure. From the T'ung Meng Hui period, the Kuomintang was dominated by a select few, chiefly from the intelligentsia, the aristocrats of Chinese society. The intelligentsia came wholly from the student class, which had been sent abroad from China at the turn of the century to study the secrets of the West. Concerned with China's future and desirous of seeing at firsthand the modern world, the students enrolled en masse in the movement to reform China. Between 1905 and 1924 the Kuomintang was governed entirely by persons from this group, and, after 1912, by the same members of the student-intelligentsia who had joined the party in the pre-Republican era.

Robert Michels' iron law of oligarchy concerning the organizational structure of political parties has thus far been examined primarily in terms of Western constitutional parties.[3] The oligarchical nature of democratic parties may be democratic in theory, but they have been found to be oligarchical in practice. If open, democratic constitutional parties have tended toward oligarchy, exiled revolutionary parties have moved even farther

---

[3] Robert Michels, *Political Parties* (New York, 1959). This work was first published in 1915.

in that direction. This is perhaps understandable. An exiled revolutionary party such as the Kuomintang demands a tight organizational structure to operate successfully, and is dependent for survival upon a dedicated and effective leadership, which is necessarily oligarchical in composition. Repeated failures are especially detrimental to a party in exile. After the loss of power to Yuan Shih-k'ai, the Kuomintang was shattered. It was saved from complete destruction only through the stubbornness of a small group of leaders. The oligarchical organizational pattern has thus been a major characteristic of the Kuomintang in exile.

Another distinctive trait of the Kuomintang has been the domination of the party by one person. Sun Yat-sen has been rightly called the Father of the Chinese Republic. He was also the creator and, more important, the builder of the new Kuomintang, which made possible the Chinese Republic.

There is no question of the close association of Sun with the origins of the Kuomintang. However, Sun's function as a party builder is less obvious. The evidence seems to argue to the contrary, for he took no active part in the founding and management of the Kuomintang in 1912. And his insistence upon reorganizing the party on a centralized basis, requiring members to declare their loyalty to him personally, badly split the party in 1914. Subsequently he ruled the party, at least what remained of it, almost single-handedly. The party became merely an institution for Sun's personal power and a grouping of his personal followers.

Yet, while the immediate consequences were detrimental, they laid the basis for a new party. This was achieved primarily through Sun Yat-sen's single-minded determination to advance the revolutionary movement. The political fortunes of the party were at their lowest ebb after 1913. The party was thoroughly defeated and its members badly divided. It was when the party was at the crossroads that Sun presented his plan for reorganization. What Sun achieved, knowingly or unknowingly, was to keep the idea of the party alive. Through his personal leadership he saved the party from disintegration. And through his personal following, Sun created a core membership for a future party. But, more important, Sun provided a rallying center around which a new party could be built. Thus Sun's personal leadership prepared the foundation for the subsequent reorganization of the Kuomintang in 1924.

Sun Yat-sen may be conceived as a charismatic leader. Max Weber defines charisma as an "extraordinary quality of a person" and charismatic authority as a rule over men "to which the governed submit because of their belief in the extraordinary quality of the specific person."[4] The charismatic leader is urged on by a sense of calling; he may address himself to the masses or to a limited group. Sun may have possessed charisma by virtue of his "extraordinary quality." He was unquestionably governed by inner determination when he demanded obedience and personal loyalty because of his mission. However, it is more difficult to measure Sun's charismatic authority. Between 1894 and 1924 he enjoyed very little mass support. No massive uprisings took place when he called upon the country to overthrow Yuan Shih-k'ai in 1913. Sun's influence over the Chinese abroad fluctuated, especially during the post-1913 period, when only a minor segment of the overseas members continued to profess faith in him. The overseas Chinese, however, do not constitute a good indicator of Sun's charismatic authority. Since they lived in a foreign world, they were not actively involved and hence were not directly affected by Sun's mission.

Sun Yat-sen elicited far greater active response from the student-intelligentsia class, the group which dominated the Kuomintang leadership. The student-intelligentsia may be said to have recognized Sun's "mission." They may also be considered the group over which Sun exercised his charismatic authority. Yet to Sun as a party leader the membership made as little response as did the masses. One of the prerequisites of a charismatic leader to gain and maintain authority is that he prove "his strength in life." For Sun this would have been success in

[4] H. H. Gerth and C. Wright Mills, *From Max Weber: Essays in Sociology* (New York, 1958), p. 295.

overthrowing the Ch'ing government *and* in capturing power. But Sun encountered repeated setbacks in his attempts to achieve his mission. In the end, the 1911 revolution was achieved apart from Sun's direct participation. When Sun returned to China after the revolution he exercised very limited authority on the new government and party. He was considered the party elder rather than the party leader. Indeed, he retired from active politics to devote his time to the economic reconstruction of China. Whatever charismatic authority Sun may have possessed all but broke down in 1914, after the party's defeat by Yuan Shih-k'ai. A majority of the members deserted him after his proposal to reorganize the party to continue the revolutionary movement. Sun's followers had refused to recognize his mission. And in 1915 party members differed with Sun in their attitude toward Yuan Shih-k'ai and Japan's Twenty-one Demands. Thereafter Sun traveled a lonely road, with only a handful of followers continuing to accept his leadership. For the most part he was "not recognized by those to whom he [felt] he [had] been sent."[5]

But whether or not Sun Yat-sen constituted a charismatic leader, the Kuomintang was primarily his creation. It was he who had served as the rallying center around which men gathered in the struggle to develop China. In assessing Sun's role in the party's development between 1894 and 1924, we may conclude that he performed the role of a catalyst, for, without Sun's foresight and determination, the party would probably not have survived.

The Kuomintang throughout the period of our investigation has been a party in search of itself. Until the 1911 revolution, the party was conceived primarily in terms of the instrument that would provide leadership in the struggle to overthrow the Ch'ing government. The 1911 revolution introduced Western institutions, among them open democratic political parties on the Western model. Overnight the Kuomintang was transformed from a secret society into a political party. But the

---

[5] *Ibid.*, p. 246.

experiences of 1912 and 1913 made clear the inapplicability of Western institutions in general, and Western-modeled political parties in particular, to China. The Western model was rejected and retreat into traditionalism ensued. The proven closed secret society model was reintroduced. Until the 1924 party reorganization, the Kuomintang was again conceived in terms of the instrument to provide leadership for the purposes of capturing power and, subsequently, guiding the nation. The success and failure of the Kuomintang must be judged accordingly.

In retrospect, the seemingly endless search of the Kuomintang for the one right method is impressive. That the party spent thirty years in overcoming a multitude of obstacles to achieve victory is a lesson to be pondered by all parties that seek political power.

Selected Bibliography

WESTERN LANGUAGES

BOOKS AND ESSAYS

Adams, R. *The People of Hawaii*. Honolulu, 1933.

Bell, H. T. Montague, and H. G. W. Woodhead. *The China Yearbook, 1913*. London, 1913.

Brain, Harrison, ed. *The First 50 Years*. Hong Kong, 1962.

Brandt, Conrad. *Stalin's Failure in China, 1924-1927*. Cambridge, Mass., 1958.

Brandt, Conrad, Benjamin Schwartz, and John K. Fairbank. *A Documentary History of Chinese Communism*. Cambridge, Mass., 1952.

Burke, Edmund. *Thoughts on the Cause of the Present Discontents*. Boston, 1950.

California, State of. Bureau of Labor Statistics. *Eleventh Biennial Report*. Sacramento, 1904.

Ch'en Kung-po. *The Communist Movement in China*. Edited with an introduction by C. Martin Wilbur. Columbia University East Asian Institute Series No. 7. New York, 1960.

Chiang Monlin. *Tides from the West.* Taipei, 1957.

Ch'ien Tuan-sheng. *The Government and Politics of China.* Cambridge, Mass., 1950.

China Year Book, The. Tientsin, 1928.

Chou Tse-tsung. *The May Fourth Movement.* Cambridge, Mass., 1960.

Coman, Katharine. "The History of Contract Labor in the Hawaiian Islands," *Publications of the American Economic Association,* Third Series, IV, No. 3 (August, 1903).

Comber, L. F. *Chinese Secret Societies in Malaya.* Monographs of the Association for Asian Studies, VI. Locust Valley, New York, 1959.

Degras, Jane. *Soviet Documents on Foreign Policy.* Vol. I. London, 1951.

Eudin, Xenia Joukoff, and Robert C. North. *Soviet Russia and the East, 1920-1927.* Stanford, 1957.

Friedrich, C. J. *Constitutional Government and Democracy.* Boston, 1950.

Gerth, H. H., and C. Wright Mills. *From Max Weber: Essays in Sociology.* New York, 1958.

Glick, C., and Hong Sheng-hwa. *Swords of Silence.* New York, 1947.

Hackett, Roger F. "Chinese Students in Japan, 1900-1910," *Paper on China.* Committee on International and Regional Studies, Harvard University, mimeographed, May, 1949, III, 134-169.

Holcombe, Arthur N. *The Chinese Revolution.* Cambridge, Mass., 1931.

Houn, Franklin W. *Central Government of China, 1912-1928.* Madison, 1957.

Hsu, Leonard Shihlien. *Sun Yat-sen, His Political and Social Ideals.* Los Angeles, 1933.

Hsueh Chun-tu. *Huang Hsing and the Chinese Revolution.* Stanford, 1961.

Huie Kin. *Reminiscences.* Peking, 1932.

Isaaca, Harold R. *The Tragedy of the Chinese Revolution.* London, 1938.

Jansen, Marius B. *The Japanese and Sun Yat-sen.* Cambridge, Mass., 1954.

Kiang Kang Hu. *China and the Social Revolution.* San Francisco, 1914.

Leng Shao Chuan and Norman D. Palmer. *Sun Yat-sen and Communism.* Foreign Policy Research Institute, University of Pennsylvania, New York, 1960.

Levenson, Joseph R. *Liang Ch'i-ch'ao and the Mind of Modern China.* Cambridge, Mass., 1953.

Li Chien-nung. *The Political History of China, 1840-1928.* Edited and translated by Ssu-yu Teng and Jeremy Ingalls. New York, 1956.

Lin, Jermyn Chi-hung. *Political Parties in China.* Peking, 1930.

Linebarger, Paul M. A. *Government in Republican China.* New York, 1938.

———. *The Political Doctrines of Sun Yat-sen.* Baltimore, 1937.

———. *Sun Yat-sen and the Chinese Republic.* New York, 1925.

MacIver, R. M. *The Web of Government.* New York, 1947.

MacNair, Harley F. *China in Revolution.* Chicago, 1931.

———, *The Chinese Abroad.* Shanghai, 1924.

Michels, Robert. *Political Parties.* New York, 1959.

Neumann, Sigmund, ed. *Modern Political Parties.* Chicago, 1955.

Nivison, David S., and Arthur F. Wright, eds. *Confucianism in Action.* Stanford, 1959.

North, Robert C. *Kuomintang and the Chinese Communist Elites.* Hoover Institute Studies, Series B: Elite Studies, No. 8. Stanford, 1952.

Ostrogorski, Moise. *Democracy and the Organization of Political Parties.* 2 vols. New York, 1902.

Scalapino, Robert A., and George T. Yu. *The Chinese Anarchist Movement.* Berkeley: Center for Chinese Studies, University of California, 1961.

Schapiro, Leonard. *The Communist Party of the Soviet Union.* New York, 1960.

Schiffrin, Harold. *The Origins and Early Development of Sun Yat-sen's Economic Policy.* Master's thesis, University of California, Berkeley, 1956.

Schwartz, Benjamin I. *Chinese Communism and the Rise of Mao.* Cambridge, 1958.

Sharman, Lyon. *Sun Yat-sen: His Life and His Meaning.* New York, 1934.

Sun Yat-sen. *Memoirs of a Chinese Revolutionary.* Taipei, 1953.

———. *Kidnapped in London.* London, 1897.

———. *Fundamentals of National Reconstruction.* Taipei, 1953.

——. *The Vital Problem of China*. Taipei, 1953.

T'ang Leang-li. *The Inner History of the Chinese Revolution*. London, 1930.

Teng Ssu-yu, John K. Fairbank, *et al. China's Response to the West*. Cambridge, Mass., 1954.

Tse Tsan-tai. *The Chinese Republic: Secret History of the Revolution*. Hong Kong, South China Morning Post, 1924.

Uchida, Naosaku. *The Overseas Chinese: A Bibliographical Essay Based on the Resources of the Hoover Institution, Stanford*. Stanford, 1959.

U. S. Department of State. *Papers Relating to the Foreign Relations of the United States, 1921*. Vol. I. Washington, D. C., 1936.

Ward, John S. M., and W. G. Stirling. *The Hung Society or the Society of Heaven and Earth*. 3 vols. London, 1925-1926.

Wilbur, C. Martin, and Julie Lien-ying How. *Documents on Communism, Nationalism, and Soviet Advisers in China, 1918-1927*. New York, 1956.

Woo, T. C. *The Kuomintang and the Future of the Chinese Revolution*. London, 1928.

Wright, Arthur F., ed. *The Confucian Persuasion*. Stanford, 1960.

Wright, Stanley F. *China's Customs Revenue since the Revolution of 1911*. 3d ed., Shanghai, 1935.

NEWSPAPERS AND PERIODICALS

China Republican. Weekly. Shanghai.
Far Eastern Political Science Review. Monthly. Canton.
The Japan Weekly Mail. Weekly. Tokyo.
The Journal of Asian Studies. Quarterly. Ann Arbor, Michigan.
Journal of the South Sea Society. Monthly. Singapore.
Millards Review of the Far East. Weekly. Shanghai.
Republican Advocate. Weekly. Shanghai.
San Francisco Chronicle. Daily. San Francisco.

CHINESE AND JAPANESE
BOOKS AND ESSAYS

Ch'ai Te-keng, ed. *Hsin-hai ke-min* (The 1911 Revolution). 8 vols. Shanghai, 1957.

Chang Chi. *Chang P'u-ch'uan hsien-sheng ch'uan-chi* (Collective Works of Mr. Chang P'u-ch'uan). Taipei, 1951.

——. *Chang P'u-ch'uan hsien-sheng ch'uan-chi pu'pien* (Supplement to the Collective Works of Mr. Chang P'u-ch'uan). Taipei, 1952.

Chang Chian t'sai. *Wang Ching-wei hsien-sheng hsing shih-lu* (A Series of True Narrations of Mr. Wang Ching-wei). Nanking, 1943.

Chang Hsiao-kan. *Chung-kuo chin-tai cheng-chih shih* (A Political History of Modern China). Taipei, 1959.

Chang Nan-hsien. *Hupeh ke-min chih-chih lu* (Record of the Hupeh Revolution). Chungking, 1945.

Chang Tzu-sheng. *Jen-shu Cheng-pien chi* (The Civil War of China in 1922). Shanghai, 1923.

Chang Wen-pe. *Chih-lao hsien-hua* (Chitchat on Old Chih). Taipei, 1952.

Ch'en Chih-mai. *Chung-kuo cheng-fu* (The Government of China). 3 vols. Chungking and Shanghai, 1944-1945.

Ch'en Ching-ts'un hsien-sheng nien-p'u (Chronology of Mr. Ch'en Ching-ts'un's Life). Hong Kong (?), n.d.

Ch'en Hsi-hao. *Kuo-ch'u san-shih-wu nien chung chih Chung-kuo Kuo-min Tang* (The Chung-kuo Kuomintang during the Past Thirty-five Years). Shanghai, 1928.

Ch'en Kung-po. *Han-feng chi* (Collective Works of the North Wind). 2d ed. Shanghai, 1944.

Chia I-chun. *Chung-hua min-kuo cheng-chih shih* (History of the Politics of the Chinese Republic). 2 vols. Peking, 1929.

——, comp. *Chung-hua min-kuo ming-jen chuan* (Biographies of Eminent Men of the Chinese Republic). 2 vols. Peking, 1932-1933.

Chin Ping-ou *et al.*, comp. *San Min Chu I tz'u-tien* (A Dictionary of San Min Chu I). Taipei, 1956.

Chou Fu-hai. *Chung-shan hsien-sheng ssu-hsiang hai-kuan* (General View of Mr. Chung-shan's Thought). 2d ed. Shanghai, 1925.

Chou Yung. *Ke-min chun* (Revolutionary Army). Shanghai, 1958.

Chu Cheng. *Chu Chio-sheng hsien-sheng ch'uan-chi* (Collective Works of Mr. Chu Chio-sheng). 2 vols. Taipei, n.d.

Chu Lin. *Hung-meng chih* (Annals of the Hung-meng). Shanghai, 1947.

Feng Tzu-yu. *Chung-hua min-kuo k'ai-kuo ch'ien ke-min shih* (History of the Revolution before the Founding of the Republic). Taipei, 1954.

——. *Hua-ch'iao ke-min tsu-chih shih-hua* (History of the Revolutionary Organization of the Overseas Chinese). Taipei, 1954.

——. *Ke-min i-shih* (Reminiscences of the Revolution). 5 vols. Taipei, 1953.

——. *She-hui chu-i yu Chung-kuo* (Socialism and China). Hong Kong, 1920.

Hirayama, Shiu. *Chung-kuo pi-mi she-hui shih* (A History of Chinese Secret Societies). Shanghai, 1934.

Hsiao I-shan, ed. *Chin-tai pi-mi she-hui shih-liao* (Historical Sources on Modern Secret Societies). 4 vols. Peking, 1935.

Hsieh Pin. *Min-kuo cheng-tang shih* (A History of the Political Parties of the Chinese Republic). Rev. 5th ed. Shanghai, 1928.

Hsu Shou-t'ang. *Chang Ping-lin.* Chungking, 1945.

Huang Chang-ku. *Kuo-fu shih-szu ch'ien wu-nien chih Chung-kuo ke-min shih-liao* (Historical Data on the Chinese Revolution Five Years before the Death of the Father of the Country). 2d ed. Taipei, 1957.

Huang Fu-luan. *Hua-ch'iao yu Chung-kuo ke-min* (The Overseas Chinese and the Chinese Revolution). Hong Kong, 1954.

Huang Hsing hsien-sheng yen-shou tz'u hui-pien (Collected Speeches of Mr. Huang Hsing). San Francisco, 1914.

Huang San-te. *Hung-meng ke-min shih* (Hung-meng Revolutionary History). N.p., 1936.

Huang Yuan-yung. *Yuan-sheng i-chu* (Posthumous Works of Huang Yuan-sheng). 4th ed., Shanghai, 1927.

Kao Liang-tso. *Sun Chung-shan hsien-sheng ch'uan* (Biography of Mr. Sun Chung-shan). Chengtu, 1945.

Kuomintang. *Ch'en Ch'i-mei ch'uan* (Biography of Ch'en Ch'i-mei). Taipei, 1949.

——. *Chu Chih-hsin ch'uan* (Biography of Chu Chih-hsin). Taipei, 1949.

——. *Chung-kuo Kuo-min Tang wu-shih chou-nien chi-nien t'i-k'an* (Special Publication for the Commemoration of the Fiftieth Anniversary of the Kuomintang). Chungking, 1944.

——. *Sung Chiao-jen ch'uan* (Biography of Sung Chiao-jen). Taipei 1949.

——. *T'an-ho Kung-ch'ang Tang liang ta-ya-an* (Two Important Cases for Impeaching the Communist Party). Nanking, 1927.

——, ed. *Kuo-fu ch'uan-chi* (Collected Works of the Father of the Country). 6 vols. Taipei, 1957.

Ku Chung-hsiu. *Chung-hua min-kuo k'ai-kuo shih* (A History of the

Founding of the Chinese Republic). Shanghai, 1914.

Li Ch'ang-fu. *Chung-kuo chin-min shih* (A History of Chinese Colonization). Shanghai, 1937.

Li Chien-nung. *Chung-kuo chin-pai-nien cheng-chih shih* (Political History of China in the Last Hundred Years). 2 vols. Taipei, 1957.

———. *Tsui-chin san-shih-nien Chung-kuo cheng-chih shih* (Political History of China in the Last Thirty Years). Shanghai, 1930.

Li Fang-ch'en. *Chung-kuo chin-tai shih* (A History of Modern China). 2 vols. 2nd ed. Taipei, 1958.

Li Lieh-chun. *Li Lieh-chun chiang-chun tzu-ch'uan* (Autobiography of General Li Lieh-chun). N.p., 1944.

Li Shu. *Hsin-hai ke-min ch'ien-hou ti Chung-kuo cheng-chih* (Chinese Politics before and after the 1911 Revolution). Peking, 1954.

Liang Ch'i-ch'ao. *Yin-ping-shih ho-chi* (Collected Works and Essays of the Ice-Drinkers Studio). 40 vols. Shanghai, 1936.

Liu K'uei-i. *Huang Hsing ch'uan-chi* (Biography of Huang Hsing). Taipei, 1952.

Liu Lien-k'o. *Pang-hui san-pai nien ke-min shih* (Three Hundred Years' Revolutionary History of Secret Societies). Macao, 1942.

Lo Chia-lun. *Chung-shan hsien-sheng Lun-tun pei-nan shih-liao k'ao-ting* (A Critical Study of the Official Documents Concerning Mr. Sun Chung-shan's Kidnap in London). Shanghai, 1930.

———, ed. *Ke-min wen-hsien* (Documents on the Revolution). Vols. I-XXII. Taipei, 1953-1960.

———, ed. *Kuo-fu nien-p'u ch'u-kao* (First Draft of the Chronological History of the Father of the Country). 2 vols. Taipei, 1958.

———. *Liu-shih nien lai chih Chung-kuo Kuo-min Tang yu Chung-kuo* (The Chung-kuo Kuomintang and China in the Last Sixty Years). Taipei, 1954.

Ou-yang Hsiu. *Ou-yang Yung-shu chi* (Collective Works of Ou-yang Hsiu). 2 vols. Shanghai, 1933.

Pao Tsun-p'eng *et al.*, eds. *Chung-kuo chin-tai shih lun-ts'ung* (Collective Essays on Modern Chinese History). Taipei, 1957.

Sa Meng-wu *et al.* *Cheng-tang cheng-chih lun-chi* (Collective Essays on Party Politics). Taipei, 1956.

Saneto Keishu. *Chukokujin Nihon ryugaku shi* (A History of Chinese Students Studying in Japan). Tokyo, 1960.

Shao Yuan-chung. *Hsuan-pu i-shu* (Posthumous Works of Paradise). 2 vols. Taipei, 1954.

Shih Hsi-sheng, ed. *Hu Han-min yen-hsing lu* (Record of the Speeches and Writings of Hu Han-min). Canton (?), 1929.

Shu Hsin-ch'eng. *Chin-tai Chung-kuo liu-hsueh shih* (A History of the Education of Students in Modern China). 3d ed. Shanghai, 1933.

Sun Chung-shan hsueh-chi (Collective Works of Sun Chung-shan). 2 vols. Peking, 1956.

Sung Chiao-jen. *Wo-chih li-shih* (My History). 6 vols. Hunan, 1920.

Ta'ao Ya-po. *Wuch'ang ke-min chen-shih* (True History of the Wuch'ang Revolution). Shanghai, 1930.

Tao Chu-yin. *Pai-yang chun-fa t'ung-chih shih-ch'i shih-hua.* (History of the Period during Control by the Pai-yang War Lords). 5 vols. 1957.

Teng Chia-yen, ed. *Chung-kuo Kuo-min Tang k'en-ch'in ta-hui shih-mo chi* (Record of the Convention of the Chinese Nationalist League in the USA). San Francisco, 1915.

Teng Tsu-ju. *Chung-kuo Kuo-min Tang erh-shih nien shih-chi* (Historical Records of the Chung-kuo Kuomintang of the Past Twenty Years). Shanghai, 1948.

Ting Wen-chiang, ed *Liang Jen-kung Hsien-sheng nien-p'u ch'ang-pien ch'u-kao* (First Draft on the Materials Gathered for a Chronological History of Mr. Liang Jen-kung). 3 vols. Taipei, 1958.

Tsou Lu. *Ch'eng-lun wen-chi* (Collective Works of the Clear Hut). 2 vols. Canton, 1934.

———. *Chung-kuo Kuo-min Tang shih-kao* (Draft History of the Chung-kuo Kuomintang). 3 vols. Chungking, 1944.

———. *Hui-i lu* (Memoirs). 2 vols. Taipei, 1951.

———. *Kwang-chou san-yueh erh-shih-chiu ke-min shih* (History of the Canton March 29 Revolution). Shanghai, 1926.

Tsui Shu-chin. *Sun Chung-shan yu Kung-ch'ang chu-i* (Sun Chung-shan and Communism). 3d ed. Hong Kong, 1956.

Tu Ch'eng-hsiang. *Ch'en Ying-shih ch'uan* (Biography of Ch'en Ying-shih). Taipei, 1958 (?).

Wang Ching-wei. *Wang Ching-wei hsien-sheng ti wen-chi* (Collective Works of Mr. Wang Ching-wei). 4 vols. Shanghai, n.d.

Wang Shih *et al. Chung-kuo Kung-ch'ang Tang li-shih chien-pien* (A Short History of the Chinese Communist Party). Shanghai, 1958.

Wang T'ung-ling. *Chung-kuo li-tai tang-cheng shih* (History of China's Historical Party Battles). 3d ed. Peking, 1931.

Wei Chu-hsien. *Chung-kuo ti pang-hui* (China's Secret Societies). Chungking, 1949.

Wen Kung-chih. *Tsui-chin san-shih-nien Chung-kuo chun-shih shih* (History of Chinese Military Affairs in the Last Thirty Years). 2 vols. 2d ed. Shanghai, 1932.

Wu Hsiang-hsiang, ed. *Chung-kuo hsien-tai shih ts'ung-k'an* (Collective Works on Contemporary Chinese History). Vols. I-XI. Taipei, 1960.

Wu T'ieh-ch'eng. *Wu T'ieh-ch'eng hsien-sheng hui-i lu* (Memoirs of Mr. Wu T'ieh-ch'eng). Taipei (?), 1957 (?).

Yang Yu-chun. *Chung-kuo cheng-tang shih* (A History of Chinese Political Parties). 2d ed. Shanghai, 1937.

Yao Yu-hsiang. *Hu Han-min hsien-sheng ch'uan* (Biography of Mr. Hu Han-min). Taipei, 1954.

Yeh Hsia-sheng. *Kuo-fu min-ch'u ke-min chi-lioh* (A Summary Record of the Revolutionary Activities in the First Five Years of the Republic of the Father of the Country). 3d private ed. Taipei, 1960.

NEWSPAPERS

Chung-kuo Jih-pao (The China Daily). Hong Kong.
Chung-sai Yat-po (The East-West Daily). San Francisco.
Min-li Pao (The People's Independence). Daily. Shanghai.

PERIODICALS

Chien-kuo Yueh-k'an (National Reconstruction Monthly). Shanghai.
Chien-she (The Construction). Monthly. Shanghai.
Ch'ien-feng (The Vanguard). Monthly. Canton.
Chung-kuo I-chou (China Weekly). Taipei.
Chung-kuo T'ung Meng Hui Yueh Chih-pu Tsa-chih (Journal of the Kwangtung Branch of the Chinese T'ung Meng Hui). Every tenth day (?). Canton.
Erh-shih Shih-chi Chih Chih-na (The Twentieth Century China). Tokyo.
Hsiang-tao (The Guide Weekly). Shanghai.
Hsin-ch'ao (The Renaissance). Monthly. Peking.
Hsin-sheng-min (New Life). Monthly. Shanghai.
Kuo-shih Kuan Kuan-k'an (Publications of the National Historical Bureau). Quarterly. Nanking.

Min-kuo (The Republic). Monthly. Tokyo.

Min-kuo Hui-pao. Weekly. Shanghai.

Min-kuo Pao (The Republican). Monthly. Shanghai.

San Min Chu I Pan-yueh K'an (The Three People's Principles Semimonthly). Taipei.

Ta-lu Tsa-chih (The Continent Magazine). Semimonthly. Taipei.

Tung-fang Tsa-chih (The Eastern Miscellany). Fortnightly. Shanghai.

Tzu-yu Ien (The Freeman). Weekly. Hong Kong.

Wen-hua Chien-she (Cultural Reconstruction). Monthly. Shanghai.

Yung-yen (The Justice). Fortnightly. Tientsin.

Index